T0226221

Lecture Notes in Computer Science 10712

Commenced Publication in 1973
Founding and Former Series Editors:
Gerhard Goos, Juris Hartmanis, and Jan van Leeuwen

More information about this series at http://www.springer.com/series/7408

Andrei Paskevich · Thomas Wies (Eds.)

Verified Software

Theories, Tools, and Experiments

9th International Conference, VSTTE 2017
Heidelberg, Germany, July 22–23, 2017
Revised Selected Papers

 Springer

Editors
Andrei Paskevich
Paris-Sud University
Orsay
France

Thomas Wies
New York University
New York, NY
USA

ISSN 0302-9743   ISSN 1611-3349 (electronic)
Lecture Notes in Computer Science
ISBN 978-3-319-72307-5   ISBN 978-3-319-72308-2   (eBook)
https://doi.org/10.1007/978-3-319-72308-2

Library of Congress Control Number: 2017961803

LNCS Sublibrary: SL2 – Programming and Software Engineering

Printed on acid-free paper

This Springer imprint is published by Springer Nature
The registered company is Springer International Publishing AG
The registered company address is: Gewerbestrasse 11, 6330 Cham, Switzerland

Preface

This volume contains the proceedings of the 9th International Working Conference on Verified Software: Theories, Tools, and Experiments (VSTTE 2017), held during July 22–23, 2017 in Heidelberg, Germany, and co-located with the 29th International Conference on Computer-Aided Verification.

The goal of the VSTTE conference series is to advance the state of the art in the science and technology of software verification, through the interaction of theory development, tool evolution, and experimental validation. We solicited contributions describing significant advances in the production of verified software, i.e., software that has been proven to meet its functional specifications. Submissions of theoretical, practical, and experimental contributions were equally encouraged, including those that focus on specific problems or problem domains. We were especially interested in submissions describing large-scale verification efforts that involve collaboration, theory unification, tool integration, and formalized domain knowledge. We also welcomed papers describing novel experiments and case studies evaluating verification techniques and technologies. The topics of interest included education, requirements modeling, specification languages, specification/verification/certification case studies, formal calculi, software design methods, automatic code generation, refinement methodologies, compositional analysis, verification tools (e.g., static analysis, dynamic analysis, model checking, theorem proving, satisfiability), tool integration, benchmarks, challenge problems, and integrated verification environments.

The inaugural VSTTE conference was held at ETH Zurich in October 2005, and the following editions took place in Toronto (2008 and 2016), Edinburgh (2010), Philadelphia (2012), Menlo Park (2013), Vienna (2014), and San Francisco (2015).

This year we received 20 submissions. Each submission was reviewed by three members of the Program Committee. The committee decided to accept 12 papers for presentation at the conference. The program also included four invited talks, given by Jan Hoffmann (CMU, USA), Shaz Qadeer (Microsoft, USA), Christoph Weidenbach (MPI for Informatics, Germany), and Santiago Zanella-Beguelin (Microsoft, UK).

We would like to thank the invited speakers and the authors for their excellent contributions to the program this year, the Program Committee and external reviewers for diligently reviewing the submissions, and the organizers of CAV 2017 for their help in organizing this event. We also thank Natarajan Shankar for his tireless stewardship of the VSTTE conference series over the years.

The VSTTE 2017 conference and the present volume were prepared with the help of EasyChair.

October 2017

Andrei Paskevich
Thomas Wies

Organization

Program Committee

June Andronick	University of New South Wales, Australia
Christel Baier	Technical University of Dresden, Germany
Sandrine Blazy	Université de Rennes 1, France
Arthur Charguéraud	Inria, France
Ernie Cohen	Amazon Web Services, USA
Rayna Dimitrova	UT Austin, USA
Carlo A. Furia	Chalmers University of Technology, Sweden
Arie Gurfinkel	University of Waterloo, Canada
Hossein Hojjat	Rochester Institute of Technology, USA
Marieke Huisman	University of Twente, The Netherlands
Bart Jacobs	Katholieke Universiteit Leuven, Belgium
Rajeev Joshi	NASA Jet Propulsion Laboratory, USA
Zachary Kincaid	Princeton University, USA
Shuvendu Lahiri	Microsoft, USA
Akash Lal	Microsoft, India
Francesco Logozzo	Facebook, USA
Peter Müller	ETH Zürich, Switzerland
Jorge A. Navas	SRI International, USA
Scott Owens	University of Kent, UK
Andrei Paskevich	Université Paris-Sud, France
Gerhard Schellhorn	Universität Augsburg, Germany
Peter Schrammel	University of Sussex, UK
Natarajan Shankar	SRI International, USA
Mihaela Sighireanu	Université Paris Diderot, France
Julien Signoles	CEA LIST, France
Michael Tautschnig	Queen Mary University of London, UK
Tachio Terauchi	Waseda University, Japan
Oksana Tkachuk	NASA Ames Research Center, USA
Mattias Ulbrich	Karlsruhe Institute of Technology, Germany
Thomas Wies	New York University, USA

Additional Reviewers

Dubslaff, Clemens	Myreen, Magnus O.
Haneberg, Dominik	Pfähler, Jörg
Kumar, Ramana	Trieu, Alix

Abstracts of Short Papers

Everest: A Verified and High-Performance HTTPS Stack

Santiago Zanella-Beguelin

Microsoft Research, UK

Abstract. The HTTPS ecosystem is the foundation of Internet security, with the TLS protocol and numerous cryptographic constructions at its core. Unfortunately, this ecosystem is extremely brittle, with frequent emergency patches and headline-grabbing attacks (e.g. Heartbleed, Logjam, Freak). The Everest expedition, joint between Microsoft Research, Inria and CMU, is a 5-year large-scale verification effort aimed at solving this problem by constructing a machine-checked, high-performance, standards-compliant implementation of the full HTTPS ecosystem. This talk is a report on the progress after just over one year into our expedition, and will overview the various verification tools that we use and their integration, including:

- F*, a dependently-typed ML-like language for programming and verification at high level;
- Low*, a subset of F* designed for C-like imperative programming;
- KreMLin, a compiler toolchain that extracts Low* programs to C;
- Vale, an extensible macro assembly language that uses F* as a verification backend.

Our flagship project is miTLS, a reference implementation of TLS using cryptographic components programmed and verified in F*, Low*, and Vale. We compile all our code to source quality C and assembly, suitable for independent audit and deployment. miTLS supports the latest TLS 1.3 standard, including Zero Round-Trip Time (0-RTT) resumption, and has been integrated in `libcurl` and the `nginx` web server.

Design Principles of Automated Reasoning Systems

Christoph Weidenbach

Max Planck Institute for Informatics, Germany

Abstract. An automated reasoning system is the implementation of an algorithm that adds a strategy to a calculus that is based on a logic. Typically, automated reasoning systems "solve" NP-hard problems or beyond. Therefore, I argue that automated reasoning system need often to be specific to a given problem. The combination of a system and a problem is called an application.

In the talk I discuss design principles based on this layered view of automated reasoning systems and their applications. I select and discuss design principles from all six layers: application, system, implementation, algorithm, calculus, and logic.

Why Verification Cannot Ignore Resource Usage

Jan Hoffmann

Carnegie Mellon University, Pittsburgh, PA, USA

Abstract. Verified programs only execute as specified if a sufficient amount of resources, such as time and memory, is available at runtime. Moreover, resource usage is often directly connected to correctness and security properties that we wish to verify. This talk will show examples of such connections and present recent work on automatic inference and verification of resource-usage bounds for functional and imperative programs. These automatic methods can be combined with other verification techniques to provide stronger guarantees at runtime.

Constructing Correct Concurrent Programs Layer by Layer

Shaz Qadeer

Microsoft Research, USA

Abstract. CIVL is a refinement-oriented verifier for concurrent programs implemented as a conservative extension to the Boogie verification system. CIVL allows the proof of correctness of a concurrent program — shared-memory or message-passing — to be described as a sequence of program layers. The safety of a layer implies the safety of the layer just below, thus allowing the safety of the highest layer to transitively imply the safety of the lowest.

The central theme in CIVL is reasoning about atomic actions. Different layers of a program describe the behavior of the program using atomic actions, higher layers with coarse-grained and lower layers with fine-grained atomic actions. The formal and automated verification justifying the connection among layers combines several techniques — linear variables, reduction based on movers, location invariants, and procedure-local abstraction.

CIVL is available in the master branch of Boogie together with more than fifty micro-benchmarks. CIVL has also been used to refine a realistic concurrent garbage collection algorithm from a simple high-level specification down to a highly-concurrent implementation described in terms of individual memory accesses.

Contents

A Formally Verified Interpreter for a Shell-Like Programming Language

Nicolas Jeannerod[1,2(✉)], Claude Marché[3], and Ralf Treinen[2]

[1] Dpt. d'Informatique, École normale supérieure, Paris, France
[2] Univ. Paris Diderot, Sorbonne Paris Cité, IRIF, UMR 8243, CNRS, Paris, France
nicolas.jeannerod@irif.fr
[3] Inria & LRI, CNRS, Univ. Paris-Sud, Université Paris-Saclay, Orsay, France

Abstract. The shell language is widely used for various system administration tasks on UNIX machines, as for instance as part of the installation process of software packages in FOSS distributions. Our mid-term goal is to analyze these scripts as part of an ongoing effort to use formal methods for the quality assurance of software distributions, to prove their correctness, or to pinpoint bugs. However, the syntax and semantics of POSIX shell are particularly treacherous.

We propose a new language called CoLiS which, on the one hand, has well-defined static semantics and avoids some of the pitfalls of the shell, and, on the other hand, is close enough to the shell to be the target of an automated translation of the scripts in our corpus. The language has been designed so that it will be possible to compile automatically a large number of shell scripts into the CoLiS language.

We formally define its syntax and semantics in Why3, define an interpreter for the language in the WhyML programming language, and present an automated proof in the Why3 proof environment of soundness and completeness of our interpreter with respect to the formal semantics.

Keywords: Posix shell · Programming language
Deductive program verification

1 Introduction

The UNIX shell is a command interpreter, originally named *Thompson shell* in 1971 for the first version of UNIX. Today, there exist many different versions of the shell language and different interpreters with varying functionalities. The most popular shell interpreter today is probably the *Bourne-Again shell* (*a.k.a.* bash) which was written by Brian Fox in 1988 for the GNU project, and which adds many features both for batch usage as an interpreter of shell scripts, and for interactive usage.

We are interested in a corpus of *maintainer scripts* which are part of the software packages distributed by the Debian project. The shell features which

This work has been partially supported by the ANR project CoLiS, contract number ANR-15-CE25-0001.

A. Paskevich and T. Wies (Eds.): VSTTE 2017, LNCS 10712, pp. 1–18, 2017.
https://doi.org/10.1007/978-3-319-72308-2_1

may be used by these scripts are described in the *Debian Policy* [18], *Sect. 10.4, Scripts.* Essentially, this is the shell described by the POSIX [12] standard. In the rest of the paper we will just speak of "shell" when we mean the shell language as defined by the POSIX standard.

Maintainer scripts are run as the *root* user, that is with maximal privileges, when installing, removing or upgrading packages. A single mistake in a script may hence have disastrous consequences. The work described in this paper is part of a research project with the goal of using formal methods to analyse the maintainer scripts, that is to either formally prove properties of scripts as required by the Debian policy, or to detect bugs. The corpus contains, even when ignoring the small number of scripts written in other languages than POSIX shell, more than 30.000 scripts.

Verifying shell scripts is a hard problem in the general case. However, we think that the restriction to Debian maintainer scripts makes the problem more manageable, since all the scripts are part of the common framework of the Debian package installation process, and the Debian policy tells us how they are called, and what they are allowed to do. For instance, the package installation process is orchestrated by the dpkg tool which guarantees that packages are not installed in parallel, which justifies our decision to completely ignore concurrency issues. The installation scripts are indeed often simple and repetitive. They are written by package developers, who have, in general, good knowledge of the shell; they try to avoid bad practices, and are quite aware of the importance of writing modular and maintainable code.

Even in that setting, the syntax and the semantics of shell is the first obstacle that we encounter during our project, since they can be treacherous for both the developer and the analysis tools. We have written a parser and a statistical analyser for the corpus of shell scripts [14] which we used in order to know which features of the shell are mostly used in our corpus, and which features we may safely ignore. Based on this, we developed an intermediate language for shell scripts, called *CoLiS*, which we will briefly define in this paper. The design of the CoLiS language has been guided by the following principles:

- It must be "cleaner" than shell: we ignore the dangerous structures (like eval allowing to execute arbitrary code given as a string) and we make more explicit the dangerous constructions that we cannot eliminate.
- It must have clear syntax and semantics. The goal is to help the analysis tools in their work and to allow a reader to be easily convinced of the soundness of these tools without having to care about the traps of the syntax or the semantics of the underlying language.
- The semantics must be less dynamic than that of the shell. This can be achieved by a better typing discipline with, for instance, the obligation of declaring the variables and functions in a header.
- An automated translation from shell must be possible. Since the correctness of the translation from shell to CoLiS cannot be proven, as we will argue in the following, one will have to trust it by reading or testing it. For this reason, the CoLiS language cannot be *fundamentally* different from shell.

This language is not conceived as a replacement of shell in the software packages. If that was our goal, we would have designed a declarative language as a replacement (similar to how systemd has nowadays mostly replaced System-V init scripts). Our mid-term goal is to analyse and, in the end, help to improve the existing shell scripts and not to change the complete packaging system. Because of this, our language shares a lot of similarities (and drawbacks) with shell.

We have formally defined the syntax and semantics of CoLiS in the Why3 verification environment [5]. It is already at this stage clear that we will be faced with an important problem when we will later write the compiler from shell to CoLiS: how can we ensure the correctness of such a compiler? The root of the problem is that there simply is no formal syntax and semantics of the shell language, even though there are recent attempts to that (see Sect. 5). In fact, if we could have clean syntax and semantics for the shell, then we wouldn't need our intermediate language, nor this translation, in the first place. An *interpreter* plays an important role when we want to gain confidence in the correctness of such a compiler, since it will allow us to compare the execution of shell scripts by real shell interpreters, with the execution of their compilation into CoLiS by the CoLiS interpreter. The main contribution of this paper is the proof of correctness and completeness of our CoLiS interpreter, with respect to the formal semantics of CoLiS.

Plan of the Paper. We present the syntax and semantics of our language in Sect. 2. We also explain some of our design choices. We describe our interpreter in Sect. 3 and the proof of its completeness in Sect. 4. This proof uses a technique that we believe to be interesting and reusable. Finally, we compare our work to other's in Sect. 5 and conclude in Sect. 6.

2 Language

2.1 Elements of Shell

Some features of the shell language are well known from imperative programming languages, like variable assignments, conditional branching, loops (both `for` and `while`). Shell scripts may call UNIX commands which in particular may operate on the file system, but these commands are not part of the shell language itself, and not in the scope of the present work. Without going into the details of the shell language, there are some peculiarities which are of importance for the design of the CoLiS language:

Expressions Containing Instructions. Expressions that calculate values may contain control structures, for instance a `for` loop, or the invocation of an external command. Execution of these instructions may of course fail, and produce exceptions.

No Static Typing. Variables are not declared, and there is no static type discipline. In principle, values are just strings, but it is common practice in shell scripts to abuse these strings as lists of strings, by assuming that the elements of a list are separated by the so-called *internal field separator* (usually the blank symbol).

Dynamic Scoping. Functions may access non-local variables, however, this is done according to the chronological order of the variables on the execution stack (dynamic scoping), not according to the syntactic order in the script text (lexical scoping).

Non-standard Control Flow. Some instructions of the shell language may signal exceptional exit, like a non-zero error-code. Different constructions of the shell language propagate or capture these exceptions in different ways. This has sometimes quite surprising consequences. For instance, `false && true` and `false` are not equivalent in shell. Furthermore, there is a special mode of the shell (the *strict* mode, in Debian parlance, obtained by the `-e` flag), which changes the way how exceptions are propagated.

2.2   Syntax of CoLiS

The shell features identified in Sect. 2.1 motivate the design of the CoLiS language, the syntax of which is shown in Fig. 1. There only is an abstract syntax because the language is meant to be the target of a compilation process from the shell language, and is not designed to be used directly by human developers.

Terms and Expressions. The mutual dependency between the categories of instructions and expressions which we have observed in the shell does not pose

String variables	$x_s \in SVar$
List variables	$x_l \in LVar$
Procedures names	$c \in \mathcal{F}$
Natural numbers	$n \in \mathbb{N}$
Strings	$\sigma \in String$
Programs	$p ::= vdecl^* \; pdecl^* \; \textbf{program} \; t$
Variables declarations	$vdecl ::= \textbf{varstring} \; x_s \mid \textbf{varlist} \; x_l$
Procedures declarations	$pdecl ::= \textbf{proc} \; c \; \textbf{is} \; t$
String expressions	$s ::= \textbf{nil}_s \mid f_s :: s$
String fragments	$f_s ::= \sigma \mid x_s \mid n \mid t$
List expressions	$l ::= \textbf{nil}_l \mid f_l :: l$
List fragments	$f_l ::= [s] \mid \textbf{split} \; s \mid x_l$
Terms	$t ::= \textbf{true} \mid \textbf{false} \mid \textbf{fatal}$
	$\mid \textbf{return} \; t \mid \textbf{exit} \; t$
	$\mid x_s := s \mid x_l := l$
	$\mid t \; ; \; t \mid \textbf{if} \; t \; \textbf{then} \; t \; \textbf{else} \; t$
	$\mid \textbf{for} \; x_s \; \textbf{in} \; l \; \textbf{do} \; t \mid \textbf{do} \; t \; \textbf{while} \; t$
	$\mid \textbf{process} \; t \mid \textbf{pipe} \; t \; \textbf{into} \; t$
	$\mid \textbf{call} \; l \mid \textbf{shift}$

Fig. 1. Syntax of CoLiS

any real problem, and shows up in the definition of the CoLiS syntax as a mutual recursion between the syntactic categories of terms (corresponding to instructions), expression fragments, and expressions.

Variables and Typing. All the variables must be declared. These declarations can only be placed at the beginning of the program. They are accompanied by a type for the variables: string or list.

CoLiS makes an explicit distinction between strings and lists of strings. Since we only have these two kinds of values, we do not use a type system, but can make the distinction on the syntactic level between the categories of string expressions, and the category of list expressions. Consequently, we have two different constructors in the abstract syntax for assignments: one for string values, and one for list values. This separation is made possible by the fact that CoLiS syntax isn't supposed to be written by humans, so that we may simply use different kinds of variables for strings and for lists. The future compiler from shell to CoLiS will reject scripts for which it is not possible to statically infer types of variables and expressions.

Arithmetical expressions, which we could have easily added at this point, are omitted here for the sake of presentation, and since we found that they are very rarely used in our corpus of scripts.

Absence of Nested Scopes. Note that variables and procedures have to be declared at the beginning of the program, and that the syntax does not provide for nested scopes. This is motivated by the fact that our corpus of scripts only very rarely uses nested shell functions, and that the rare occurrences where they are used in our corpus can easily be rewritten. Hence, we have circumvented the problem of dynamic binding which exists in the shell. The future compiler from shell to CoLiS will reject scripts which make use of dynamic scoping.

Control Structures and Control Flow. Proper handling of exceptions is crucial for shell scripts since in principle any command acting on the file system may fail, and the script should take these possible failures into account and act accordingly. Debian policy even stipulates that fatal errors of commands should usually lead to abortion of the execution of a script, but also allows the maintainer to capture exceptions which he considers as non-fatal. Hence, we have to keep the exception mechanism for the CoLiS language. This decision has an important impact on the semantics of CoLiS, but also shows in the syntax (for instance via the **fatal** term).

The terms **true**, **false**, **return** t and **exit** t correspond to shell built-ins; **fatal** raises a fatal exception which in real shell scripts would be produced by a failing UNIX command. Note that **return** t and **exit** t take a term instead of a natural number. In fact, these commands transform a normal behaviour (of the term t) into an exceptional one for the complete construct. This does only provide for distinction between null or non-null exit codes, which is sufficient for us since we found that the scripts of our corpus very rarely distinguish between different non-null exit codes.

Some shell-specific structures remain. The **shift** command, for instance, removes the first element of the argument list if it exists, and raises an error otherwise.

Note that the procedure invocation, **call**, does not work on a procedure name with arguments, but on a list whose first element will be considered as the name of the procedure and the remaining part as the arguments. This makes a difference when dealing with empty lists; in that case, the call is a success.

The **pipe** command (the | character in shell) takes the standard output of a term and feeds it as input to a second term. The **process** construct corresponds to the invocation of a sub-shell (backquotes, or $(...) in shell).

2.3 Semantics

All the elements (that is terms, string fragments and expressions, and list fragments and expressions) of the language are evaluated (see semantic judgements in Fig. 2) in a context that contains the file system (left abstract in this work), the standard input, the list of arguments from the command line and the variable environments. They produce a new context, a *behaviour* and a string or a list. In particular, terms produce strings, which is their standard output. For instance, a judgement

$$t_{/\Gamma} \quad \Downarrow \quad \sigma \star b_{/\Gamma'}$$

means that the evaluation of the term t in the context Γ terminates with behaviour b, produces the new context Γ', and the standard output σ.

Note that the file system as well as the built-ins of the shell are left abstract in this work. We focus only on the structure of the language.

Behaviours. We inherit a quite complex set of possible behaviours of terms from the shell: True, False, Fatal, Return True, Return False, Exit True, Exit False and None. The case of expressions is simpler, their behaviour can only be True for success, Fatal for error, and None for the cases that do not change the behaviour. A term behaviour b can be converted to an expression behaviour $\overline{b}$ as follows:

$$\overline{b} := \text{True} \qquad \text{if } b \in \{\text{True}, \text{Return True}, \text{Exit True}\}$$
$$\mid \text{Fatal} \qquad \text{otherwise}$$

The composition $\beta\beta'$ of two expression behaviours β and β' is defined as :

$$\beta\beta' := \beta \qquad \text{if } \beta' = \text{None}$$
$$\mid \beta' \qquad \text{otherwise}$$

Values: strings	$\sigma \in String$
Values: lists	$\lambda \in StringList \triangleq \{\sigma^* \mid \sigma \in String\}$
Behaviours: terms	$b \in \{\text{True}, \text{False}, \text{Fatal}, \text{Return True}$
	$\quad\quad \text{Return False}, \text{Exit True}, \text{Exit False}\}$
Behaviours: expressions	$\beta \in \{\text{True}, \text{Fatal}, \text{None}\}$
File systems	$\mathcal{FS}$
Environments: strings	$SEnv \triangleq [SVar \rightharpoonup String]$
Environments: lists	$LEnv \triangleq [LVar \rightharpoonup StringList]$
Contexts	$\Gamma \in \mathcal{FS} \times String \times StringList \times SEnv \times LEnv$
Judgments: terms	$t_{/\Gamma} \Downarrow \sigma \star b_{/\Gamma'}$
Judgments: string fragment	$f_{s/\Gamma} \Downarrow_{sf} \sigma \star \beta_{/\Gamma'}$
Judgements: string expression	$s_{/\Gamma} \Downarrow_{s} \sigma \star \beta_{/\Gamma'}$
Judgements: list fragment	$f_{l/\Gamma} \Downarrow_{lf} \lambda \star \beta_{/\Gamma'}$
Judgements: list expression	$l_{/\Gamma} \Downarrow_{l} \lambda \star \beta_{/\Gamma'}$

Fig. 2. Semantics of CoLiS

Expressions. The semantics of string fragments and expressions are defined by the derivation rules of Fig. 3, operating on the judgements defined on Fig. 2. Each expression or fragment is evaluated with respect to a context and produces a value of type string or list, an expression behaviour and a new context. An expression behaviour can be True, Fatal or the absence of behaviour None. Roughly, the behaviour of an expression is the last success or failure of a term observed when evaluating the expression. Expression fragments other than terms do not contribute to the behaviour of a term, this is modeled by giving them the dummy behaviour None.

$$\frac{}{\mathbf{nil}_{s/\Gamma} \Downarrow_{s} \epsilon \star \text{None}_{/\Gamma}} \qquad \frac{f_{s/\Gamma} \Downarrow_{sf} \sigma \star \beta_{/\Gamma'} \qquad s_{/\Gamma'} \Downarrow_{s} \sigma' \star \beta'_{/\Gamma''}}{f_s :: s_{/\Gamma} \Downarrow_{s} \sigma \cdot \sigma' \star \beta\beta'_{/\Gamma''}}$$

$$\frac{}{\sigma_{/\Gamma} \Downarrow_{sf} \sigma \star \text{None}_{/\Gamma}} \qquad \frac{}{x_{s/\Gamma} \Downarrow_{sf} \Gamma.\mathbf{senv}[x_s] \star \text{None}_{/\Gamma}}$$

$$\frac{}{n_{/\Gamma} \Downarrow_{sf} \Gamma.\mathbf{args}[n] \star \text{None}_{/\Gamma}} \qquad \frac{t_{/\Gamma} \Downarrow \sigma \star b_{/\Gamma'}}{t_{/\Gamma} \Downarrow_{sf} \sigma \star \overline{b}_{/\Gamma[\mathbf{fs} \leftarrow \Gamma'.\mathbf{fs};\, \mathbf{input} \leftarrow \Gamma'.\mathbf{input}]}}$$

Fig. 3. Semantic rules for the evaluation of string expressions and fragments

In the semantics of Fig. 3, we write $\Gamma.\mathbf{senv}$, $\Gamma.\mathbf{lenv}$ and $\Gamma.\mathbf{args}$ for the fields of the context Γ containing the string environment, the list environments and the argument line respectively, and we write $\Gamma[\text{input} \leftarrow \sigma]$ for the context Γ in which the field **input** has been changed to σ.

Figure 4 gives the rules for the evaluation of a "do while" loop, and spells out how the possible behaviours observed when evaluating the condition and the body determine the behaviour of the complete loop.

$$\frac{t_{1/\Gamma} \Downarrow \sigma_1 \star b_{1/\Gamma_1} \qquad b_1 \in \{\text{Fatal}, \text{Return}\ \_, \text{Exit}\ \_\}}{(\mathbf{do}\ t_1\ \mathbf{while}\ t_2)_{/\Gamma} \Downarrow \sigma_1 \star b_{1/\Gamma_1}} \ \text{T\scriptsize RANSMIT-B\scriptsize ODY}$$

$$\frac{t_{1/\Gamma} \Downarrow \sigma_1 \star b_{1/\Gamma_1} \qquad b_1 \in \{\text{True}, \text{False}\}}{t_{2/\Gamma_1} \Downarrow \sigma_2 \star \text{True}_{/\Gamma_2} \quad (\mathbf{do}\ t_1\ \mathbf{while}\ t_2)_{/\Gamma_2} \Downarrow \sigma_3 \star b_{3/\Gamma_3}}{(\mathbf{do}\ t_1\ \mathbf{while}\ t_2)_{/\Gamma} \Downarrow \sigma_1\sigma_2\sigma_3 \star b_{3/\Gamma_3}} \ \text{T\scriptsize RUE}$$

$$\frac{t_{1/\Gamma} \Downarrow \sigma_1 \star b_{1/\Gamma_1} \qquad b_1 \in \{\text{True}, \text{False}\}}{t_{2/\Gamma_1} \Downarrow \sigma_2 \star b_{2/\Gamma_2} \qquad b_2 \in \{\text{False}, \text{Fatal}\}}{(\mathbf{do}\ t_1\ \mathbf{while}\ t_2)_{/\Gamma} \Downarrow \sigma_1\sigma_2 \star b_{1/\Gamma_2}} \ \text{F\scriptsize ALSE}$$

$$\frac{t_{1/\Gamma} \Downarrow \sigma_1 \star b_{1/\Gamma_1} \qquad b_1 \in \{\text{True}, \text{False}\}}{t_{2/\Gamma_1} \Downarrow \sigma_2 \star b_{2/\Gamma_2} \qquad b_2 \in \{\text{Return}\ \_, \text{Exit}\ \_\}}{(\mathbf{do}\ t_1\ \mathbf{while}\ t_2)_{/\Gamma} \Downarrow \sigma_1\sigma_2 \star b_{2/\Gamma_2}} \ \text{T\scriptsize RANSMIT-C\scriptsize OND}$$

Fig. 4. Semantic rules for the "do while"

The pipe construct completely ignores the behaviour of the first term. Finally, the **process** protects part of the context from modifications. Changes to variables and arguments done inside a **process** are not observable. The modifications on the file system and the standard input are kept. Their semantics is given in Fig. 5.

$$\frac{t_{1/\Gamma} \Downarrow \sigma_1 \star b_{1/\Gamma_1} \qquad t_{2/\Gamma_1[\text{input}\leftarrow\sigma_1]} \Downarrow \sigma_2 \star b_{2/\Gamma_2}}{\mathbf{pipe}\ t_1\ \mathbf{into}\ t_{2/\Gamma} \Downarrow \sigma_2 \star b_{2/\Gamma_2[\text{input}\leftarrow\Gamma_1.\text{input}]}} \ \text{P\scriptsize IPE}$$

$$\frac{t_{/\Gamma} \Downarrow \sigma \star b_{/\Gamma'}}{\mathbf{process}\ t_{/\Gamma} \Downarrow \sigma \star \overline{b}_{/\Gamma[\text{fs}\leftarrow\Gamma'.\text{fs},\ \text{input}\leftarrow\Gamma'.\text{input}]}} \ \text{P\scriptsize ROCESS}$$

Fig. 5. Semantics of the evaluation for **pipe** and **process**

2.4   Mechanised Version

We have formalised the syntax and semantics of CoLiS using the proof environment Why3 [5]. Why3 is an environment dedicated to deductive program verification. It provides both a specification language, and a programming language. The theorems and annotated programs (in fact, everything that needs to be proven) are converted by Why3 into proof obligations and passed to external

```
inductive eval_term term context string behaviour context =

  | EvalT_DoWhile_Transmit_Body : ∀ t₁ Γ σ₁ b₁ Γ₁ t₂.

    eval_term t₁ Γ σ₁ b₁ Γ₁ →
    (match b₁ with BNormal _ → false | _ → true end) →

    eval_term (TDoWhile t₁ t₂) Γ σ₁ b₁ Γ₁

  | EvalT_DoWhile_True : ∀ t₁ Γ σ₁ b₁ Γ₁ t₂ σ₂ Γ₂ σ₃ b₃ Γ₃.

    eval_term t₁ Γ σ₁ (BNormal b₁) Γ₁ →
    eval_term t₂ Γ₁ σ₂ (BNormal True) Γ₂ →
    eval_term (TDoWhile t₁ t₂) Γ₂ σ₃ b₃ Γ₃ →

    eval_term (TDoWhile t₁ t₂) Γ (concat (concat σ₁ σ₂) σ₃) b₃ Γ₃
```

Fig. 6. Term evaluation judgement as an inductive predicate in Why3 (excerpt with two rules for the "do while")

provers. Its programming language, WhyML, is a language of the ML family containing imperative constructs such as references and exceptions. These elements are well handled in the proof obligations, allowing the user to write programs in a natural way.

The semantics of CoLiS is expressed in the Why3 specification language as a so-called inductive predicate, defined by a set of Horn clauses. The translation is completely straightforward, for instance a fragment of the translation of the semantic rules from Fig. 4 to Why3 is shown in Fig. 6. Formalising the semantics in Why3 this way has the immediate advantage of syntax and type checks done by the Why3 system, and is of course indispensable for proving the correctness of the interpreter.

3   Interpreter

The interpreter is written in WhyML, the programming language of the Why3 environment, as a set of mutually recursive functions. The functions are written in a standard style combining functional and imperative features. The main interpreter function has the following signature in Why3:

```
let rec interp_term (t: term) (Γ: context) (stdout : ref string)
                                            : (bool, context)
```

There are some fundamental differences between the interpreter on the one hand, and the specification of the semantics on the other hand:

– The function `interp_term` returns normally only in case of normal behaviours.

- The exceptional behaviours Fatal, Return b and Exit b are signaled by raising Why3 exceptions, respectively of the form Fatal(Γ), Return (b, Γ) and Exit (b, Γ) where Γ is the resulting context.
- The standard output is modelled by the mutable variable `stdout` of type string, to which characters are written. This makes the code closer to a standard interpreter which displays results as it produces them.
- The composition of expression behaviours is done by an auxiliary function with an accumulator: instead of yielding the behaviours as a component of a complex result type and then composing them (what corresponds to the semantic rules), we transmit to the recursive call the current behaviour, and let it update it if needed.

```
match t with
| TFatal → raise (EFatal Γ)
| TIf t₁ t₂ t3 →
  let (b₁, Γ₁) =
    try
      interp_term t₁ Γ stdout
    with
      EFatal Γ' → (false, Γ')
    end
  in
  interp_term (if b₁ then t₂ else t3) Γ₁ stdout
  ...
```

Fig. 7. Code of the interpreter for the **if** construct

To illustrate theses differences we present in Fig. 7 an excerpt of the interpreter code for the case of **fatal** command, and the conditional command. Note that exceptions, other that `EFatal`, potentially raised by the interpretation of t_1 are naturally propagated. This implicit propagation makes the code of the interpreter significantly simpler than the inductive definition of the semantics.

Due to while loops in particular, this interpreter does not necessarily terminate. Yet, we prove that this interpreter is sound and complete with respect to the semantics, as expressed by the two following theorems. We define a notation for executions of the interpreter. For any term t, contexts Γ and Γ', string σ and behaviour b,

$$t_{/\Gamma} \mapsto \sigma \star b_{/\Gamma'}$$

states that when given the term t, the context Γ and a string reference as its input, the interpreter terminates, writing the string σ at the end of the reference. It terminates

- normally when b is True or False, returning the boolean b and the new context Γ';
- with an exception EFatal(Γ'), EReturn(b', Γ') or EExit(b', Γ') when b is Fatal, Return b' or Exit b' respectively.

Theorem 1 (Soundness of the interpreter). *For all t, Γ, σ, b and Γ': if $t_{/\Gamma} \mapsto \sigma \star b_{/\Gamma'}$ then $t_{/\Gamma} \Downarrow \sigma \star b_{/\Gamma'}$*

Theorem 2 (Completeness of the interpreter). *For all t, Γ, σ, b and Γ': if $t_{/\Gamma} \Downarrow \sigma \star b_{/\Gamma'}$ then $t_{/\Gamma} \mapsto \sigma \star b_{/\Gamma'}$*

Due to the mutual recursion in the definition of the abstract syntax, and in the functions of the interpreter, we need of course analogous theorems for string and list fragments and expressions, which are omitted here.

3.1 Proof of Soundness

Soundness is expressed in Why3 as a set of post-conditions (see Fig. 8) for each function of the interpreter. Why3 handles the recursive functions pretty well and splits the proof into many simpler sub-goals. However, some of these subgoals still require up to 30 s to be proven by the E prover.

One difficulty in the proof comes from the fact that the interpreter uses an additional argument to pass the behaviour of the previous term. This makes the annotations of the functions harder to read and the goals harder to prove, with post-conditions of the form:

```
(eval_sexpr_opt s Γ σ None Γ' ∧ b = previous)
    ∨  eval_sexpr_opt s Γ σ (Some b) Γ
```

for an output (σ, b, Γ') of the expression interpreter.

The choice to have an interpreter with imperative feature (and thus different from the declarative semantics) makes the proof hard. The most disturbing feature for provers is the use of a reference to model the standard output. This causes proof obligations of the form:

```
∃ σ. !stdout = concat (old !stdout) σ ∧ eval_term t Γ σ b Γ'
```

An existential quantification is hard for SMT solvers; it is a challenge for them to find the right instance of the existentially quantified variable that makes the proof work. This is in general a weak point of SMT solvers and requires provers like the E prover which is based on the superposition calculus.

```
let rec interp_term (t: term) (Γ: context) (stdout : ref string)
                                          : (bool, context)
    diverges
    returns { (b, Γ') → ∃ σ. !stdout = concat (old !stdout) σ
                        ∧ eval_term t Γ σ (BNormal b)   Γ' }
    raises  { EFatal Γ' → ∃ σ. !stdout = concat (old !stdout) σ
                        ∧ eval_term t Γ σ BFatal Γ' }
    ...
```

Fig. 8. Contract of the sound interpreter. There are similar post-conditions for other exceptions raised.

4   Proof of Completeness

We show completeness of the interpreter (Theorem 2) by proving two intermediary lemmas. The first lemma states the functionality of our semantic predicates:

Lemma 1 (Functionality of the semantic predicates). *For all t, Γ, Γ_1, Γ_2, σ_1, σ_2, b_1, and b_2: if $t_{/\Gamma} \Downarrow \sigma_1 \star b_{1/\Gamma_1}$ and $t_{/\Gamma} \Downarrow \sigma_2 \star b_{2/\Gamma_2}$, then $\sigma_1 = \sigma_2$, $b_1 = b_2$ and $\Gamma_1 = \Gamma_2$.*

This lemma is quite straightforward to prove.

The second lemma states the termination of the interpreter in case one can prove a judgement about the semantics for the same input:

Lemma 2 (Termination of the interpreter). *For all t, Γ, Γ_1, σ_1 and b_1: if $t_{/\Gamma} \Downarrow \sigma_1 \star b_{1/\Gamma_1}$, then the interpreter terminates when given t, Γ.*

It is not obvious how to prove this lemma in the Why3 framework. The difficulty of the proof will be discussed below in Sect. 4.1, and our solution to the problem is presented in Sect. 4.2.

Theorem 2, stating the completeness of the interpreter, follows immediately from the above two lemmas, together with Theorem 1 stating the soundness of the interpreter:

Proof. Let t be a term, Γ and Γ_1 contexts, σ_1 a string and b_1 a behaviour. Let us assume that there exists a proof of the judgement $t_{/\Gamma} \Downarrow \sigma_1 \star b_{1/\Gamma_1}$. By Lemma 2 (termination of the interpreter), there exists some results σ_2, b_2 and Γ_2 computed by the interpreter. By Theorem 1 (soundness of the interpreter), we have $t_{/\Gamma} \Downarrow \sigma_2 \star b_{2/\Gamma_2}$. By Lemma 1 (functionality of the semantics), we obtain $\sigma_1 = \sigma_2$, $b_1 = b_2$ and $\Gamma_1 = \Gamma_2$, which allows us to conclude.

4.1   Proving (or not Proving) Termination with Heights and Sizes

A first naive idea to prove the two lemmas is to use induction on the structure of the terms. This does, of course, not work since one premise of the rule TRUE for the **do while** construct (see Fig. 4) uses the same term as its conclusion.

In fact, what does decrease at every iteration is the proof of the judgement itself. A common way in by-hand proofs to exploit that fact is to use the *size* of the proof (*i.e.* the number of rules involved), or alternatively the *height* of the proof tree.

These numbers could then be passed to the interpreter as a new argument along with a pre-condition specifying that this number corresponds to the size (resp. the height) of the proof. It is then easy to prove that it decreases at each recursive call, and since this value is always positive, we obtain termination of the program. These solutions, however, have drawbacks that make them unsuitable for use in the Why3 environment:

- On the one hand, back-end SMT solvers can reason about arithmetic, but have only incomplete strategies for handling quantifiers; on the other hand superposition provers are good with quantifiers but do not support arithmetic. One could think of replacing an axiomatised arithmetic by a simple successor arithmetic, that is using only *zero* and the *successor* function. This would not solve the problem since when using the size one still needs addition and subtraction, and when using the height one needs the maximum function, and handling of inequalities.
- When we know the size of a proof, we cannot deduce from it the size of the proofs of the premises, which makes the recursive calls complicated.

   A way to solve this problem is to modify the interpreter so that it returns the "unused" size (a technique, sometimes referred to as the *credit* or *fuel*, which can be useful for proving the complexity of a program). This does imply a major modification of the interpreter, though: the exceptions would have to carry that number as well, and the interpreter would have to catch them every time, just to decrement the size and then raise them again.
- We have a similar problem with the height: we cannot deduce from the height of a proof the heights of the premises, but only an upper bound.

   We could solve this problem by using inequalities either in the pre- and post-conditions or in the predicate itself. Nevertheless, it makes the definition of the predicate and the pre- and post-conditions more onerous, and the work of the SMT solvers more complicated.

4.2   Proving Termination with Ghosts and Skeletons

The proof of termination of the interpreter would be easy if we could use an induction on the proof tree of the judgement. The problem is that the proof tree is (implicitly) constructed during the proof, and is not available as a first-class value in the specification. The solution we propose is to modify the predicates specifying the semantics of CoLiS to produce a lightweight representation of the proof tree. This representation, which we call a *skeleton*, contains only the shape of the proof tree. The idea is that a complete proof tree could be abstracted to a skeleton just be ignoring all the contents of the nodes, and just keeping the outline of the tree. This avoids the use of arithmetic, since provers only have to work with a simple algebraic data type.

The definition of the type of skeletons in Why3 is shown in Fig. 9. There is one constructor for every number of premises of rules in the definition of the semantics, that is in our case, 0, 1, 2 and 3. We then have alternative definitions of our predicates including their skeleton (see Fig. 10).

We can now prove the properties of the semantic predicates by induction on the skeletons. Skeletons make proofs by induction possible when nothing else than the proof is decreasing. In fact, it also has an other interesting advantage: we often need to conduct inductions on our semantic predicates. However, these predicates are mutually recursive and do not work on the same data types, which makes our proofs verbose and annoying. Now, we can run our induction on the

```
type skeleton =
  | S0
  | S1 skeleton
  | S2 skeleton skeleton
  | S3 skeleton skeleton skeleton
```

Fig. 9. The data type for skeletons

```
inductive eval_term term context string behaviour context skeleton =
```

| EvalT_DoWhile_True : $\forall$ t_1 Γ σ_1 b_1 Γ_1 t_2 σ_2 Γ_2 σ_3 b_3 Γ_3 s_1 s_2 s_3.

```
eval_term t₁ Γ σ₁ (BNormal b₁) Γ₁ s₁ →
eval_term t₂ Γ₁ σ₂ (BNormal True) Γ₂ s₂ →
eval_term (TDoWhile t₁ t₂) Γ₂ σ₃ b₃ Γ₃ s₃ →

eval_term (TDoWhile t₁ t₂) Γ
          (concat (concat σ₁ σ₂) σ₃) b₃ Γ₃ (S3 s₁ s₂ s₃)
```

Fig. 10. (Part of the) inductive predicates with skeletons

skeletons, and that makes the definitions and proofs of the theorems much easier. This is, for instance, the case for the Theorem 1.

There remains the question how to connect the interpreter to the skeletons produced by the predicates. This is where *ghost* arguments come in. In the context of deductive program verification, ghost code [9] is a part of a program that is added solely for the purpose of specification. Ghost code cannot have any impact on the execution of the code: it must be removable without any observable difference on the program. In this spirit, we extend the functions of the interpreter with a ghost parameter which holds the skeleton (see Fig. 11).

```
let rec interp_term (t: term) (g: context) (stdout : ref string)
                                (ghost sk: skeleton) : (bool, context)

  requires { ∃ s b g'. eval_term t g s b g' sk }
  variant { sk }
  returns { (b, g') → ∃ s. !stdout = concat (old !stdout) s
                      ∧ eval_term t g s (BNormal b)  g' sk }
```

Fig. 11. Contract for the terminating interpreter. There are similar post-conditions for exceptions raised.

We also add ghost code in the body of the function (see Fig. 12) in order to give indications to the provers, using some auxiliary destructor functions for skeletons. The function skeleton23, for instance, takes a skeleton that is required to have a head of arity 2 or 3, and returns its direct subtrees. The fact that it

```
| TDoWhile t₁ t₂ →
  let ghost sk1 = skeleton123 sk in
  (* At this point, we know that the rules
     that might apply can have 1, 2 or 3 premises. *)
  let (b₁, g₁) = interp_term t₁ g stdout sk1 in
  let (b₂, g₂) =
    try
      let ghost (_, sk2) = skeleton23 sk in
      (* At this point, we know that the rule
         with 1 premise cannot be applied anymore. *)
      interp_term t₂ g₁ stdout sk2
    with
      EFatal g₂ → (false, g₂)
    end
  in
  if b₂ then
    let ghost (_, _, sk3) = skeleton3 sk in
    (* And finally, only the rule with 3 premises can be applied. *)
    interp_term (TDoWhile t₁ t₂) g₂ stdout sk3
  else
    (b₁, g₂)
```

Fig. 12. Excerpt of the body of the terminating interpreter

requires the skeleton to have a head of arity 2 or 3 adds the right axioms and goals to the proof context, thus helping the provers.

This works well because we wrote the semantics in a specific way: the order of the premises always corresponds to the order in which the computation must happen. This means that we can take the skeleton of the first premise and give it to the first recursive call. After that call, either an exception is raised which interrupts the control flow, or we take the skeleton of the second premise and give it to the second recursive call.

It would have been tempting to match on the term and the skeleton at the same time (to have something like |TDoWhile t_1 t_2, S1 sk_1 → .). This, however, does not work, since it would make the execution of the code dependent on a ghost parameter, which is rejected by the type checker of Why3 as a forbidden effect of ghost code on non-ghost code [9].

4.3 Reproducibility

Using the technique of skeletons, all the proof obligations are proven by automated provers. The proof takes some time because there are a many cases (we obtain 207 subgoals), but none of those takes more than 4 s to our provers.

The Why3 code for the syntax, semantics, the interpreter and all the proofs is available online [13]. The proofs need of course Why3 [5], and at least the provers Alt-Ergo [4] (1.30), Z3 [16] (4.5.0) and E [17] (1.9.1). One may in addition use CVC3 [3], CVC4 [2] and SPASS [19] in order to gain additional confirmation.

5   Related Work

Formalising the semantics of programming language is most of the time done using interactive proof assistants like Coq or Isabelle. Yet, formalising semantics and proving complex properties, with automatic provers only, was already shown possible by Clochard et al. [8], who also use the Why3 environment. The difficulty of proving completeness was not addressed in that work, though. Interestingly, the issues we faced regarding completeness and inductive predicates was present in other work conducted within the CoLiS project by Chen et al. [7], for proving a shell path resolution algorithm. They solve completeness by indexing their inductive predicates with heights. We would like to investigate whether an approach with skeletons instead of heights would make the proofs easier. To our knowledge, the idea of using proof skeletons is new, even though the idea seems quite close to the concept of step-indexing for reasoning on operational semantic rules [1].

Several tools can spot certain kinds of errors in shell scripts. The tool `checkbashisms` [6], for instance, detects usage of bash-specific constructs in shell scripts. It is based on regular expressions. The `ShellCheck` [11] tool detects error-prone usages of the shell language. This tool is written in Haskell and analyses the scripts on-the-fly while parsing.

There have been few attempts to formalize the shell. Recently, Greenberg [10] has presented elements of formal semantics of POSIX shell. The work behind Abash [15] contains a formalization of the part of the semantics concerned with variable expansion and word splitting. The Abash tool itself performs abstract interpretation to analyze possible arguments passed by Bash scripts to UNIX commands, and thus to identify security vulnerabilities in Bash scripts.

6   Conclusion and Future Work

We presented a Why3 implementation of the semantics of an imperative programming language. This formalisation is faithful to the semantic rules written by hand. Our main contribution is an interpreter for this language proven both sound and complete. The proof of completeness uses an original technique involving what we call skeletons: an abstraction of the proof tree for an inductive predicate, that decreases on recursive call, allowing us to use induction on the proof itself.

Future work. In the near future, we would like to try a more direct proof of completeness (*i.e.* without separating it into the soundness, the functionality of the semantic predicates and the termination of the algorithm). Such a proof would be interesting in cases where the functionality can not be proven (when we can derive the same judgement in different manners, for instance).

To fulfil our mid-term goal to verify shell scripts in Debian packages, we will need to formalise the file system as well as its built-ins. We will also have to write the automated translation from shell to CoLiS. This translation will have to analyse the scripts statically to determine, among other things, the type of the variables. The first step of this compiler, the parser of POSIX shell scripts, is described in [14].

Acknowledgements. We would like to thanks Mihaela Sighireanu, Ilham Dami, Yann Régis-Gianas, and the other members of the CoLiS project, for their contributions and feedback on the design of the CoLiS language.

References

1. Appel, A.W., McAllester, D.: An indexed model of recursive types for foundational proof-carrying code. ACM Trans. Program. Lang. Syst. **23**(5), 657–683 (2001). http://doi.acm.org/10.1145/504709.504712
2. Barrett, C., Conway, C.L., Deters, M., Hadarean, L., Jovanović, D., King, T., Reynolds, A., Tinelli, C.: CVC4. In: Gopalakrishnan, G., Qadeer, S. (eds.) CAV 2011. LNCS, vol. 6806, pp. 171–177. Springer, Heidelberg (2011). https://doi.org/10.1007/978-3-642-22110-1_14. http://cvc4.cs.stanford.edu/web/
3. Barrett, C., Tinelli, C.: CVC3. In: Damm, W., Hermanns, H. (eds.) CAV 2007. LNCS, vol. 4590, pp. 298–302. Springer, Heidelberg (2007). https://doi.org/10.1007/978-3-540-73368-3_34
4. Bobot, F., Conchon, S., Contejean, E., Iguernelala, M., Lescuyer, S., Mebsout, A.: The Alt-Ergo automated theorem prover (2008). https://alt-ergo.ocamlpro.com/
5. Bobot, F., Filliâtre, J.C., Marché, C., Paskevich, A.: Why3: Shepherd your herd of provers. In: First International Workshop on Intermediate Verification Languages, Boogie 2011, Wrocław, Poland, pp. 53–64, August 2011. http://proval.lri.fr/publications/boogie11final.pdf
6. Braakman, R., Rodin, J., Gilbey, J., Hobley, M.: Checkbashisms. https://sourceforge.net/projects/checkbaskisms/
7. Chen, R., Clochard, M., Marché, C.: A formal proof of a UNIX path resolution algorithm. Research Report RR-8987, Inria Saclay Ile-de-France, December 2016
8. Clochard, M., Filliâtre, J.-C., Marché, C., Paskevich, A.: Formalizing semantics with an automatic program verifier. In: Giannakopoulou, D., Kroening, D. (eds.) VSTTE 2014. LNCS, vol. 8471, pp. 37–51. Springer, Cham (2014). https://doi.org/10.1007/978-3-319-12154-3_3
9. Filliâtre, J.-C., Gondelman, L., Paskevich, A.: The spirit of ghost code. In: Biere, A., Bloem, R. (eds.) CAV 2014. LNCS, vol. 8559, pp. 1–16. Springer, Cham (2014). https://doi.org/10.1007/978-3-319-08867-9_1. https://hal.inria.fr/hal-00873187
10. Greenberg, M.: Understanding the POSIX shell as a programming language. In: Off the Beaten Track 2017, Paris, France, January 2017
11. Holen, V.: Shellcheck. https://github.com/koalaman/shellcheck
12. IEEE and The Open Group: POSIX.1-2008/Cor 1–2013. http://pubs.opengroup.org/onlinepubs/9699919799/
13. Jeannerod, N.: Full Why3 code for the CoLiS language and its proofs. http://toccata.lri.fr/gallery/colis_interpreter.en.html
14. Jeannerod, N., Régis-Gianas, Y., Treinen, R.: Having fun with 31.521 shell scripts. Working paper, April 2017. https://hal.archives-ouvertes.fr/hal-01513750
15. Mazurak, K., Zdancewic, S.: ABASH: finding bugs in bash scripts. In: Proceedings of the 2007 Workshop on Programming Languages and Analysis for Security, PLAS 2007, San Diego, CA, USA, pp. 105–114, June 2007

16. de Moura, L., Bjørner, N.: Z3: an efficient SMT solver. In: Ramakrishnan, C.R., Rehof, J. (eds.) TACAS 2008. LNCS, vol. 4963, pp. 337–340. Springer, Heidelberg (2008). https://doi.org/10.1007/978-3-540-78800-3_24. https://github.com/Z3Prover/z3

17. Schulz, S.: System description: E 0.81. In: Basin, D., Rusinowitch, M. (eds.) IJCAR 2004. LNCS (LNAI), vol. 3097, pp. 223–228. Springer, Heidelberg (2004). https://doi.org/10.1007/978-3-540-25984-8_15. http://wwwlehre.dhbw-stuttgart.de/~sschulz/E/E.html

18. The Debian Policy Mailing List: Debian policy manual. https://www.debian.org/doc/debian-policy/

19. Weidenbach, C., Dimova, D., Fietzke, A., Kumar, R., Suda, M., Wischnewski, P.: SPASS version 3.5. In: Schmidt, R.A. (ed.) CADE 2009. LNCS (LNAI), vol. 5663, pp. 140–145. Springer, Heidelberg (2009). https://doi.org/10.1007/978-3-642-02959-2_10. http://www.mpi-inf.mpg.de/departments/automation-of-logic/software/spass-workbench/classic-spass-theorem-prover/

A Formal Analysis of the Compact Position Reporting Algorithm

Aaron Dutle[1](✉), Mariano Moscato[2], Laura Titolo[2], and César Muñoz[1]

[1] NASA Langley Research Center, Hampton, VA, USA
{aaron.m.dutle,cesar.a.munoz}@nasa.gov
[2] National Institute of Aerospace, Hampton, VA, USA
{mariano.moscato,laura.titolo}@nianet.org

Abstract. The Compact Position Reporting (CPR) algorithm is a safety-critical element of the Automatic Dependent Surveillance - Broadcast (ADS-B) protocol. This protocol enables aircraft to share their current states, i.e., position and velocity, with traffic aircraft in their vicinity. CPR consists of a collection of functions that encode and decode aircraft position data (latitude and longitude). Incorrect position decoding from CPR has been reported to the American and European organizations responsible for the ADS-B standard. This paper presents a formal analysis of the CPR algorithm in the Prototype Verification System (PVS). This formal analysis shows that the published requirements for correct decoding are insufficient, even if computations are assumed to be performed using exact real arithmetic. As a result of this analysis tightened requirements are proposed. These requirements, which are being considered by the standards organizations, are formally proven to guarantee correct decoding under exact real arithmetic. In addition, this paper proposes mathematically equivalent, but computationally simpler forms to several expressions in the CPR functions in order to reduce imprecise calculation.

1 Introduction

Automatic Dependent Surveillance - Broadcast (ADS-B) is arguably the most important change to the operation of aircraft in national and international airspace since the introduction of radar. The Federal Aviation Administration has mandated that ADS-B out capability be installed on almost all general aviation aircraft for most classes of airspace before the year 2020 [3]. ADS-B allows for a wide variety of information to be broadcast from an aircraft to any nearby receiver, enabling many new capabilities, including increased situational awareness for pilots. To enable this technology, the industry and regulatory agencies agreed on a standard message format based on an existing transponder[1]; the 1090 Mhz Mode-S Extended Squitter. The broadcast message is 112 bits, of which 56 bits are the data frame, the rest being aircraft identification, message

---

[1] In fact, there are several allowable transponders and formats, though the majority of current applications use the 1090 ES message described here.

A. Paskevich and T. Wies (Eds.): VSTTE 2017, LNCS 10712, pp. 19–34, 2017.
https://doi.org/10.1007/978-3-319-72308-2_2

type, and parity check information. When the data frame is a position message, 21 bits go to transmitting status information and altitude, leaving 35 bits total for latitude and longitude. If raw latitude and longitude data were taken and approximated to 17 bits each, the resulting precision would be worse than 300 m, which would not be useful for precise navigation.

To remedy this, an algorithm referred to as Compact Position Reporting (CPR) was developed to allow for more accurate position reporting. The general idea is as follows. Each direction (latitude and longitude) is divided into zones approximately 360 nautical miles long, and each zone into 2^{17} bins. The position broadcast corresponds to the centerline of the bin where the aircraft is currently located in. This corresponds to one position in each zone. Depending on the type of decoding being performed, the correct zone is then determined from either a previously known position (for local decoding) or from a matched pair of messages (for global decoding). This allows for position accuracy of approximately 5 m in airborne applications. It should be noted that because the number of longitude degrees in 360 nautical miles differs based on latitude, the number of zones used for calculating the longitude message also depends on the latitude. The function that determines the number of longitude zones, named NL, can be calculated directly from the latitude, but in practice is determined from a pre-calculated lookup table.

Anecdotal evidence from pilots and manufacturers suggests that decoding of CPR messages can lead to incorrect position reports for target aircraft. A priori, these errors could stem from any number of places, including issues with the functions themselves, issues with the requirements under which the functions may be used, numerical computation errors, environmental factors, or any other number of unknown causes. The work described here addresses the first three of these possibilities.

On the practical side, this paper has two significant contributions that are presented in the form of recommendations to the standards organizations in charge of the ADS-B protocol.[2] These recommendations aid in more reliable usage and implementation of the CPR algorithm and do *not* alter the logic of the algorithm in its pure mathematical form. Hence, they do not impact implementations that are already in place and operating reliably. The first recommendation is a tightening of the requirements on conditions for reliable decoding. These strengthened requirements were discovered during the interactive construction of the proof of correctness, during which a class of examples meeting the published requirements for correct decoding were found to give significantly incorrect answers. The second recommendation consists of a collection of simplified expressions for computations performed in the algorithm. These simplifications reduce the numerical complexity of the expressions. This second class of results are intended to aid future implementors of the algorithm in producing simpler and more reliable code.

From the theoretical standpoint, the main contribution of this work is a formal analysis of the CPR algorithm in the Prototype Verification System

---

[2] These organizations are RTCA in the US and EUROCAE in Europe.

(PVS) [6]. The analysis includes a mechanically verified proof that the encoding and decoding functions work as designed under the proposed tightened requirements, and with the assumption of real number computation. This formal analysis is meant to increase confidence that the functions themselves, in their pure mathematical forms, are correct. In addition, the formal specification itself is done in a way that allows the CPR algorithm to be executed in a number of different computational modes. By instantiating a parameter, any of the CPR functions can be evaluated in single precision floating-point, double precision floating-point, or exact rational arithmetic. Transcendental functions that occur in the algorithm can be evaluated in either one of the floating-point implementations or to a user specified precision. This allows for simple comparison of the algorithm's results under different computation models, without the need to write separate versions of the algorithm for each model.

The remainder of the paper is organized as follows. Section 2 presents the formal development of the CPR algorithm, including its main properties and some rationale for how the requirements for proper decoding arise. Section 3 details the main practical results from the formal analysis, including the tightened requirements for proper decoding and a number of computational simplifications or the CPR algorithm. Section 4 discusses a method used to animate the specification of CPR in different computational modes. Finally, Sect. 5 concludes this work.

The formulas and theorems presented in this paper are written in PVS. For readability, this paper uses mathematical notation as opposed to PVS syntax. The formal development is available at http://shemesh.larc.nasa.gov/fm/CPR and requires the latest version the NASA PVS Library, which is available at http://github.com/nasa/pvslib.

2   The Compact Position Reporting Algorithm

This section presents the formal development of the CPR algorithm, which closely follows its standard definition in [7]. The CPR algorithm allows for three different classes of position messages known as *coarse*, *airborne*, and *surface*, which provide accuracies of approximately 165 m, 5 m, and 1.3 m, respectively. For simplicity, the analysis presented in this paper only considers airborne messages. The analysis of the NL function, as well as the mathematical simplifications of computations, apply to all three versions. The requirement tightening, as well as the formal verification of correct decoding, applies only to the airborne version. Generalization to the other classes of messages is not theoretically challenging but would require a non-trivial amount of work.

The principle of the CPR encoding and decoding functions is that transmitting the entire latitude and longitude measurement of a target would be (a) a prohibitively large message for sufficient precision, and (b) wasteful, as the higher order bits of such a transmission are very unlikely to change over a short period of time. To remedy both of these issues, CPR transmits a version of the lower order bits, and uses two different techniques to recover the higher order bits.

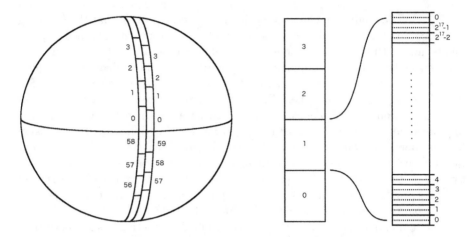

Fig. 1. CPR coordinates for latitude. Latitude is divided into 60 or 59 zones, depending on the format to be broadcast (left). Each zone is then divided into 2^{17} bins (right). The bin the aircraft lies in determines the message.

To accomplish this, CPR divides each of latitude and longitude into a number of equally sized zones. The number of these zones depends on if the message is an *even* or *odd* format, and when encoding longitude, on the current latitude of the target. Each zone is then divided into 2^{17} bins (see Fig. 1). The transmitted information is the number corresponding to the bin that the target is currently in. The difficult part of the process is then determining the correct zone. This is done in the *local* decoding case by identifying a reference position close enough to the target that only one of the possible bins is feasible, and in the *global* decoding case by using an odd and an even message, and employing the difference in size of odd versus even zones.

2.1   Number of Longitude Zones

As previously stated, the number of longitude zones depends on both the format (even or odd) and the present latitude of the target. Note that if the number of zones used for longitude encoding were a constant with respect to latitude, the size of one such zone would vary significantly between the poles and the equator. This would make decoding much more difficult at the poles, since the zone number would change more rapidly at high latitudes. In order to alleviate this, the number of longitude zones is variable depending on the latitude. This NL value is meant to keep the size of a zone nearly constant.

For latitude, the size of an even zone is 6°, while the odd zone is slightly larger, at 360°/59°. To keep longitude similarly spaced, there are 59 even longitude zones at the equator, and one fewer odd zones (the number of odd zones is always one fewer than the number of even zones). This even zone is approximately 360 NMI wide. The number of even zones drops to 58 at the circle of latitude where 58 zones of size 360 NMI suffice to cover the circular latitude distance (assuming a spherical earth). More precisely, the number of longitude zones (or NL value) corresponding to a specific latitude *lat* is given by

$$
NL(lat) = \begin{cases} 59 & \text{if } lat = 0, \\ \left\lfloor 2\pi \left(\arccos\left(1 - \frac{1-\cos\left(\frac{\pi}{30}\right)}{\cos^2\left(\frac{\pi}{180}|lat|\right)} \right) \right)^{-1} \right\rfloor & \text{if } |lat| < 87, \\ 1 & \text{if } |lat| > 87, \\ 2 & \text{otherwise.} \end{cases} \tag{1}
$$

In practice, computing this function is inefficient and would be burdensome to perform each time an encoding is done. Instead, a lookup table of *transition latitudes* is pre-calculated, and the NL value is determined from this table. In PVS, the NL table is specified as follows.

$$
\begin{aligned}
NL\_Table(lat) = \ &\texttt{if } |lat| > transition(2) \texttt{ then } 1 \\
&\texttt{elsif } |lat| > transition(3) \texttt{ then } 2 \\
&\texttt{elsif } |lat| > transition(4) \texttt{ then } 3 \\
&\qquad\vdots \\
&\texttt{elsif } |lat| > transition(59) \texttt{ then } 58 \\
&\texttt{else } 59 \\
&\texttt{endif.}
\end{aligned}
$$

The transition latitudes are given for a value *nl* from 2 to 59 by the following formula.

$$
transition(nl) = \frac{180}{\pi} \arccos\left(\sqrt{\frac{1 - \cos(\pi/30)}{1 - \cos(2\pi/nl)}} \right). \tag{2}
$$

The following theorem about the correctness of this table is proven in PVS.

Theorem 1. *For every latitude value lat,*

$$
NL(lat) = NL\_Table(lat).
$$

During the process of encoding, extra precaution must be taken to ensure that the NL value used for the longitude encoding is consistent with the latitude broadcast. To do so, the latitude message to be broadcast is decoded onboard, and *this* latitude is used to determine the NL value, ensuring that the receiver can decode the longitude message consistently with the broadcaster.

2.2 Encoding

As mentioned in Sect. 1, the position message consists of 35 bits of information. The first bit is used to describe the *format* of the message. The message is called even if the bit is 0, and odd if the bit is 1.

Here, and throughout all computation in CPR, the mod function is defined by

$$\mod(x, y) = x - y \left\lfloor \frac{x}{y} \right\rfloor. \tag{3}$$

While this is fairly standard for mathematics, it differs from the version used in practice in standard programming languages, where the function is generally restricted to integers.

Let $dlat_i = 360/(60 - i)$, where i is the format bit of the message to be sent. The value of $dlat_i$ is the size of a latitude zone. Next, for a latitude value lat, compute

$$YZ_i = \left\lfloor 2^{17} \frac{\mod(lat, dlat_i)}{dlat_i} + \frac{1}{2} \right\rfloor. \tag{4}$$

The latitude message, $\widehat{YZ}_i$, is then the last 17 bits of this value. That is,

$$\widehat{YZ}_i = \mod(YZ_i, 2^{17}). \tag{5}$$

In Formula (4), $\mod(lat, dlat_i)$ corresponds to the distance that lat is from the bottom of a zone edge. Thus $\frac{\mod(lat, dlat_i)}{dlat_i}$ denotes the fractional amount that lat is into this zone. Multiplying by 2^{17} gives a value between 0 and 2^{17}, while $\lfloor x + \frac{1}{2} \rfloor$ rounds a number x to the nearest integer. The interval of latitudes inside a zone that are mapped to a particular number is referred to as a *bin*, and the number they map to as the *bin number*. The latitude to be recovered is in the center of this interval, and is referred to as the *bin centerline*. The final truncation to 17 bits to determine $\widehat{YZ}_i$ may appear to discard some information, but in actuality only affects half of a bin at the top of a zone, and is accounted for by the adjacent zone.

In order to compute the longitude portion of the message, the NL value of the encoded latitude must be determined. To do so, the latitude that is intended to be decoded is computed as

$$rlat = dlat_i \left(\left\lfloor \frac{lat}{dlat_i} \right\rfloor + \frac{YZ_i}{2^{17}} \right).$$

The NL value of $rlat$ is then used to compute the longitude equivalent of $dlat_i$ as follows.

$$dlon_i = 360/\max\{1, NL(rlat) - i\}. \tag{6}$$

Note that the denominator in the above expression uses the max operator for the case of latitudes beyond $\pm 87°$, where there is only one longitude zone. In this case the even and odd longitude encodings are identical.

With $dlon_i$ calculated, the encoding of a longitude lon is nearly identical to that of latitude.

$$XZ_i = \left\lfloor 2^{17} \frac{\text{mod}(lon, dlon_i)}{dlon_i} + \frac{1}{2} \right\rfloor . \tag{7}$$

The longitude message is the final 17 bits of this value.

$$\widehat{XZ}_i = \text{mod}(XZ_i, 2^{17}). \tag{8}$$

The final message to be broadcast is then the concatenated string of bits $(i, \widehat{YZ}_i, \widehat{XZ}_i)$ (see Fig. 2). In theory, it would be desirable to have the messages sent strictly alternate between odd and even. In practice, the format for broadcast is chosen by any number of methods (including randomly) to ensure an equiprobable distribution.

Format 1 bit	Latitude 17 bits	Longitude 17 bits

Fig. 2. The 35 bit CPR message. One bit determining the format, and 17 each for latitude and longitude.

It is worth noting that every latitude lat can be exactly and uniquely determined by the following formula.

$$lat = dlat_i \left(\left\lfloor \frac{lat}{dlat_i} \right\rfloor + \frac{2^{17} \text{mod}(lat, dlat_i)/dlat_i}{2^{17}} \right) . \tag{9}$$

The only difference between this and the value intended to be recovered is in the rounding of $2^{17} \text{mod}(lat, dlat_i)/dlat_i$ to the nearest integer, which induces an error of at most $1/2$. Hence the upper bound for the difference between a latitude and its correctly encoded and decoded value is $dlat_i/2^{18}$. Similarly, a longitude and its recovered value should differ by no more than $dlon_i/2^{18}$.

The formal development includes specification of the encoding algorithm as a single function $encode$ that takes as parameters the format i, and lat, lon, the latitude and longitude to encode, and returns the pair $(\widehat{YZ}_i, \widehat{XZ}_i)$ containing the encoded latitude and longitude. The following lemma, formally proven in PVS, ensures that the encoding fits into the available space for broadcast.

Theorem 2. *For all* $i \in \{0, 1\}$, *latitudes* lat *and longitudes* lon, *if* $(Y, X) = encode(i, lat, lon)$, *then* Y *and* X *are integers and*

$$0 \le X, Y < 2^{17}.$$

2.3   Local Decoding

Since a broadcast message corresponds to a position inside each zone, in order to recover the correct position, one needs only to determine which zone is the correct one, and in the case of longitude, how many zones there are.

Local decoding does this using a reference position that is known to be near the broadcast position. This can be a previously decoded position, or known by some other means. The concept is simple, and uses the observation that the interval one zone wide centered around any position contains exactly one point corresponding to each bin centerline.

From this reasoning, it would seem to follow that if the target and the reference position are separated by at most half the length of a zone, the decoding should be reliable. This is the requirement given in the standards document [7] for local decoding. However, during the formal analysis, it was discovered that this is too generous, as proven in Theorem 3 below.

The local decoding uses the following formula to calculate the zone index number j of the target using the format i, the latitude message $\widehat{YZ}_i$, and a reference latitude lat_{ref}.

$$j = \left\lfloor \frac{lat_{\mathrm{ref}}}{dlat_i} \right\rfloor + \left\lfloor \frac{1}{2} + \frac{\mathrm{mod}(lat_{\mathrm{ref}}, dlat_i)}{dlat_i} - \frac{\widehat{YZ}_i}{2^{17}} \right\rfloor. \tag{10}$$

The first term in this sum calculates which zone the reference latitude lies in, while the second term adjusts it by -1, 0, or 1 based on the difference between the reference latitude and the broadcast message. This value is then used to compute the recovered latitude $rlat$ using the following formula.

$$rlat = dlat_i \left(j + \frac{\widehat{YZ}_i}{2^{17}} \right). \tag{11}$$

This decoded latitude is used to determine the NL value used for encoding the longitude, which is then used to determine the value of $dlon_i$ by Formula (6). Using $dlon_i$, a reference longitude lon_{ref}, and the longitude message $\widehat{XZ}_i$, the longitude zone index m and recovered longitude $rlon$ are determined nearly identically to the latitude case.

$$m = \left\lfloor \frac{lon_{\mathrm{ref}}}{dlon_i} \right\rfloor + \left\lfloor \frac{1}{2} + \frac{\mathrm{mod}(lon_{\mathrm{ref}}, dlon_i)}{dlon_i} - \frac{\widehat{XZ}_i}{2^{17}} \right\rfloor. \tag{12}$$

$$rlon = dlon_i \left(m + \frac{\widehat{XZ}_i}{2^{17}} \right). \tag{13}$$

Local decoding is specified as a pair of functions $Rlat_i$ and $Rlon_i$. The function $Rlat_i$ takes as input a reference latitude lat_{ref}, a format i, and a non-negative integer Y less than 2^{17} meant to be an encoded latitude. The function $Rlon_i$ takes an entire reference position $lat_{\mathrm{ref}}, lon_{\mathrm{ref}}$, a format i and a pair Y, X of non-negative integers at most 2^{17} meant to be the encoded pair. The longitude decoding requires the latitude input in order to calculate the correct NL value to decode with.

The two main theorems concerning local decoding are with respect to the requirements for correct decoding. The first states that the published requirements are not sufficient for local decoding.

Theorem 3. *For each format i, there exist latitudes lat, lat_{ref} with $|lat - lat_{\text{ref}}| < \frac{dlat_i}{2}$, but*

$$|lat - Rlat_i(lat_{\text{ref}}, i, \widehat{YZ_i})| > 5.9,$$

where $(\widehat{YZ_i}, \widehat{XZ_i}) = encode(i, lat, lon)$.

The value of 5.9 is in degrees latitude, which at a longitude of 0 is more than 300 nautical miles. This theorem is formally proven in PVS by giving actual latitude values that decode incorrectly. One such pair, for even encoding, is

$$lat = 71582788 * 360/2^{32} \approx 5.99999997765,$$

$$lat_{ref} = 35791394 * 360/2^{32} \approx 2.99999998882.$$

The next theorem states that local decoding does work properly for the set of tightened requirements, which reduce the bound between position and reference by $1/2$ bin.

Theorem 4. *For all pairs of positions $(lat, lon), (lat_{\text{ref}}, lon_{\text{ref}})$, let $(\widehat{YZ_i}, \widehat{XZ_i}) = encode(i, lat, lon)$. If*

$$|lat - lat_{\text{ref}}| < \frac{dlat_i}{2} - \frac{dlat_i}{2^{18}},$$

then

$$|lat - Rlat_i(lat_{\text{ref}}, i, \widehat{YZ_i})| \leq \frac{dlat_i}{2^{18}},$$

Furthermore, if $dlon_i$ is calculated using this decoded latitude, and

$$|lon - lon_{\text{ref}}| < \frac{don_i}{2} - \frac{dlon_i}{2^{18}},$$

then

$$|lon - Rlon_i(lat_{\text{ref}}, lon_{\text{ref}}, i, \widehat{YZ_i}, \widehat{XZ_i})| \leq \frac{dlon_i}{2^{18}}.$$

2.4   Global Decoding

Global decoding is used when an approximate position for the target is unknown. This can occur when a target is first encountered, or when messages have not been received for a significant amount of time.

Similar to local decoding, the receiver must determine the correct zone in which the broadcast message lies, as well as (for longitude) the number of zones. Global decoding does this through means of a pair of messages, one of each format type. Using a method that is essentially the Chinese Remainder Theorem, the algorithm determines the number of *zone offsets* (the difference between an odd zone length and an even zone length) from the origin (either equator or prime meridian) to the broadcast position. This can be used to determine the zone for either message type, and hence used to decode either message. The most recently received message is used to provide more accurate information. Similar to the local decoding, it seems that this should tolerate pairs of positions separated by no more than half of a zone offset, since this is the critical parameter in the computation. The formal analysis shows that this is too generous, as proven in Theorem 5 below.

The first step in global decoding is to determine j, which is the number of zone offsets between the southern boundaries of the two encoded latitudes.

$$j = \left\lfloor \left| \frac{59\,\widehat{YZ}_0 - 60\,\widehat{YZ}_1}{2^{17}} + \frac{1}{2} \right| \right\rfloor.$$

In order to convert this into the correct zone index number for the even or odd message to be decoded, the positive value modulo $60 - i$ is calculated. This is then used to determine the recovered latitude, as follows.

$$rlat = dlat_i \left(\mod(j, 60 - i) + \frac{\widehat{YZ}_i}{2^{17}} \right). \tag{14}$$

For global decoding of longitude, care must be taken that both the even and odd messages being used were calculated with the same number of zones. As such, *both* even and odd latitude messages are decoded, and the NL values for each are determined. If they differ, the messages are discarded and not decoded until further broadcast meet this criterion. In the case both recovered latitudes have the same NL value, longitude decoding proceeds as follows, where nl is the common NL value computed, $dlon_i$ is calculated according to Formula (6), and $n_i = \max\{nl - i, 1\}$.

Calculate m, the number of zone offsets between the western zone boundaries of the messages.

$$m = \left\lfloor \left| \frac{(nl - 1)\,\widehat{XZ}_0 - nl\,\widehat{XZ}_1}{2^{17}} + \frac{1}{2} \right| \right\rfloor.$$

Convert this value to a zone index number by taking the positive value modulo n_i, and use this to determine the recovered longitude.

$$rlon = dlon_i \left(\mod(m, n_i) + \frac{\widehat{XZ}_i}{2^{17}} \right). \tag{15}$$

Global decoding is specified as a pair of functions $Rlat_g$ and $Rlon_g$. The function $Rlat_g$ takes as inputs a format i and natural numbers Y_0, Y_1 meant to be odd and even latitude messages. The function $Rlon_g$ takes as inputs a format i and four numbers Y_0, Y_1, X_0, X_1 meant to describe odd and even messages of latitude and longitude. Each latitude message is decoded, and the NL value computed. If the values do not match, the computation is aborted. If they do, the function returns both the even and odd decoded longitude.

As with local decoding, there are two accompanying theorems. In the following, the latitude zone offset is denoted by ZO_{lat}. This is calculated as $ZO_{lat} = dlat_1 - dlat_0$. Similarly, $ZO_{lon} = dlon_1 - dlon_0$ where it is assumed that the NL value used is known from the context.

Theorem 5. *For each format i, there exist latitudes lat_0, lat_1 with $|lat_0 - lat_1| < \frac{ZO_{lat}}{2}$, but*

$$|lat - Rlat_g(i, \widehat{YZ}_0, \widehat{YZ}_1)| > 5.9,$$

where $(\widehat{YZ}_j, \widehat{XZ}_j) = encode(j, lat, lon)$ for $j \in \{0, 1\}$.

Again, the units of 5.9 are degrees latitude, which corresponds to over 300 nautical miles at longitude 0. This theorem is formally proven in PVS by giving actual latitude values that decode incorrectly. One such pair, which decodes incorrectly using either format, is

$$lat_0 = 363373617 * 360/2^{32} \approx 30.4576247279,$$
$$lat_1 = 363980245 * 360/2^{32} \approx 30.5084716994.$$

The next theorem states that the tightened requirements, given by shrinking the bound by the size of one odd bin, suffice for proper global decoding.

Theorem 6. *For all pairs of positions $(lat_0, lon_0), (lat_1, lon_1)$, let $(\widehat{YZ}_j, \widehat{XZ}_j) = encode(j, lat, lon)$ for $j \in \{0, 1\}$. If*

$$|lat_0 - lat_1| < \frac{ZO_{lat}}{2} - \frac{dlat_1}{2^{17}},$$

then

$$|lat - Rlat_g(i, \widehat{YZ}_0, \widehat{YZ}_1)| \le \frac{dlat_i}{2^{18}},$$

for each $i \in \{0, 1\}$. Furthermore, if these decoded latitudes have a common NL value, $dlon_i$ is calculated using this value, and

$$|lon - lon_{\text{ref}}| < \frac{ZO_{lon}}{2} - \frac{dlon_1}{2^{17}},$$

then

$$|lon - Rlon_g(i, \widehat{YZ}_0, \widehat{YZ}_1, \widehat{XZ}_0, \widehat{XZ}_1)| \le \frac{dlon_i}{2^{18}}$$

for each $i \in \{0, 1\}$.

These correctness theorems, while lacking the need for groundbreaking mathematical insight to formulate, are nonetheless long and difficult proofs to develop in an interactive proof system. For example, the proof of the correctness for only the longitude portion of the global correctness theorem is composed of 763 individual proof commands.

3   Practical Results

The main practical results of the formal analysis conducted are essentially in two categories. The first set of results, presented in Sect. 3.1, concerns the requirements for both local and global decoding. As discussed in Sects. 2.3 and 2.4, the formal analysis led to the discovery of examples that meet the stated algorithmic requirements for decoding, but decode incorrectly. A set of tightened requirements were discovered that are formally proven to guarantee correct decoding. In addition to the algorithmic requirements, an arguably *less* restrictive operational requirement is developed for global decoding. This proposed requirement allows for CPR applications for aircraft with a much wider performance envelope than the original specification, as well as a longer possible time delay between received messages.

The second set of results, in Sect. 3.2, examine expressions in the CPR algorithm, and give mathematically equivalent, but in a simpler or numerically more stable form. These equivalent expressions are meant to assist implementors of the CPR algorithm in creating more reliable code.

3.1   Decoding Requirements

The requirement stated in [7] for local decoding is that the reference position and the encoded position must be within $1/2$ of a zone to guarantee correct decoding. As mentioned in Sect. 2, this stems from the fact that an interval one zone long, centered at the reference position, encounters exactly one bin centerline for each possible broadcast message, so only one recovered position is possible. While this statement is true, it is not necessarily true that the position being within $1/2$ zone from the reference position ensures that the corresponding *bin centerline* is within $1/2$ zone of the reference position. For example, if the reference position is slightly above a bin centerline, then the half-bin at the bottom of the 1 zone length interval centered around the reference position is mapped to a bin centerline that occurs *outside* of this one zone region. The bin centerline with the same number, but lying inside the one zone region, occurs at the *top* of this region. Hence local decoding in this case is inaccurate by the size of one zone, approximately 360 nautical miles, as is the case in the example after Theorem 3.

During the formal analysis, several examples illustrating this phenomenon were discovered, and this discovery led to the tightened requirement of the target position and reference position being required to be separated by no more than half a zone minus half of a bin for reliable local decoding.

For global decoding, the requirement in [7] is that the two messages used are received within ten seconds of each other. This is based on two conditions. The first condition is a restriction on the performance limits of the aircraft to which the standard applies. The second condition is an algorithmic restriction. The document states that the positions for the odd and even messages be separated by no more than half of a zone offset to ensure reliable decoding. As with local decoding, this algorithmic condition is nearly correct, but fails to account for the positions not being on the bin centerline. The *correct* requirement is that the bin centerlines of the encoded positions be within 1/2 zone offset. Since a position is at most half of a bin size away from the corresponding centerline, shrinking the original requirement by one odd bin size is sufficient to guarantee correct global decoding. As with the local decoding, examples were discovered that meet the published algorithmic requirement, but decode incorrectly by the length of one zone, approximately 360 nautical miles, as is the case in the example after Theorem 5.

The published global decoding requirement enforces the closeness of the original positions of the two messages by means of a limit on the time between two messages, paired with a limit on the speed of the aircraft. While this is a testable and practical method of enforcing the algorithmic requirements, it limits the applications that can be correctly decoded due to speed assumptions[3], while artificially limiting the time between messages for slow moving targets.

To loosen this restriction, while still providing a testable and practical method for guaranteeing that the even and odd pair of messages meet the global decoding algorithmic requirements, the following alternative requirement is proposed.

The receiver waits for three alternating messages, either even-odd-even or odd-even-odd, where it is known (through a time restriction or some other means) that the first and last messages were broadcast without having travelled more than 1/2 zone. In addition, the difference between the values of the first and last messages transmitted should be less than 1000 (modulo 2^{17}). The second condition ensures that the bookend messages were broadcast within 1/2 zone offset (minus an odd zone) of each other, unless they are separated by a full zone, which is impossible by the first condition. For longitude decoding, the NL value of all three latitudes messages must also stay constant. The proposed requirement allows for a much longer time frame to collect messages, even with an increased performance threshold for the target. It also more directly enforces the actual algorithmic requirement.

3.2   Numerical Simplifications

In addition to the formal specification and proof of the algorithm with the tightened requirements, the formal analysis revealed several expressions in the CPR algorithm that can be simplified or rewritten in a way that is mathematically equivalent, but numerically simpler. Each pair of equivalent formulas was specified in PVS, and proven to be equal.

The formula for calculating the NL table, used as a lookup-table for calculating NL values for a latitude is given in Formula (2). An equivalent version, removing four operations in total, is defined as follows.

$$lat_{NL}(nl) = \frac{180}{\pi} \arccos \left(\frac{\sin(\pi/60)}{\sin(\pi/nl)} \right). \tag{16}$$

---

[3] This is an issue that affects the usability of ADS-B for hypersonic aircraft and for sub-orbital applications, both of which are poised to become more ubiquitous in the near future.

The remainder of the simplifications essentially rely on two observations. The first observation is that when the mod operator is divided by its second argument, a cancellation can be made instead of a division. That is,

$$\frac{\text{mod}(a, b)}{b} = \frac{a - b * \lfloor \frac{a}{b} \rfloor}{b} = \frac{a}{b} - \lfloor \frac{a}{b} \rfloor. \tag{17}$$

The second observation is that the floor function and addition of integers are commutative. That is, for any number x and any integer z,

$$\lfloor z + x \rfloor = z + \lfloor x \rfloor. \tag{18}$$

Using the simplifications of Formula (17) and Formula (18) on the local decoding formulas (10) and (12) yields

$$j = \left\lfloor \frac{1}{2} + \frac{lat_{\text{ref}}}{dlat_i} - \frac{\widehat{YZ}_i}{2^{17}} \right\rfloor, \tag{19}$$

and

$$m = \left\lfloor \frac{1}{2} + \frac{lon_{\text{ref}}}{dlon_i} - \frac{\widehat{YZ}_i}{2^{17}} \right\rfloor. \tag{20}$$

The most significant simplification is in the encoding algorithm, and applies to both latitude and longitude. Let x denote the position, either latitude or longitude, and let dl denote $dlat_i$ or $dlon_i$ accordingly, then Formula (4) and Formula (7) can be simplified as follows.

$$\left\lfloor 2^{17} \frac{\text{mod}(x, dl)}{dl} + \frac{1}{2} \right\rfloor = \left\lfloor 2^{17} \frac{x}{dl} + \frac{1}{2} \right\rfloor - 2^{17} \left\lfloor \frac{x}{dl} \right\rfloor. \tag{21}$$

The simplifications presented in this section reduce the number of operations overall and remove computation of several expressions that strictly cancel mathematically. For instance, on the right hand side of Formula (21), once the term x/dl is computed, the subtracted term can be calculated exactly as an integer.

4   Animation of the CPR Specification

In contrast to a programming language, PVS is designed to manipulate and reason about real numbers. For example, the value of π in PVS is the real, irrational, transcendental number that exactly relates a diameter to a circumference. In this paper, the exact, ideal version of an algorithm or quantity is referred to as the *platonic* version. For instance, the functions presented in Sect. 2 correspond to the platonic version of CPR. However, since the CPR algorithm is implemented on actual hardware, numerical imprecisions are unavoidable. In addition to the formal verification of the CPR algorithm, the formal specification of CPR was used to compare on a set of inputs the evaluation of the platonic algorithm versus the algorithm implemented in both single and double precision floating-point.

To achieve this goal, the CPR specification is written in a way that arithmetic operators can be ground-evaluated in PVSio [5] using *semantic attachments* [1]. PVSio allows for the evaluation of PVS functional specifications using the ground evaluator. A semantic attachment is a Lisp function that is called by the ground evaluator when a particular function is not evaluable in PVS, e.g., square root, trigonometric functions, etc. Since semantic attachments are external to the PVS logic, ground evaluations in PVSio may not be logically sound. However, PVSio provides a practical way to quickly test a PVS specification on concrete values. See [2] for more details.

PVSio and, in particular, semantic attachments enable the evaluation of CPR functions on concrete inputs using different computation models, e.g., real arithmetic, single or double floating-point arithmetic, etc. Using this method on the latitude encoding, it has been checked that the right-hand side of Formula (21) performed in double precision floating-point agrees with the platonic calculation for all angular weighted binary (AWB) latitudes [4]. These are latitudes of the form $n \cdot \frac{360}{2^{32}}$ with n a whole number, and are a widely used format for providing position. Furthermore, a test of the standard formulation of the latitude encoding using Formula (4) revealed that when performed with double precision floating-point, the encoding differed from the correct value by 1 in 27,259 cases. While this is a relatively small number compared to the 2^{32} test cases, it shows how different expressions of the same quantity may lead to numerical errors in calculation.

The animation of the CPR specification also confirmed reported observations that a straightforward implementation of CPR in single precision floating-point arithmetic is unsound. The Appendix T of [7] includes several tables containing the expected output of the CPR algorithm on a reduced set of AWB latitudes. Encoding these latitudes in a single precision implementation of Formula (4), resulted in 162 wrong encodings (with respect to the expected output in Appendix T) over a total of 232 input AWB latitudes. In the case of local decoding, 46 encoded positions over a total of 116 were wrongly decoded by using single precision floating-point numbers. Finally, in the case of global decoding, the number of wrong cases detected was 28 out of 116.

5   Conclusion

This paper presents a formal analysis of the CPR algorithm used for encoding and decoding position messages for ADS-B broadcast. The formal analysis includes a formal specification in PVS and a proof of the correctness of the algorithm for a set of tightened requirements from those originally proposed. These tightened requirements are also shown to be necessary, by proving that there exist positions meeting the original requirements, but not decoding to a correct position.

The paper also presents a collection of simplifications of some the mathematical expressions used in the algorithm, which are proven to be mathematically equivalent to the original expressions, but also shown to be numerically simpler in the sense that the expressions evaluate in floating-point to values closer to the platonic computation. The evaluation of these simplifications was aided by an approach in the formal specification that allowed for the evaluation of arithmetic operators in a variety of computation models. This approach may be useful outside of the current work to examine the effect of numerical imprecision on the floating-point implementation of a platonic algorithm.

A possible further direction is the completion of the formal analysis for the two types of CPR messages, coarse and surface, that were not addressed in this work. This would not be theoretically difficult, as the existing specification and proofs would serve as a clear roadmap, but would take a significant amount of work. An area of current research is the formal numerical analysis of fixed-point and floating-point implementations of CPR. This analysis will enable the development of formally verified CPR implementations that could serve as reference implementations of the standard mathematical definition.

References

1. Crow, J., Owre, S., Rushby, J., Shankar, N., Stringer-Calvert, D.: Evaluating, testing, and animating PVS specifications. Technical report, Computer Science Laboratory, SRI International, Menlo Park, CA, March 2001. http://www.csl.sri.com/users/rushby/abstracts/attachments
2. Dutle, A.M., Muñoz, C.A., Narkawicz, A.J., Butler, R.W.: Software validation via model animation. In: Blanchette, J.C., Kosmatov, N. (eds.) TAP 2015. LNCS, vol. 9154, pp. 92–108. Springer, Cham (2015). https://doi.org/10.1007/978-3-319-21215-9_6
3. Code of Federal Regulations: Automatic Dependent Surveillance-Broadcast (ADS-B) out equipment and use, 91 C.F.R., Sect. 225 (2015)
4. ICAO: Manual on the Universal Access Transceiver (UAT). Doc (International Civil Aviation Organization), vol. 9861 (2012)
5. Muñoz, C.: Rapid prototyping in PVS. Contractor Report NASA/CR-2003-212418, NASA, Langley Research Center, Hampton, VA, USA, May 2003
6. Owre, S., Rushby, J.M., Shankar, N.: PVS: a prototype verification system. In: Kapur, D. (ed.) CADE 1992. LNCS, vol. 607, pp. 748–752. Springer, Heidelberg (1992). https://doi.org/10.1007/3-540-55602-8_217
7. RTCA SC-186: RTCA-DO-260B, minimum operational performance standards for 1090 MHz extended squitter Automatic Dependent Surveillance - Broadcast (ADS-B) and Traffic Information Services - Broadcast (TIS-B), December 2009

Proving JDK's Dual Pivot Quicksort Correct

Bernhard Beckert, Jonas Schiffl, Peter H. Schmitt, and Mattias Ulbrich(✉)

Karlsruhe Institute of Technology, Karlsruhe, Germany
mattias.ulbrich@kit.edu

Abstract. Sorting is a fundamental functionality in libraries, for which efficiency is crucial. Correctness of the highly optimised implementations is often taken for granted. De Gouw et al. have shown that this certainty is deceptive by revealing a bug in the Java Development Kit (JDK) implementation of TimSort.

We have formally analysed the other implementation of sorting in the JDK standard library: A highly efficient implementation of a dual pivot quicksort algorithm. We were able to deductively prove that the algorithm implementation is correct. However, a loop invariant which is annotated to the source code does not hold.

This paper reports on how an existing piece of non-trivial Java software can be made accessible to deductive verification and successfully proved correct, for which we use the Java verification engine KeY.

1 Introduction

Sorting is an important functionality in every standard library. But implementing sorting efficiently is a non-trivial task. Algorithms found in state-of-the-art runtime libraries are highly optimised for cache-efficient execution on multi-core platforms. De Gouw et al. [9] attempted to prove termination and absence of runtime exceptions of the TimSort implementation used in the Java Development KIT (JDK) for sorting object arrays. In the course of that attempt, they detected a bug in the implementation, attracting a considerable amount of public attention. TimSort is not the only sorting implementation in the JDK: Arrays of primitive data types, such as int, float, or char, are sorted using an implementation of the Dual Pivot Quicksort (DPQS) algorithm [21], a very efficient variation of traditional quicksort. This paper reports on the successful verification of the highly optimised Java routine that implements the DPQS algorithm in the JDK (both oracle's JDK and OpenJDK). We used the deductive verification engine KeY [3] for the task. In this paper, we show how we were able to accommodate the code, which is not at all designed in a verification-friendly fashion, for interactive program verification. The techniques used to make the proof feasible can be transferred to other verification scenarios for real code.

We were able to fully verify correctness of the algorithm and did not find a bug in the code. We found, however, like the authors of the TimSort investigation, that a loop invariant annotated as a comment to the code does actually not hold.

© Springer International Publishing AG 2017
A. Paskevich and T. Wies (Eds.): VSTTE 2017, LNCS 10712, pp. 35–48, 2017.
https://doi.org/10.1007/978-3-319-72308-2_3

Contributions. We present a mechanised formal proof that the dual pivot quick-sort implementation used in the JDK *does* sort an array in ascending order. This consists of proving two properties: The resulting array is sorted, and it is a permutation of the original input. In the course of the verification, lemmas about array permutations have been identified, formulated and proved correct. These can also be used, e.g., for the verification of other permutation-based sorting implementations. Moreover, the paper lists refactoring mechanisms which maintain the semantics of a program but make it more accessible to formal verification. The specifications in the form of annotations to the source code and the proofs in KeY can be obtained from the companion webpage [1].

Structure of the paper. First we present the algorithm and its implementation (Sect. 2) and the employed technologies – the Java Modeling Language and the KeY system (Sect. 3). Then, in the main part of the paper, we describe the specification and report on how the program was made more accessible to the KeY tool and how it was proven correct (Sect. 4). The required effort for the specification and verification is discussed in Sect. 5. In Sect. 6, we discuss our discovery of an invariant contained as comment in the implementation that is not always satisfied by the code. We draw conclusions in Sect. 7.

Related work. We did not find many publications, let alone high profile publications, specifically on formal machine-assisted verification of efficient sorting implementations. But, what we found shows a marked line of development in sorting algorithm verification that parallels the development in the field of program verification in general. Before 2000, subsets or even idealised versions of programming languages were targeted and machine support was mostly restricted to proof checking. The verification of merge sort by Black et al. [5] may serve as an example. A next stage was reached by using an interactive verification system to verify single-thread programs in a real programming language, but written by the people doing the verification. An example is the verification of a counting sort and radix sort program [8]. Another kind of programs written for verification uses a programming language designed for this purpose. As described in a lab report [2], a whole array of sorting programs (selection, bubble, insertion, and quick sort) written in Dafny are proved correct; Leino and Lucio [16] report on the verification of merge sort in Dafny. In the final and challenging stage, programs are verified as they are implemented and employed by a great number of users, as has been done in the much acclaimed paper by de Gouw et al. [9]. One should notice, however, that only normal termination of the TimSort program was analysed. Galeotti et al. [7] successfully applied their verification framework, which automatically infers loop invariants using a combination of different static and dynamic techniques, to implementations of less complex algorithms from the JDK package java.util. Sorting algorithms were, however, not considered in this approach.

2   Dual Pivot Quicksort

2.1   The Abstract Algorithm

While the worst-case runtime complexity of comparison-based sorting algorithms is known to be in the class $\mathcal{O}(n \log(n))$, there have been numerous attempts to reduce their "practical" complexity. In 2009, Vladimir Yaroslavskiy [21] suggested a variation of the quicksort algorithm [10] that uses two pivot elements. In conventional quicksort, one element – the pivot – of the array is chosen, and the array elements are rearranged into two sections according to how they compare against the pivot. In the dual pivot variant, the partition separates the elements into the three sections according to their comparison against both pivots. Figure 1 exemplarily illustrates the arrangement of the array elements after the partitioning step. The pivot elements are shown as hatched bars. The first part (green in the figure) contains all elements smaller than the smaller pivot element, the middle part (blue) contains all elements between the pivots (inclusively), and the third part (red) consists of all elements greater than the larger pivot. The algorithm proceeds by sorting the three parts recursively by the same principle.

Extensive benchmarking gave empirical evidence that dual pivot sorting performs substantially better on the Java VM than the originally supplied sorting algorithms. This led to the adoption of Yaroslavskiy's Dual Pivot Quicksort implementation as the OpenJDK 7 standard sorting function for primitive data type arrays in 2011. Conclusive explanations for its superior performance appear to be surprisingly hard to find, but evidence points to cache effects [13]. Wild et al. [20] conclude: *"The efficiency of Yaroslavskiy's algorithm in practice is caused by advanced features of modern processors. In models that assign constant cost contributions to single instructions – i.e., locality of memory accesses and instruction pipelining are ignored – classic Quicksort is more efficient."*

2.2   JDK's Implementation

Like many modern programming languages, the standard library of Java uses a portfolio of various sorting algorithms in different contexts. The standard sorting

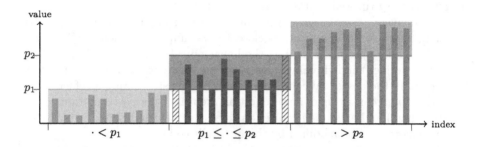

Fig. 1. Illustration of a dual pivot partition (Colour figure online)

algorithm for object arrays in general is TimSort, an optimised version of merge sort. Calling `sort()` for a primitive data type array, however, leads to the Dual Pivot Quicksort class.

This class, consisting of more than 3000 lines of code, makes use of no less than four different algorithms: Merge sort, insertion sort, counting sort, and quicksort. For the `byte`, `char`, or `short` data types, counting sort is used. Arrays of other primitive data types are first scanned once to determine whether they consist of a small number of already sorted sequences; if that is the case, merge sort is used, taking advantage of the existing sorted array parts. For arrays with less than 47 entries, insertion sort is used – in spite of its worse average-case performance – to avoid the comparatively large overhead of quicksort or merge sort.

In all other cases, quicksort is used (e.g., for large integer arrays that are not partially sorted). This "default" option is the subject of our correctness proof. The algorithm itself uses two different partitioning schemes. First, five elements are drawn evenly distributed from the array range and compared; if they are distinct, the range is partitioned with two pivot elements; otherwise, the classical single-pivot three-way partition introduced by Hoare [10] is applied.

The method realising the central part of dual-pivot sorting comprises some 340 lines of Java code containing many optimisations that make the code less comprehensible and more susceptible to oversights. One example of such an optimisation is the approximation of `len / 7` by `(len >> 3) + (len >> 6) + 1`.

Our verification shows that despite these intricacies, the implementation correctly sorts its input. An indication for the fact that the algorithm is difficult to understand is a loop invariant added as a comment to the source code which is not always preserved by the implementation (see Sect. 6).

3   Background

3.1   Java Modeling Language

The Java Modeling Language (JML) [14] is a behavioural interface specification language which follows the principle of design by contract. It is the de facto standard language for the formal specification of Java programs. JML specifications are added to the program source code as special comments beginning with `/*@`. An introductory tutorial to JML can be found in [11].

The language possesses several means for structuring data on more abstract levels, but also for a specification close to the implementation. JML allows method-modular specifications, i.e., the behaviour of each method is described (and later verified) individually. This keeps the complexity of the verification task down. In the design by contract philosophy, the structuring artefact is the *method contract* consisting of a precondition (`requires`), a postcondition condition (`ensures`) and a *framing clause* (`assignable`), which describes which part of the memory may be modified by the method's code.

All side-effect-free Java expressions may be used in specifications, in addition to specification-specific constructs like the implication connective `==>`, or the quantifiers \forall and \exists. The expression (\forall T x; ϕ; ψ) evaluates to true iff ψ is true for all elements of the type T that satisfy ϕ. It is equivalent to (\forall T x; ϕ ==> ψ).

Besides the concept of method contracts, loop specifications are particularly important for this verification project. Loop specifications are comprised of a loop invariant (loop_invariant), a termination measure or variant (decreases), and a loop framing clause (assignable). Moreover, JML supports *block contracts*, i.e., the specification of (non-loop) statement blocks with local postconditions (ensures). Block contracts can be used to abstract from the effects of a block. This allows breaking down larger methods into smaller code pieces as the code block can be analysed separately from the enclosing method context.

JML is exception- and termination-aware, and we annotated all methods as "normal_behavior" indicating that they are expected to terminate normally when called with a satisfied precondition.

The JML dialect that we consider in this work has a built-in data type \seq for finite sequences (of values or object references). We also make use of an extension to JML that allows marking specification clauses as "free". Such clauses are assumed to hold like their normal counterparts; but unlike them, need not be proved. A free method precondition is hence assumed at method entry without being proved at the method callsite. This mechanism has to be used with care since it allows the introduction of arbitrary assumptions and could make specifications inconsistent. We used this feature (in a sound fashion) to reuse previously verified program properties without reproving them. The theorem prover KeY has built in support for these language extensions.

3.2 The Program Verification System KeY

KeY is an interactive theorem prover for verifying the correctness of Java programs w.r.t. their formal JML specifications. The KeY tool is available at the site www.key-project.org; more information may be found in the KeY Book [3].

KeY is designed as an interactive tool but has a powerful built in automatic verification engine which can solve many proof obligations automatically. Moreover, state of the art satisfiability modulo theories (SMT) solvers like Z3 or Yices can be called to discharge verification conditions. User interaction is relevant for the most important decision points within the course of a proof, which include quantifier instantiation, definition expansion, or reconfiguration of the strategy.

KeY uses a program logic called Java Dynamic Logic to formalise proof obligations for program properties. It possesses a sequent calculus for that logic that can be used to verify program properties both interactively and automatically.

The JML data type of sequences has its logical counterpart in the theory of sequences in KeY [19]. For the verification of dual-pivot quicksort, the abstract data type of sequences is used to abstract from arrays. This is important for verification, as Java arrays are objects on the heap, which makes them susceptible to effects like aliasing.

KeY usually treats integral primitive data types as unbounded mathematical integers. Yet, it also supports the bounded bit vector semantics of Java using

Listing 1. Top-level specification of the sort() method

```
1   class DualPivotQuicksort {
2     // ...
3
4     /*@ public normal_behavior
5       @     ensures (\forall int i; 0 <= i && i < a.length;
6       @               (\forall int j; 0 < j && j < a.length;
7       @                 i < j ==> a[i] <= a[j]));
8       @     ensures \seqPerm(\array2seq(a), \old(\array2seq(a)));
9       @     assignable a[*];
10      @*/
11    void sort(int[] a) { ... }
12  }
```

modulo operations and overflow checks, but is less efficient in these modes. In the presented case study, the verification was first completed using unbounded integer semantics. Only after finishing this simpler task did we prove that this verification was sound since no integer operation ever overflows.

4   Specification and Verification

Usually, the first challenge of a verification endeavour is to come up with a suitable and concise specification. Sorting algorithms have the neat property that the top-level specification can be stated very concisely and comprehensibly, which is not the case for specifications in general.

The top-level specification for the sort method, which is the top-level method to be verified for our verification task, is shown in Listing 1. This JML specification covers the following aspects of the behaviour of the method sort:

(a) On termination, the array is sorted in increasing order (lines 5–7).
(b) On termination, the array contains a permutation of the initial array content (line 8).
(c) The implementation does not modify any existing memory location except the entries of the array (line 9).
(d) The method always terminates (this is the default for JML if a diverges clause has not been specified).
(e) The method does not throw an exception. This is implied since the contract is declared normal_behavior.

Stability of the sorting algorithm is not a relevant issue here as dual-pivot quicksort is applied only to arrays of primitive values.

More specification constructs have to be provided for the verification task, like invariants and contracts for helper methods. These are "auxiliary" specifications that guide the proof but are not part of the requirement specification.

4.1 Proof Management by Gentle Problem Adaptation

The dual-pivot quicksort implementation to be verified is embedded into the portfolio solver of the JDK that is used to sort primitive values. In order to treat it with the formal verification tool KeY, we have slightly adapted the code to accommodate it to the style of programs that KeY can deal with comfortably.

Most importantly, our work focuses on the verification of the dual pivot implementation. The other sorting schemes from which the JDK's portfolio sorting mechanism may choose were not the main goal of this verification (for insights regarding the other schemes, see Sect. 6).

While we claim that we verified the actual JDK implementation, a few semantics-preserving refactorings were necessary to make the code accessible for verification with KeY. A few of these changes were due to the less-supported Java features, but more often they were needed due to a high complexity of the implementation:

- The single-pivot and dual-pivot implementations were encapsulated in separate classes. The part of the dual-pivot partition code that swaps all elements equal to the pivots to the sides of the sorted array range was encapsulated in its own class as well.
- Bit shift operations like x >>> k were replaced by divisions x / 2^k, which are semantically equivalent when applied to non-negative values of x.
- We extracted various code blocks into new private methods. Local variables became fields of the class.

For an interactive verification project, it is more important to structure the endeavour into more manageable parts than for an automatic one since the human operator needs to be able to keep an overview. We employed two mechanisms to achieve this: *modularisation* (by splitting the code into smaller units) and *separation of concerns* (by considering only one aspect of the specification at a time).

To modularise the problem, we broke down the code into smaller units by refactoring the large sort method into smaller new methods. Besides disentangling the different sorting algorithms, it significantly reduced the complexity of the individual proof obligations. The parts of the code that suggested themselves for method extraction were the partitioning implementation, the initial sorting of the five chosen elements, and several small loops for moving the indices used in the partitioning algorithm.

Besides this modularisation into smaller sub-problems, we also reduced complexity by separating three parts of the requirement specification (a) the sortedness property, (b) the permutation property, and (c) the absence of integer overflows.

Each aspect of the specification contains particular (auxiliary) specification clauses, but the aspects also share common elements. It is desirable that the common elements need not be reproved in every verification step. To achieve this, we added annotations verified for an earlier specification part as assumptions for the following parts by using the mechanism of free JML clauses. Since these

Listing 2. Specification of the partitioning method `split`

```
1    static int less, great;        // static variables introduced during method extraction to reflect
2    static int e1,e2,e3,e4,e5;     // local variables of the enclosing method.
3
4    /*@ normal_behaviour
5    @ requires right - left + 1 > 46 && 0 <= left && right < a.length;
6    @ requires (\exists int x; left < x && x < right; a[x] < pivot1);
7    @ requires (\exists int y; left < y && y < right; a[y] > pivot2);
8    @ requires a[e1] < a[e2] && a[e2] < a[e3] && a[e3] < a[e4] && a[e4] < a[e5];
9    @ requires left < e1 && e1 < e2 && e2 < e3 && e3 < e4 && e4 < e5 && e5 < right;
10   @ requires a[e2] == pivot1 && a[e4] == pivot2;
11   @ requires (\forall int i; 0 <= i < left; (\forall int j; left <= j && j < a.length; a[i] <= a[j]));
12   @ requires (\forall int i; 0 <= i && i <= right; (\forall int j; right < j && j < a.length; a[i] <= a[j]));
13   @ ensures (\forall int i; left <= i && i < less-1; a[i] < pivot1);
14   @ ensures a[less-1] == pivot1;
15   @ ensures (\forall int j; less <= j && j <= great; pivot1 <= a[j] && a[j] <= pivot2);
16   @ ensures a[great+1] == pivot2;
17   @ ensures (\forall int l; great+1 < l && l <= right; a[l] > pivot2);
18   @ ensures left < less-1;
19   @ ensures great < right-1;
20   @ ensures (\forall int i; 0 <= i && i < left; (\forall int j; left <= j && j < a.length; a[i] <= a[j]));
21   @ ensures (\forall int i; 0 <= i && i <= right; (\forall int j; right < j && j < a.length; a[i] <= a[j]));
22   @ assignable less, great, a[left..right];
23   @*/
24   private static void split(int[] a, int left, int right, int pivot1, int pivot2) {...}
```

clauses had been proven correct previously, reusing them later as assumptions is sound.

The absence of implicit exceptions (e.g., division by zero or a `null` dereference) cannot be switched off in KeY and was thus checked thrice.

The atomic units for contract-based modular verification systems like KeY are the methods of a program. The target method `sort` has about 340 lines of code which causes difficulties concerning the resources required by the prover, and, moreover, makes the interactive verification task unmanageable. To modularise the task, we annotated relevant blocks (in particular the elementary steps of the algorithm and the loop bodies) of the methods using block contracts and then (manually) extracted the blocks as synthetic new methods using the block contracts as their method contracts. Local variables of the enclosing method became new class fields in the process such that they can be accessed from more than one method. This method extraction preserves the program semantics for single-threaded execution cases; the extracted fields would be shared between threads which makes the code no longer reentrant. For future work we plan to perform such extraction automatically.

4.2 The Sortedness Property

Proving sortedness is quite straight forward by means of assertions on the elements in the array. Quantification and arithmetic over integers are all that is needed. Due to space limitations, we cannot show all intermediate loop invariants and method contracts here, but they can be found in the sources available on the companion web page [1].

Exemplarily, we show in Listing 2 the precondition of the method `split` which implements the partitioning part of the algorithm. The actual partitioning property as illustrated in Fig. 1 is covered in lines 13–17. The remainder encodes auxiliary properties needed for the recursive verification to be inductive, and to facilitate proof automation (e.g., lines 3 and 4 provide a direct witness that ensures the termination of the inner loop, which could also be derived from lines 8 and 10, but giving the witness in the precondition minimises the need for interaction).

4.3   The Permutation Property

The textbook quicksort algorithm orders an array by continued swapping of its elements. The resulting array is thus easily proved to be a permutation of the original. However, in the optimised Java implementation, the two pivot elements get special treatment: they are exchanged for the boundary elements during the split phase and excluded from the recursive calls. As a consequence, there are intermediate states where the array is only a permutation of the initial array if the pivots are restored to their place.

Let us recall that a sequence b is called a permutation of sequence a iff a and b have the same length n and there is an injective mapping σ from $[0, \ldots, n-1]$ onto itself such that $b[i] = a[\sigma(i)]$ for all $0 \le i < n$. The mapping σ is called a *witness* of the permutation property.

The theory of sequences in KeY contains a predicate `seqPerm(a,b)`, which is true if and only if the sequence a is a permutation of sequence b. Already in Listing 1, the function `array2seq` occurred. It transforms the (heap-dependent) content of Java arrays into (heap-independent) mathematical sequences. This frees us from the burden to incorporate the heap in all statements and allows us to make use of the rich theory of the JML data type **\seq** of finite sequences built into the KeY theorem prover. Besides the possibility to expand the definition of \seqPerm using the permutation witness, KeY has calculus rules that allow one to reason about the predicate exploiting its reflexivity, symmetry and transitivity and the fact that it is maintained by a transposition.

The following lemma helps to deal with the problem described in the previous paragraph (see [18, Corollary 1] for a proof).

Lemma 1. *Let a, b be two arrays such that b is a permutation of a and such that there are two indices i, j with $a[i] = b[i]$ and $a[j] = b[j]$.*
Then there is a witness σ such that $\sigma(i) = i$ and $\sigma(j) = j$.

The lemma was needed to show in KeY that there exists a witness to establish the permutation invariant of the main loop of the partitioning algorithm. The used fixed points are the left- and right-most element of the currently sorted subarray. Only if the pivot values are stored to these places do we obtain a permutation of the original input array.

Lemma 1 and, in fact, a much more general statement have been proved using KeY. Further background material and full proofs of related lemmas and theorems on permutations can also be found in the technical report [18].

4.4   Absence of Integer Overflow

For the verification of the sortedness and permutation properties, we treated the int data type in Java as mathematical integers. This made the deductive verification tasks more accessible, both to the user and to the theorem prover. Afterwards we switched the integer mode of KeY to overflow checking: All operations are still on mathematical integers, but for every operation in the code, an additional assertion is added that the result of the operation is not beyond the limits of the Java primitive data type. If these assertions can be discharged, it is ensured that the proof conducted on mathematical integers is also valid for the bounded data types of Java.

Moreover, since all clauses formulated over mathematical integers still hold, the statements proved in earlier passes can soundly be used for this task as assumptions (again using free JML clauses).

We were able to prove absence of overflows in the implementation. Most proofs were comparatively simple. Only the code that computes the indices for the pivot candidates was a challenge. Here, quantiles of the possible array indices are considered, and this computation relies on bit shift operations. The deductive engine of KeY was overwhelmed by the arithmetic used in this loop-free piece of code, and the verification did not succeed. For this single obligation, we hence employed the bounded verification engine CBMC [6] (which encodes C and Java verification challenges as SAT problems). This proof obligation was discharged fully automatically in a few seconds by CBMC. Since the bounded verifier did make any bounding assumptions, this instance of bounded verification implies full correctness.

4.5   Sorting Pivot Candidates

The pivot elements used by the quicksort algorithms are chosen as quantiles from a set of five elements taken from the array. These five elements are sorted using an insertion sort algorithm whose loops have been manually unrolled for performance reasons yielding four consecutive nested if-statements. This if-cascade is a real-world example of a piece of code where conventional weakest precondition computation results in exponentially many paths to be considered. We employed manually annotated block contracts to bring complexity back to linear. Alternatively, we could have used KeY's ability to recombine proof goals into one if they represent the same node in the control-flow graph reached on different paths [17]. Similar effects can be obtained by using an efficient weakest precondition calculus [15] after transforming the program into a sequence of assumptions and assertions.

5   Verification Effort

The first part of the proof consisted of verifying the sortedness property and termination without exceptional behaviour. Including the rather complex process of identifying and implementing suitable adaptations of the problem to a scale where the proof became feasible in KeY, the proof took about two person months.

Similarly, the permutation proof required some effort outside the actual work with KeY, including the design of the lemma described in Sect. 4.3, its incorporation into the KeY rule set, and improving the proof work-flow by making it possible to use the loop invariants that were already proven in the sortedness proof. Apart from these tasks, the proof of the permutation property required roughly two weeks.

The proof of the sortedness property required a total of 510,439 sequent calculus rule applications on the 1892 proof branches created by symbolic execution. KeY's automatic mode takes about 20 min to conduct this proof. Most of the rule applications were automatic, but in 132 cases, calculus rules had to be applied manually. 186 proof branches were closed by appeal to the SMT solver Z3, while the others were discharged by KeY's native theorem prover.

The proof of the permutation property required more interaction than the sortedness proof, since the rules on sequences and permutation are not usually included in the automatic mode of KeY. The proof of the permutation property of the dual pivot partitioning, which was by far the hardest part, was achieved using a proof script to automate interactive rule applications; the script takes roughly 20 min to execute on a machine with a core i7 and 8 GB of memory.

Pair Insertion Sort. Besides the different quicksort variants, JDK's portfolio sorting engine uses a variation of insertion sort if there are less than 47 elements to be sorted. Instead of the standard algorithm, a more efficient scheme called *pair insertion sort* has been implemented that inserts two elements at a time.

During the latest VerifyThis verification competition [12] at ETAPS 2017, this variation of insertion sort has been put up as specification and verification challenge. During the event, one competitor succeeded in verifying a pseudo code version of the algorithm within the given 90 min. In the aftermath of the event, a full verification of the actual Java implementation using KeY has been carried out and is available on the webpage [1].

6   Invalid Invariant in Single Pivot Quicksort

If there are two or more equal elements among the initially chosen five, the sorting engine resorts to a single pivot partition. While we concentrated on dual-pivot quicksort for the case study reported in this paper, we also verified the implementation of single-pivot quicksort under a slight simplification.[1]

In the course of this verification, we discovered that a loop invariant, stated as a comment in the source code, is not valid. This invariant is attached to the loop for partitioning the array. It states that the array is divided into three parts

---

[1] The first element of the array range to be sorted acts as the pivot element, instead of choosing the median of the initially chosen five elements, as in the JDK implementation.

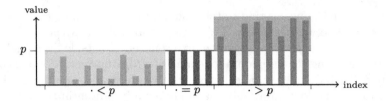

Fig. 2. After a single pivot partition, the array can be in a state where the invariant does not hold as the last part contains one misplaced element at the second position.

according to the general quicksort paradigm: (1) elements less than the pivot, (2) elements equal to the pivot, and (3) elements greater than the pivot.

Due to the efficient implementation, this invariant may not hold when the partitioning is finished. In many cases, the single pivot partition terminates in a state as shown in Fig. 2, where the last part contains an element that should have been placed in the central part because it is equal to the pivot.

This violation does not lead to incorrect sorting. The part violating the invariant will itself be sorted recursively, leaving the offending element in the leftmost place, which guarantees a correct order on termination. Since smaller parts of the array with less than 47 elements will eventually be sorted using insertion sort, the violation of the invariant does not persist.

The code can easily been modified such that the violated invariant becomes valid by addition of an extra comparison. A non-representative statistical analysis with random arrays showed that the algorithm is more efficient without the correction.

7   Conclusions

What conclusions can be drawn from this successful verification attempt? It confirms that a real-world optimised algorithm implementation covering more than 300 lines can be verified using existing verification technology if ...

1. ... *the property to be verified can be concisely specified and formulated.* The specification language and verification technology must possess the right data structures to speak about the program at the right abstraction level – or it must be possible to define them effectively.
2. ... *sensible modularising refactorings can be made.* In the case of this verification, the nature both of the portfolio solver and the sorting algorithm had points at which modularisation was natural. In the present case we were also able to separate concerns by considering the sortedness, permutation and overflow properties separately. The challenges of verifying code that has not been written with verification in mind is also discussed in [4], where modularisation and separation of concerns are identified as being indispensable for interactive post-hoc verification.

3. *... one is willing to add auxiliary specifications.* The modularisation introduced by splitting and extraction of individual methods reduces the complexity of individual proof tasks at the price of a considerable amount of intermediate specifications. In the case of KeY, additional user interaction is required to guide the proof. Other tools do this using even more code annotations.

References

1. Proving JDK's dual pivot quicksort correct. Blog post, companion website. https://www.key-project.org/2017/08/17/dual-pivot/
2. Abano, C., Chu, G., Eiseman, G., Fu, J., Yu, T.: Lab report, Rutgers University
3. Ahrendt, W., Beckert, B., Bubel, R., Hähnle, R., Schmitt, P.H., Ulbrich, M. (eds.): Deductive Software Verification: The KeY Book. From Theory to Practice. LNCS, vol. 10001. Springer, Heidelberg (2016). https://doi.org/10.1007/978-3-319-49812-6
4. Beckert, B., Bormer, T., Grahl, D.: Deductive verification of legacy code. In: Margaria, T., Steffen, B. (eds.) ISoLA 2016. LNCS, vol. 9952, pp. 749–765. Springer, Cham (2016). https://doi.org/10.1007/978-3-319-47166-2_53
5. Black, P.E., Becker, G., Murray, N.V.: Formal verification of a merge sort program with static semantics. ACM SIGPLAN Not. **30**(4), 51–60 (1995)
6. Clarke, E., Kroening, D., Lerda, F.: A tool for checking ANSI-C programs. In: Jensen, K., Podelski, A. (eds.) TACAS 2004. LNCS, vol. 2988, pp. 168–176. Springer, Heidelberg (2004). https://doi.org/10.1007/978-3-540-24730-2_15
7. Galeotti, J.P., Furia, C.A., May, E., Fraser, G., Zeller, A.: Inferring loop invariants by mutation, dynamic analysis, and static checking. IEEE Trans. Softw. Eng. **41**(10), 1019–1037 (2015)
8. de Gouw, S., de Boer, F.S., Rot, J.: Verification of counting sort and radix sort. In: Ahrendt, et al. [3], pp. 609–618
9. de Gouw, S., Rot, J., de Boer, F.S., Bubel, R., Hähnle, R.: OpenJDK's Java.utils.Collection.sort() is broken: the good, the bad and the worst case. In: Kroening, D., Păsăreanu, C.S. (eds.) CAV 2015. LNCS, vol. 9206, pp. 273–289. Springer, Cham (2015). https://doi.org/10.1007/978-3-319-21690-4_16
10. Hoare, C.A.R.: Quicksort. Comput. J. **5**(1), 10–16 (1962)
11. Huisman, M., Ahrendt, W., Grahl, D., Hentschel, M.: Formal specification with the Java modeling language. In: Ahrendt et al. [3], pp. 193–241
12. Huisman, M., Monahan, R., Mostowski, W., Müller, P., Ulbrich, M.: VerifyThis 2017: A program verification competition. Technical Report Karlsruhe Reports in Informatics 2017–10, Karlsruhe Institute of Technology (2017)
13. Kushagra, S., López-Ortiz, A., Munro, J.I., Qiao, A.: Multi-pivot quicksort: Theory and experiments. In: Proceedings of the Meeting on Algorithm Engineering and Experiments, pp. 47–60. Society for Industrial and Applied Mathematics (2014)
14. Leavens, G.T., Poll, E., Clifton, C., Cheon, Y., Ruby, C., Cok, D., Müller, P., Kiniry, J., Chalin, P., Zimmerman, D.M., Dietl, W.: JML Reference Manual (2013). draft Revision 2344
15. Leino, K.R.M.: Efficient weakest preconditions. Inf. Process. Lett. **93**(6), 281–288 (2005). https://doi.org/10.1016/j.ipl.2004.10.015
16. Leino, K.R.M., Lucio, P.: An assertional proof of the stability and correctness of natural mergesort. ACM Trans. Comput. Log. **17**(1), 6:1–6:22 (2015)

17. Scheurer, D., Hähnle, R., Bubel, R.: A general lattice model for merging symbolic execution branches. In: Ogata, K., Lawford, M., Liu, S. (eds.) ICFEM 2016. LNCS, vol. 10009, pp. 57–73. Springer, Cham (2016). https://doi.org/10.1007/978-3-319-47846-3_5

18. Schmitt, P.H.: Some notes on permutations. Technical Report 7, Department of Informatics, Karlsruhe Institute of Technology (2017). http://publikationen.bibliothek.kit.edu/1000068624

19. Schmitt, P.H., Bubel, R.: Theories. In: Ahrendt et al. [3], pp. 149–166

20. Wild, S., Nebel, M.E., Neininger, R.: Average case and distributional analysis of Java 7's dual pivot quicksort. CoRR abs/1304.0988 (2013). http://arxiv.org/abs/1304.0988

21. Yaroslavskiy, V.: Dual-pivot quicksort algorithm (2009). http://codeblab.com/wp-content/uploads/2009/09/DualPivotQuicksort.pdf. published online

A Semi-automatic Proof of Strong Connectivity

Ran Chen[1,2] and Jean-Jacques Lévy[3(✉)]

[1] Inria Saclay, Saclay, France
chenr@ios.ac.cn
[2] ISCAS Beijing, Beijing, China
[3] Inria Paris, Paris, France
jean-jacques.levy@inria.fr

Abstract. We present a formal proof of the classical Tarjan-1972 algorithm for finding strongly connected components in directed graphs. We use the Why3 system to express these proofs and fully check them by computer. The Why3-logic is a simple multi-sorted first-order logic augmented by inductive predicates. Furthermore it provides useful libraries for lists and sets. The Why3 system allows the description of programs in a Why3-ML programming language (a first-order programming language with ML syntax) and provides interfaces to various state-of-the-art automatic provers and to manual interactive proof-checkers (we use mainly Coq). We do not claim that this proof is new, although we could not find a formal proof of that algorithm in the literature. But one important point of our article is that our proof is here completely presented and human readable.

1 Introduction

Formal proofs about programs are often very long and have to face a huge amount of cases due to the multiplicity of variables, the details of programs, and the description of their meta-theories. This is very frustrating since we would like to explain these formal proofs and publish them in scientific articles. However if one considers simple algorithms, we would expect to explain their proofs of correctness in the same way as we explain a mathematical proof for a not too complex theorem. This surely can be done on algorithms dealing with simple recursive structures [5,19,29]. But we take here the example of an algorithm on graphs where sharing and combinatorial properties holds.

Tarjan-1972's algorithm for finding strongly connected components in directed graphs is very magic [1,24,26]. It consists in an efficient depth-first search in graphs which traces the bases of the strongly connected components. It computes in linear time the strongly connected components. In textbooks, the presentation uses an imperative programming style that we will refresh in Sect. 2, but for the sake of the simplicity of the proof, we will describe this algorithm in a functional programming style with abstract values for vertices in graphs,

---

R. Chen—Partly supported by ANR-13-LAB3-0007, http://www.spark-2014.org/ proofinuse and National Natural Science Foundation of China (Grant No. 61672504).

A. Paskevich and T. Wies (Eds.): VSTTE 2017, LNCS 10712, pp. 49–65, 2017.
https://doi.org/10.1007/978-3-319-72308-2_4

with functions between vertices and their successors, and with data types such that lists (representing immutable stacks) and sets. This programming style will much ease the readability of our formal proof.

We use the Why3 system [3,14] and the Why3-logic to express these proofs. Our proof is rather short, namely 235 lines (38 lemmas) including the program texts. Most of the lemmas and the 74 proof obligations generated by the Why3 system for our program are proved automatically using Alt-Ergo (1.30), CVC3 (2.4.1), CVC4 (1.5-prerelease), Eprover (1.9), Spass (3.5), Yices (1.0.4), Z3 (4.4.0) except 2 of them which are manually checked by Coq (8.6) with a few ssreflect features [13,15]. Coq proofs are 233-line long (65 + 168).

Our claim is that the details of our proof are human readable and intuitive. The proof will be fully described in our paper. Therefore it could be an example of teaching algorithms with their formal proofs. Finally our article can present a useful step to compare with other formal methods, for instance within Isabelle or Coq [2,6–8,16,18,20–22,27,28].

The next section will present the algorithm; Sects. 3 and 4 present the invariants and pre-/post-conditions, Sect. 5 describes the formal proof. We conclude in Sect. 6.

2   The Algorithm

A strongly connected component in a directed graph is a nonempty maximal set of vertices in which any pair of vertices can be joined by a path. Therefore when two vertices x and y are in such a component, there exist paths from x to y and from y to x. In the rest of the paper we shall just say connected components for strongly connected components.

Tarjan-1972 algorithm [1,24,26] for finding (strongly) connected components in a directed graph performs a single depth-first search traversal. It maintains a stack of visited vertices and a numbering of vertices. Initially the stack is empty and the serial number of all vertices is -1. Then vertices get increasing serial numbers in the order of their visit. Each vertex is visited once. The search is realized by a recursive function which starts from any unvisited vertex x, pushes it on the stack, visits the directly reachable vertices from x, and returns the minimum value of the numbers of all vertices accessible from x by at most one cross-edge. A cross-edge is an edge between an unvisited vertex and an already visited vertex. If there is no such edge, the returned value is $+\infty$. When the returned value is equal to the number of x, a new component cc containing x is found and all vertices of cc are then at top of the stack, x being the lowest. Therefore the stack is popped until x and the numbers of the component members are set to $+\infty$, which withdraws them from further calculations in the following visits of vertices.

To make this algorithm more explicit, we consider the below recursive function $printSCC$ which prints the connected components reachable from any given vertex x and returns an integer. It works with a given stack s, an array num of numbers, and a current serial number sn. The program written in two columns

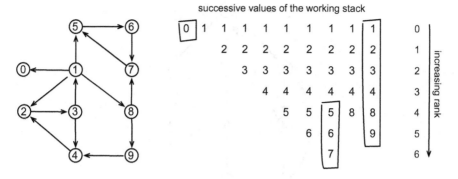

Fig. 1. An example: in the graph on left, vertices are numbered and pushed onto the stack in the order of their visit by the recursive function *printSCC*. When the first component {0} is discovered, vertex 0 is popped; similarly when the second component {5, 6, 7} is found, its vertices are popped; finally all vertices are popped when the third component {1, 2, 3, 4, 8, 9} is found. Notice that there is no cross edge to a vertex with a number less than 5 when the second component is discovered. Similarly in the first component, there is no edge to a vertex with a number less than 0. In the third component, there is no edge to a vertex less than 1 since we then set the number of vertex 0 to $+\infty$.

adopts a syntax close to the one of (Why3-)ML. The set of vertices directly reachable from vertex x by a single edge is represented by the set *(successors x)*. This set can be implemented by a list of integers. We suppose that initially sn is set to 0 and that all entries in *num* are equal to -1. The constant *max_int* represents $+\infty$. Figure 1 provides an example of execution of that function.

```
let rec printSCC (x: int) (s: stack int)        if !min = num[x] then begin
    (num: array int) (sn: ref int) =               repeat
Stack.push x s;                                         let y = Stack.pop s in
num[x] ← !sn; sn := !sn + 1;                            Printf.printf "%d " y;
let min = ref num[x] in                                 num[y] ← max_int;
foreach y in (successors x) do                          if y = x then break;
    let m = if num[y] = -1                          done;
        then printSCC y s num sn                     Printf.printf "\n";
        else num[y] in                              min := max_int;
    min := Math.min m !min                      end;
done;                                           return !min;
```

The proof of correctness of this algorithm in original Tarjan's article relies on the structure of the connected components with respect to the spanning tree (forest) corresponding to the recursive calls of *printSCC*. A first lemma (Lemma 10 in the paper) states that if x and y are in a same component, their smallest common ancestor (i.e. the one with highest number) in the spanning tree is also in the same component. Therefore a connected component is always contained in one subtree of the spanning forest. The root of that minimum subtree is called the base of the component (Tarjan named it the root). Therefore the algorithm

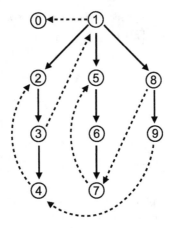

Fig. 2. Spanning forest: $LOWLINK(x)$ is $0, 1, 1, 1, 2, 5, 5, 5, 4, 4$ for $0 \leq x \leq 9$

is designed to discover the bases of connected components. Lemma 12 proves that a vertex x is a base of a connected component if and only if the number of x is equal to the value of so-called $LOWLINK(x)$, which corresponds to the value computed by *printSCC* with x as input.

$$LOWLINK(x) = \min (\{num[x]\} \ \cup \ \{num[y] \mid x \stackrel{*}{\Longrightarrow} z \hookrightarrow y$$
$$\wedge \ x \text{ and } y \text{ are in the same connected component}\})$$

where $x \stackrel{*}{\Longrightarrow} z$ means that z is a descendant of x in the spanning forest and $z \hookrightarrow y$ means that there is a cross-edge from z to y (that is either an edge to an ancestor y of x, or to a cousin y of x, or to a descendant y of a child of x). Notice that in the second case, cousin y could only be at left of x in the spanning tree. The trick of the algorithm is that the $LOWLINK$ function can be simply calculated through a single depth-first-search.

The proof of that Lemma 12 is about spanning trees and not about the recursive function which implements the depth-first-search. In order to make a formal proof of the algorithm, we may either formalize spanning trees and extract a program from these formal specifications, or directly manipulate the program and adapt the previous abstract proof to the various steps of this program. We prefer the latter alternative which is more speaking to a programmer and maybe easier to understand.

Our program will be expressed in a functional programming style. Thus we avoid side-effects and mutable variables. This Why3-ML program is based on two mutually recursive functions *dfs1* and *dfs* which respectively take as arguments a vertex x and a set of vertices *roots*, and which return the number n of the oldest vertex accessible by at most one cross-edge. Both functions work with an environment represented by a record with four fields: *stack* for the working stack, *sccs* for the set of already computed connected components, *sn* for the current available serial number and *num* for the numbering mapping. The environment at end of both functions is also returned in their results. Thus the result of *dfs1* and *dfs* is a pair (n, e') where n is the number of the oldest vertex accessible by at most one cross-edge and e' is the environment at end of these functions. The main program *tarjan* calls *dfs* with all vertices as roots and an empty environment, i.e. an empty stack, an empty set of connected components, a null serial number and a constant mapping of vertices to -1.

```
let rec dfs1 x e =
  let n = e.sn in
  let (n1, e1) = dfs (successors x) (add_stack_incr x e) in
  let (s2, s3) = split x e1.stack in
  if n1 < n then (n1, e1) else
    (max_int(), {stack = s3; sccs = add (elements s2) e1.sccs;
      sn = e1.sn; num = set_max_int s2 e1.num})

with  dfs roots e = if is_empty roots then (max_int(), e) else
  let x = choose roots in
  let roots' = remove x roots in
  let (n1, e1) = if e.num[x] ≠ -1 then (e.num[x], e) else dfs1 x e in
  let (n2, e2) = dfs roots' e1 in (min n1 n2, e2)

let tarjan () =
  let e0 = {stack = Nil; sccs = empty; sn = 0; num = const (-1)} in
  let (_, e') = dfs vertices e0 in e'.sccs
```

The data structures used by these functions are the ones of the Why3 standard library. For lists we have the constructors *Nil*, *Cons* and the function *elements* which returns the set of elements of a list. For finite sets, we have the empty set *empty*, and functions *add* to add an element to a set, *remove* to remove an element from a set, *choose* to pick an element in a set, and *cardinal*, *is_empty* with intuitive meanings. We also use maps (instead of mutable arrays) with functions *const* denoting the constant function, [] to get the value of an element and [←] to create a new map with an element set to a given value. Thus we can define an abstract type *vertex* for vertices and a constant *vertices* for the finite set of all vertices in the graph. The type *env* of environments is a record with the four fields *stack*, *sccs*, *sn* and *num* whose meanings were stated above.

```
type vertex
constant vertices: set vertex
function successors vertex : set vertex
function max_int (): int = cardinal vertices
type env = {stack: list vertex; sccs: set (set vertex);
            sn: int; num: map vertex int}
```

Finally the functions *dfs1* and *dfs* use the following three functions. Two of them handle environments: *add_stack_incr* pushes a vertex on the stack and sets its number to the value of the current serial number which is then incremented, *set_max_int* sets all the elements of a stack to *max_int()*. The polymorphic function *split* returns the pair of sublists produced by decomposing a list with respect to the first occurrence of an element.

```
let add_stack_incr x e = let n = e.sn in
  {stack = Cons x e.stack; sccs = e.sccs; sn = n+1; num = e.num[x ← n]}

let rec set_max_int (s : list vertex)(f : map vertex int) =
  match s with
  | Nil → f
  | Cons x s' → (set_max_int s' f)[x ← max_int()]
  end

let rec split (x : α) (s: list α) : (list α, list α) =
  match s with
  | Nil → (Nil, Nil)
  | Cons y s' → if x = y then (Cons x Nil, s') else
      let (s1', s2) = split x s' in ((Cons y s1'), s2)
  end
```

We will assume that the imperative program *printSCC* behaves as the functions *dfs1* and *dfs*. Our formal proof will only work on these two functions. We experimented several formal proofs of imperative versions, but they always looked over-complex (that complexity is mainly notational, since one always has to refer to the value of a variable at a given point of the program). To be convinced that the functions *dfs1* and *dfs* follow the algorithm in the original paper, we notice that instead of printing the connected components, we accumulate them in the *sccs* field of environments and produce them as the result of the main function *tarjan*. We also use *dfs* to recursively execute the iterative loop of *printSCC*. The heart of the algorithm is in the body of function *dfs1* where we split the working stack with respect to the vertex x giving two lists *s2* and *s3* (the last element of *s2* is x). Then we test if the elements of *s2* forms a new connected component. In fact this test could be done before splitting, but the formal proof looks clearer if we keep them in that order.

Notice a small modification between our presentation and the one of the original version. In *dfs1*, we test $n1 < n$ instead of $n1 \neq n$. In the imperative program, the minimum is initialized to the number of x. Thus this initial value is used for two distinct purposes: the case when x is the root of a new connected component and the case when x is the top of the working stack. In the latter case we prefer returning $+\infty$ for *dfs* which corresponds to the simpler formula $\mathcal{E}$.

$$LOWLINK(x) = \min \{num[y] \mid x \overset{*}{\Longrightarrow} z \hookrightarrow y \qquad\qquad (\mathcal{E})$$
$$\wedge \ x \text{ and } y \text{ are in the same connected component}\}$$

A final remark is that we could have inlined *dfs1* in *dfs* or transformed the call to *dfs1* into a call to *dfs* with a singleton set of roots as argument. Both alternatives do not simplify the proof, nor the invariants. Altogether we feel our presentation easier to read.

3   Invariants

This algorithm collects connected components in the *sccs* field of environments and we have to maintain that property along the execution of the program.

Partial connected components are contained in the working stack, and as soon as they are complete, they are moved from the stack to the *sccs* field. These partial connected components are connected components of the graph restricted to the elements of the stack and the *sccs* field, that is up to the already explored subgraph. These partial connected components are merged as soon as a back edge may access to an older ancestor in the spanning tree. This notion is not easy to manipulate since we would have also to mark the edges that we have visited. Therefore we break that property into several smaller pieces.

First we have to speak of the explored vertices. The *num* field marks visited vertices when their *num* value is not −1. There are two kinds of visited vertices as in any depth-first-search algorithm. The black vertices are fully explored by the algorithm, namely the call of *dfs1* has been totally performed on them. The gray vertices are partially explored by that function, and the algorithm has still to visit several of its descendants in the spanning tree. The gray vertices represent the call stack of the recursive function *dfs1*. The non-visited vertices are said white, they correspond to a *num* field equals to −1 in the environment.

The connected components are either fully black and are then members of the *sccs* field, or they contain a gray vertex, or are fully white. A gray vertex can access to any vertex pushed after it in the working stack (i.e. before in the list representing the stack). Conversely any vertex in the stack can access to a gray vertex pushed in the stack before it (i.e after in the list representing the stack). This invariant property of the stack and environment is illustrated in Fig. 3 and can be checked on the example of Figs. 1 and 2.

We now define formally the invariants. The graph is defined with an abstract type *vertex* for the type of vertices, a constant *vertices* for the set of all vertices in the graph, a function *successors* giving the set of vertices directly reachable by a single edge (see Sect. 2). We also have the following axiom and definition:

```
axiom successors_vertices:
  ∀x. mem x vertices → subset (successors x) vertices
predicate edge (x y: vertex) = mem x vertices ∧ mem y (successors x)
```

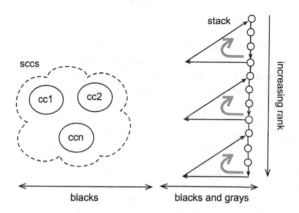

Fig. 3. Invariants on colors and stack

where *mem* and *subset* are the predicates denoting the membership in a set and the subset relation between two sets. Therefore *edge* is the binary relation defining the graph. The Why3 standard library defines paths in graphs as an inductive predicate and we also use a reachability predicate:

```
inductive path vertex (list vertex) vertex =
  | Path_empty: ∀x: vertex. path x Nil x
  | Path_cons: ∀x y z: vertex, l: list vertex.
       edge x y → path y l z → path x (Cons x l) z
```

```
predicate reachable (x y: vertex) = ∃l. path x l y
```

Strongly connected components are naturally defined as non-empty maximal sets of vertices connected in both ways by paths.

```
predicate in_same_scc (x y: vertex)  =  reachable x y ∧ reachable y x
predicate is_subscc (s: set vertex) =
  ∀x y. mem x s → mem y s → in_same_scc x y
predicate is_scc (s: set vertex) = not is_empty s ∧
  is_subscc s ∧ (∀s'. subset s s' → is_subscc s' → s == s')
```

The colors of vertices are defined by membership to two sets: *blacks* and *grays* for the set of black and gray vertices. A white vertex is neither in *blacks*, nor in *grays*. (The *grays* set can also be implicit, since gray vertices are the non-black elements of the working stack, but we feel simpler to keep it explicit). These two sets *blacks* and *grays* are ghost variables for the Why3-ML program. They are used inside the logic of the proof, but they affect neither the control flow, nor the result of the program. We will treat them differently since *blacks* will be a new ghost field in environments and *grays* will be an extra ghost argument to the functions *dfs1*, *dfs* and *tarjan*. Adding the gray set as another new field of environments was intractable in the proof. We will discuss that point later. Thus the new type of environments is as follows:

```
type env = {ghost blacks: set vertex; stack: list vertex;
            sccs: set (set vertex); sn: int; num: map vertex int}
```

and the main invariant $(\mathcal{I})$ of our program will be: $(\mathcal{I})$

```
  wf_env e grays  ∧ ∀cc. mem cc e.sccs ↔ subset cc e.blacks ∧ is_scc cc
```

where *wf_env* defines a well formed environment and the other conjunct specifies that the black connected components are exactly the elements of the *sccs* field.

The definition of a well formed environment is done in three steps. First we define a well formed coloring: the *grays* and *blacks* sets are disjoint subsets of vertices in the graph; the elements of the stack is the union of grays and the difference of blacks and the union of elements of *sccs*; the elements of *sccs* are all black. The operations *union, inter, diff* on sets are defined in the Why3 standard library. But we had to define the big union *set_of* axiomatically.

```
predicate wf_color (e: env) (grays: set vertex) =
  let {stack = s; blacks = b; sccs = ccs} = e in
  subset (union grays b) vertices ∧ inter b grays == empty ∧
  elements s == union grays (diff b (set_of ccs)) ∧
  subset (set_of ccs) b
```

In the next two steps, we use two new predicates and a new definition. The *no_black_to_white* predicate states that there is no edge from a black vertex to a white vertex. Any depth-first search respects that property since the black set is saturated by reachability. The *simplelist* predicate says that a list has no repetitions i.e. there is no more than one occurrence of any element. Our working stack satisfies that predicate since any vertex is visited no more than once. (The *num_occ* function belongs to the Why3 standard library)

```
predicate no_black_to_white (blacks grays: set vertex) =
  ∀x x'. edge x x' → mem x blacks → mem x' (union blacks grays)
```

```
predicate simplelist (l: list α) = ∀x. num_occ x l ≤ 1
```

The *rank* function gives the position of an element in a list starting from the end of the list. In a working stack of length ℓ, the ranks of the bottom and top of the stack are 0 and $\ell - 1$ (see Figs. 1 and 3). The *rank* function allows to order vertices in the stack with respect to their positions. It could be done just with numbers of the vertices, but we shall discuss that point later. (*lmem* and *length* are the Why3 functions for membership in and length of a list)

```
function rank (x: α) (s: list α): int =
 match s with
 | Nil → max_int()
 | Cons y s' → if x = y && not (lmem x s') then length s' else rank x s'
 end
```

The well formed numbering is a bit long to state formally, but is quite easy to understand. Numbers of vertices can be -1, non-negative or $+\infty$ (i.e. *max_int*()). Finite numbers range between -1 and *sn* (excluded). The serial number *sn* is the number of non-white vertices. A vertex has number $+\infty$ if and only if it is in the set of already discovered connected components. It has number -1 exactly when it is a white vertex. Finally numbers of vertices in the stack are ordered as their ranks.

A well-formed environment is well colored, well numbered, respects the non-black-to-white property, contains a stack without repetitions and the partial connected components property described above. Thus there should be a path between any gray vertex and any higher-ranked vertex in the stack, and conversely any vertex in the stack can reach a lower-ranked gray vertex (see Fig. 3).

```
predicate wf_num (e: env) (grays: set vertex) =
  let {stack = s; blacks = b; sccs = ccs; sn = n; num = f} = e in
  (∀x. -1 ≤ f[x] < n ≤ max_int() ∨ f[x] = max_int())  ∧
  n = cardinal (union grays b) ∧
  (∀x. f[x] = max_int() ↔ mem x (set_of ccs)) ∧
  (∀x. f[x] = -1 ↔ not mem x (union grays b)) ∧
  (∀x y. lmem x s → lmem y s → f[x] < f[y] ↔ rank x s < rank y s)
```

```
predicate wf_env (e: env) (grays: set vertex) = let s = e.stack in
  wf_color e grays ∧ wf_num e grays ∧
  no_black_to_white e.blacks grays ∧ simplelist s ∧
  (∀x y. mem x grays → lmem y s → rank x s ≤ rank y s → reachable x y)
  ∧
  (∀y. lmem y s → ∃x. mem x grays ∧ rank x s ≤ rank y s ∧ reachable y x)
```

4   Pre-/Post-conditions

The previous invariant ($\mathcal{I}$) of Sect. 3 is surely a pre-condition and a post-condition of the *dfs1* and *dfs* functions. We have several simple extra pre-conditions, namely the argument x of *dfs1* should be a white vertex and all gray vertices must reach x. Similarly for *dfs*, the vertices in *roots* can all be accessed by all gray vertices.

The post-conditions are more subtle. The simplest one is the monotony property *subenv* which relates the environments at the beginning and at the end of the function. It states that the working stack is extended by a new black area, that the black set of vertices and the set of discovered connected components are augmented, and that the numbers of vertices in the initial stack are unchanged. Vertices whose numbers change are either the new white vertices pushed onto the stack or the vertices moved to the *sccs* field; in the latter case they do not belong to the initial stack. (++ is the infix append operator)

```
predicate subenv (e e': env) =
   (∃s. e'.stack = s ++ e.stack ∧ subset (elements s) e'.blacks) ∧
   subset e.blacks e'.blacks ∧ subset e.sccs e'.sccs ∧
   (∀x. lmem x e.stack → e.num[x] = e'.num[x])
```

There are four main post-conditions. For *dfs1*, the last one $\mathcal{P}_4$ tells that the white vertex x argument of *dfs1* is blackened at the end of the function. The other post-conditions give properties of the number n returned in the resulting pair. One way of specifying n is to give its definition by equation ($\mathcal{E}$) of Sect. 2. Then we would have to handle white paths which are not easy to handle. Instead of paths we will only consider edges with the following three post-conditions which describe implicit properties of the result n. Post-condition $\mathcal{P}_1$ says that n cannot be greater than the number of x. Then n is either $+\infty$ and then x is also numbered $+\infty$, or n is the number of some vertex in the stack reachable from x (post-condition $\mathcal{P}_2$). Thirdly if an edge starts from the new part of the resulting stack to a vertex y in the old stack, then n is smaller than the number of that y (post-condition $\mathcal{P}_3$). For *dfs*, all roots are either black or gray at the end of the function (post-condition $\mathcal{P}_1'$). The other post-conditions $\mathcal{P}_2'$, $\mathcal{P}_3'$, $\mathcal{P}_4'$ are the natural extension to sets of the post-conditions of *dfs1*. These post-conditions use the following predicates.

```
predicate num_reachable (n: int) (x: vertex) (e: env) =
   ∃y. lmem y e.stack ∧ n = e.num[y] ∧ reachable x y


predicate xedge_to (s1 s3: list vertex) (y: vertex) =
   (∃s2. s1 = s2 ++ s3 ∧ ∃x. lmem x s2 ∧ edge x y) ∧ lmem y s3


predicate access_to (s: set vertex) (y: vertex) =
   ∀x. mem x s → reachable x y
```

The function *dfs1* can now be written as follows.

```
let rec dfs1 x e (ghost grays)   =
requires{mem x vertices}
requires{access_to grays x}
requires{not mem x (union e.blacks grays)}
```

```
(* invariants *)
requires{wf_env e grays}
requires{∀cc. mem cc e.sccs ↔ subset cc e.blacks ∧ is_scc cc}
returns{(_, e') → wf_env e' grays}
returns{(_, e') → ∀cc. mem cc e'.sccs ↔ subset cc e'.blacks ∧ is_scc cc}
(* post-conditions *)
returns{(n, e') → n ≤ e'.num[x]}                                    (*P₁*)
returns{(n, e') → n = max_int() ∨ num_reachable n x e'}             (*P₂*)
returns{(n, e') → ∀y. xedge_to e'.stack e.stack y → n ≤ e'.num[y]} (*P₃*)
returns{(_, e') → mem x e'.blacks}                                  (*P₄*)
(* monotony *)
returns{(_, e') → subenv e e'}
  let n = e.sn in
  let (n1, e1) = dfs (successors x) (add_stack_incr x e) (add x grays) in
  let (s2, s3) = split x e1.stack in
  if n1 < n then (n1, add_blacks x e1) else
     (max_int(), {blacks = add x e1.blacks; stack = s3;
       sccs = add (elements s2) e1.sccs; sn = e1.sn;
       num = set_max_int s2 e1.num})
```

(The keywords "requires" and "returns" represent pre- and post-conditions; "returns" allows pattern matching on the result). The functions *dfs* and *tarjan* have similar pre-/post-conditions.

```
with  dfs roots e (ghost grays) =
requires{subset roots vertices}
requires{∀x. mem x roots → access_to grays x}
(* invariants *)
requires{wf_env e grays}
requires{∀cc. mem cc e.sccs ↔ subset cc e.blacks ∧ is_scc cc}
returns{(_, e') → wf_env e' grays}
returns{(_, e') → ∀cc. mem cc e'.sccs ↔ subset cc e'.blacks ∧ is_scc cc}
(* post-conditions *)
returns{(n, e') → ∀x. mem x roots → n ≤ e'.num[x]}
returns{(n, e') → n = max_int() ∨ ∃x. mem x roots ∧ num_reachable n x e'}
returns{(n, e') → ∀y. xedge_to e'.stack e.stack y → n ≤ e'.num[y]}
returns{(_, e') → subset roots (union e'.blacks grays)}
(* monotony *)
returns{(_, e') → subenv e e'}
  if is_empty roots then (max_int(), e) else
  let x = choose roots in
  let roots' = remove x roots in
  let (n1, e1) = if e.num[x] ≠ -1 then (e.num[x], e)
    else dfs1 x e grays in
  let (n2, e2) = dfs roots' e1 grays in (min n1 n2, e2)

let tarjan () =
returns{r → ∀cc. mem cc r ↔ subset cc vertices ∧ is_scc cc}
  let e0 = {blacks = empty; stack = Nil; sccs = empty;
            sn = 0; num = const (-1)} in
  let (_, e') = dfs vertices e0 empty in e'.sccs
```

5   The Formal Proof

The proof of these post-conditions relies on three main remarks inside *dfs1*. In the function *dfs*, proofs are more routine and could be treated automatically.

First as we already discussed about partial connected components, it is clear that when the stack *e1.stack* is split into two pieces *s2* and *s3* with *x* as the last element in *s2*, the elements of *s2* form a subset of a connected component. Any vertex *y* in *s2* has higher rank than *x* and since *x* is gray in the call of *dfs* on the successors of *x*, invariant $(\mathcal{I})$ at end of *dfs* says that *x* reaches *y*. Conversely, we remark that the extension of the stack *s3* appended with *x* is black by the monotony condition at end of *dfs*. Therefore the elements of *s2* are either black or *x*. So invariant $(\mathcal{I})$ at end of *dfs* says that vertex *y* in *s2* can reach a gray vertex *z* of lower rank, since *s2* only contains black vertices and *x*, the rank of *z* is smaller than or equal to the rank of *x*. Therefore again by invariant $(\mathcal{I})$ at end of *dfs*, there is a path from *z* to *x*. Hence any element of *s2* is connected both ways to *x* and therefore the elements of *s2* form a subset of a connected component.

In *dfs1*, in case we have $n1 < n$, we prove that there is a gray vertex in the connected component of *x* (i.e. the same component as all elements in *s2*). Therefore the connected component is not fully black and it cannot be inserted in the *sccs* field of the environment. By post-condition $\mathcal{P}_2'$ of *dfs*, we know than *x* can reach a vertex *y* in the stack with number *n1* (*n1* cannot be $+\infty$ since $n1 < n = e.sn \leq +\infty$). We also have by the monotony condition in *dfs*:

```
e1.num[y] = n1 < n = e.sn
          = (add_stack_incr x e}).num[x]
          = e1.num[x]
```

By invariant $(\mathcal{I})$, the vertex *y* has a strictly smaller rank than *x*. Again by $(\mathcal{I})$, the vertex *y* can reach a gray vertex *z* with rank lower than *y* in the stack at end of *dfs*. Therefore *x* can reach *z* gray with lower rank. Thus *z* can also reach *x* by invariant $(\mathcal{I})$. We indeed proved there is a gray vertex *z* in the same connected component as *x*.

In *dfs1*, in case we have $n1 \geq n$, we prove that *s2* is the connected component of *x*. Let us consider a vertex *y* in the same connected component as *x*. We show that *y* belongs to *s2*. We proceed by contradiction. Suppose *y* is not in *s2*. Since there is a path from *x* in *s2* to *y* not in *s2*, there is an edge from *x'* to *y'* on that path such that *x'* is in *s2* and *y'* is not in *s2*. Moreover *x'* and *y'* are in the same component as *x*. We have three subcases:

- *y'* is in the set union of all members of *sccs*. This means that *x* is also in that big union. Therefore *x* would be black. Impossible since *x* is white.
- *y'* is in the working stack *e1.stack* but not in the *s2* part. Therefore *y'* is in *s3* (the other part of the split) and has rank strictly lower than the one of *x*. By $(\mathcal{I})$ at end of *dfs*, we have that the number of *y'* is strictly less than the number of *x*. Then there are two cases. When *x'* is *x*, Then *y'* is a successor of *x*. Post-condition $\mathcal{P}_1'$ states that *n1* is smaller than the number of *y'*. Then $n1 < n$. Impossible. When *x'* is not *x*, the vertex *x'* is not the last element of *s2* and the edge from *x'* to *y'* crosses the border between the

stacks *e1.stack* and *Cons x s3*, which are the stacks at end and beginning of *dfs*. Hence $n1$ is less than the number of y' in $e1$ by post-condition $\mathcal{P}'_3$. Thus $n1 < n$. Impossible.

- y' is white. When $x' = x$, then y' is in the successors of x. It cannot be white by post-condition $\mathcal{P}'_4$. When x' is not x, vertex x' is in the black extension of the stack at end of *dfs*. Therefore x' is black. This is impossible since there is no edge from a black vertex to a white vertex.

Thus the elements of *s2* form a complete connected component. At end of *dfs1*, the vertex x is turned to black and therefore the component can be inserted in the field *sccs* of the current environment.

The three main above remarks are implemented in the Why3-ML program by adding intermediate assertions in the body of *dfs1*. Namely the body is now:

```
let n = e.sn in
let (n1, e1) = dfs (successors x) (add_stack_incr x e) (add x grays) in
let (s2, s3) = split x e1.stack in
assert{is_last x s2 ∧ s3 = e.stack ∧
        subset (elements s2) (add x e1.blacks)};
assert{is_subscc (elements s2)};
if n1 < n then begin
  assert{∃y. mem y grays ∧ lmem y e1.stack ∧ e1.num[y] < e1.num[x] ∧
        reachable x y};
  (n1, add_blacks x e1) end
else begin
  assert{∀y. in_same_scc y x → lmem y s2};
  assert{is_scc (elements s2)};
  assert{inter grays (elements s2) = empty};
  (max_int(), {blacks = add x e1.blacks; stack = s3;
    sccs = add (elements s2) e1.sccs; sn = e1.sn;
    num = set_max_int s2 e1.num}) end
```

where the polymorphic predicate *is_last* is defined by:

```
predicate is_last (x: α) (s: list α) = ∃s'. s = s' ++ Cons x Nil
```

These assertions are proved automatically except for the third and the fourth ones manually proved in Coq along the lines of the second and the third remarks explained above. All pre-conditions and post-conditions are automatically proved (see Table 1 or the detailed session at [9]). These Coq proofs use the compact ssreflect syntax, several lemmas proved in Why3 and are $65 + 168$ line-long. The body of the functions *dfs* and *tarjan* is unchanged except for two assertions which ease the behaviour of the automatic provers. In *dfs*, one adds

```
assert{e.num[x] ≠ -1 ↔ (lmem x e.stack ∨ mem x e.blacks)};
```

before the -1 test for the number of x. In *tarjan* we add this assertion

```
assert{subset vertices e'.blacks};
```

which ensures the blackness of all vertices before returning the result. Notice finally the sixth assertion in *dfs1* which caused us many problems and eases the automatic proof of properties about sets.

There is no space here to fully describe the lemmas that we added in our proof. We have 8 lemmas about ranks in lists, 4 about simple lists, 12 about sets, 3 about sets of sets, 2 about paths, 5 about connected components, 4 special ones to show proof obligations. We present three typical lemmas. The first one states that when the vertex x is in the list s, the rank of x in s is invariant by the extension of s.

```
lemma rank_app_r:
  ∀x:α, s s'. lmem x s → rank x s = rank x (s' ++ s)
```

The second lemma shows that when a path l joins x to y and the vertex x is in a set s and the vertex y is not in s, then there is an edge from vertex x' in s to vertex y' not in s such that x reaches x' and y' reaches y. In fact x' and y' are on that path l. This lemma is critical to reduce properties on paths to properties on edges.

```
lemma xset_path_xedge:
  ∀x y l s. mem x s → not mem y s → path x l y →
  ∃x' y'. mem x' s ∧ not mem y' s ∧ edge x' y' ∧
           reachable x x' ∧ reachable y' y
```

The third lemma is used in the second assertion in the body of *dfs1*. The statement is not interesting by itself and this lemma is part of the four specialized lemmas. It shows the use of the by logical connector in Why3 [11]. This operator is no more than an explicit cut-rule meaning that in order to prove A with A by B, one can prove B and $B \to A$ in current environment.

```
lemma subscc_after_last_gray:
  ∀x e.g. s2 s3. wf_env e (add x g) →
  let {blacks = b; stack = s} = e in
  s = s2 ++ s3 → is_last x s2 →
  subset (elements s2) (add x b) → is_subscc (elements s2)
     by (access_to (add x g) x
           by inter (add x g) (elements s2) == add x empty)
     ∧ access_from x (elements s2)
```

Table 1. These are the provers results in seconds on a 3.3 GHz Intel Core i5 processor. The two last columns contains the numbers of verification conditions and proof obligations. Notice that there could be several VCs per proof obligation.

Provers	Alt-Ergo	CVC3	CVC4	Coq	E-prover	Spass	Yices	Z3	All	#VC	#PO
38 lemmas	2.35	0.23	5.79		0.66	0.75	0.21		9.99	77	38
split	0.09	0.2							0.29	6	6
add_stack_incr	0.01								0.01	1	1
add_blacks	0.01								0.01	1	1
set_max_int	0.02								0.02	1	1
dfs1	53.52	12.88	36.39	3.06	28.06			9.01	142.92	218	24
dfs	4.6	0.23	11.63					0.31	16.77	51	35
Tarjan	0.44								0.44	16	6
Total	61.04	13.54	53.81	3.06	28.72	0.75	0.21	9.32	170.45	371	112

6   Conclusion

We presented a formal proof of Tarjan's algorithm for computing strongly connected components in a graph. There are other (less efficient) algorithms. We did prove the two-passes Kosaraju's algorithm in a similar way, but the proof for Tarjan is more involved. Many of the lemmas in our proof can be used for other algorithms on graphs such as acyclicity test, articulation points, or biconnected components. We had to fight with properties on sets, maybe because of a misusage of the Why3 library and the distinction between == (membership in both directions) and the extensional equality =.

In our presentation, we treated differently the *blacks* and *grays* sets. The main reason is that the automatic provers have difficulties when the data is too structured. We indeed started with flat formalizations where environment fields were passed as arguments of the functions. Then the automatic provers worked splendidly. But the presentation was uglier [10]. As soon as you have structures such as records, the automatic proofs are more complex and we had to help them with the inlining strategies of the Why3 ide. At time of writing this article, we could not succeed in introducing the *grays* set in the environment.

We also use the *rank* function and it is unclear if reasoning with the *num* field could be sufficient. Indeed if you want to escape painful properties about spanning trees and white paths, you have to speak about positions in the working stack. The ranks are an explicit expression of these positions. Moreover we had versions of Tarjan algorithm with just ranks and no numbers. The properties are then simpler, since there are less many variables in the algorithm: *stack*, *blacks*, *grays*, *sccs* and functions return ranks. But we experienced that the presentation is further from the initial sequential algorithm and therefore was less convincing.

We also said that white paths are difficult to handle and we then took an implicit description of the results of functions *dfs1* and *dfs*. One of the reasons is that a white path is a volatile notion, since its color could be modified on its intermediate vertices. The proofs are indeed longer than with simple edges.

Notice also that we only prove partial correctness. Total correctness is very easy since a variant with lexicographic ordering on the pair made of the number of white vertices and the number of roots is clearly decreasing.

This comes to the comparison with other formalisms. We have a similar proof fully in Coq/ssreflect [12] with the Mathematical Components library. The proof is 920-line long and a version with explicit expression of the results is 951-line long for the version of our algorithm with just ranks and no numbers depending upon the accounting of the Coq parts. Notice that the use of Mathematical Components makes Coq proofs much shorter. Still our proof is between two or four times shorter (up to the accounting of our Coq proofs), and we think that our proof is also much more readable. Coq demanded some agility to follow the same partial correctness proof. It would also be interesting to redo our proof in Isabelle or another system. In the literature, many articles are about graph concurrent algorithms, either embedded in Coq [25] or in separation logic [17, 23] or both. None of them treat strong connectivity except [22] by Kosaraju method and with reasoning more on spanning trees than on the effective program.

Hence, for a non-obvious algorithm, Why3 allowed us to achieve a not too long formal proof, not much sophisticated, as simple-minded as first-order logic, and fully described in this article. The system is easy to use, but very unstable which makes uneasy incremental development, although the replay function [4] of the Why3 ide greatly helps. But we gained in readability, which seems to us a very important criterion in formal proofs of programs. Thus we were able to present here the full details of this formal proof.

Acknowledgments. Thanks to the Why3 group at Inria-Saclay/LRI-Orsay for very valuable advices, to Cyril Cohen and Laurent Théry for their fantastic expertise in Coq proofs, to Claude Marché and the reviewers for many corrections.

References

1. Aho, A.V., Hopcroft, J.E., Ullman, J.D.: The Design and Analysis of Computer Algorithms. Addison-Wesley, Boston (1974)
2. Appel, A.W.: Verified Functional Algorithms, August 2016. www.cs.princeton.edu/~appel/vfa/
3. Bobot, F., Filliâtre, J.C., Marché, C., Melquiond, G., Paskevich, A.: The Why3 platform, version 0.86.1. LRI, CNRS and Univ. Paris-Sud and INRIA Saclay, version 0.86.1 edn., May 2015. why3.lri.fr/download/manual-0.86.1.pdf
4. Bobot, F., Filliâtre, J.-C., Marché, C., Melquiond, G., Paskevich, A.: Preserving user proofs across specification changes. In: Cohen, E., Rybalchenko, A. (eds.) VSTTE 2013. LNCS, vol. 8164, pp. 191–201. Springer, Heidelberg (2014). https://doi.org/10.1007/978-3-642-54108-7_10. hal.inria.fr/hal-00875395
5. Bobot, F., Filliâtre, J.C., Marché, C., Paskevich, A.: Let's verify this with Why3. Softw. Tools Technol. Transf. (STTT) **17**(6), 709–727 (2015). hal.inria.fr/hal-00967132
6. Charguéraud, A.: Program verification through characteristic formulae. In: Hudak, P., Weirich, S. (eds.) Proceeding of the 15th ACM SIGPLAN International Conference on Functional Programming (ICFP), pp. 321–332. ACM (2010). arthur.chargueraud.org/research/2010/cfml
7. Charguéraud, A.: Higher-order representation predicates in separation logic. In: Proceedings of the 5th ACM SIGPLAN Conference on Certified Programs and Proofs, pp. 3–14, CPP 2016. ACM, New York, January 2016
8. Charguéraud, A., Pottier, F.: Machine-checked verification of the correctness and amortized complexity of an efficient union-find implementation. In: Proceedings of the 6th International Conference on Interactive Theorem Proving (ITP), August 2015
9. Chen, R., Lévy, J.J.: Full script of Tarjan SCC Why3 proof. Technical report, Iscas and Inria (2017). jeanjacqueslevy.net/why3/graph/abs/scct/2/scc.html
10. Chen, R., Lévy, J.J.: Une preuve formelle de l'algorithme de Tarjan-1972 pour trouver les composantes fortement connexes dans un graphe. In: JFLA (2017)
11. Clochard, M.: Preuves taillées en biseau. In: vingt-huitièmes Journées Francophones des Langages Applicatifs (JFLA). Gourette, France, January 2017. hal.inria.fr/hal-01404935
12. Cohen, C., Théry, L.: Full script of Tarjan SCC Coq/ssreflect proof. Technical report, Inria (2017). github.com/CohenCyril/tarjan

13. Coq Development Team: the coq 8.5 standard library. Technical report, Inria (2015). coq.inria.fr/distrib/current/stdlib
14. Filliâtre, J.-C., Paskevich, A.: Why3 — where programs meet provers. In: Felleisen, M., Gardner, P. (eds.) ESOP 2013. LNCS, vol. 7792, pp. 125–128. Springer, Heidelberg (2013). https://doi.org/10.1007/978-3-642-37036-6_8
15. Gonthier, G., Mahboubi, A., Tassi, E.: A small scale reflection extension for the Coq system. Rapport de recherche RR-6455, INRIA (2008). hal.inria.fr/inria-00258384
16. Gonthier, G., et al.: Finite graphs in mathematical components (2012). ssr.msr-inria.inria.fr/ jenkins/current/Ssreflect.fingraph.html. The full library is available at www.msr-inria.fr/projects/mathematical-components-2
17. Hobor, A., Villard, J.: The ramifications of sharing in data structures. In: Proceedings of the 40th Annual ACM SIGPLAN-SIGACT Symposium on Principles of Programming Languages, pp. 523–536, POPL 2013. ACM, New York (2013). doi.acm.org/10.1145/2429069.2429131
18. Lammich, P., Neumann, R.: A framework for verifying depth-first search algorithms. In: Proceedings of the 2015 Conference on Certified Programs and Proofs, pp. 137–146, CPP 2015. ACM, New York (2015). doi.acm.org/10.1145/2676724.2693165
19. Lévy, J.J.: Essays for the Luca Cardelli Fest. In: Simple Proofs of Simple Programs in Why3. Microsoft Research Cambridge, MSR-TR-2014-104 (2014)
20. Mehta, F., Nipkow, T.: Proving pointer programs in higher-order logic. In: CADE (2003)
21. Poskitt, C.M., Plump, D.: Hoare logic for graph programs. In: VSTTE (2010)
22. Pottier, F.: Depth-first search and strong connectivity in Coq. In: Journées Francophones des Langages Applicatifs (JFLA 2015), January 2015
23. Raad, A., Hobor, A., Villard, J., Gardner, P.: Verifying concurrent graph algorithms. In: Igarashi, A. (ed.) APLAS 2016. LNCS, vol. 10017, pp. 314–334. Springer, Cham (2016). https://doi.org/10.1007/978-3-319-47958-3_17
24. Sedgewick, R., Wayne, K.: Algorithms, 4th edn. Addison-Wesley, Boston (2011)
25. Sergey, I., Nanevski, A., Banerjee, A.: Mechanized verification of fine-grained concurrent programs. In: Proceedings of the 36th ACM SIGPLAN Conference on Programming Language Design and Implementation, pp. 77–87, PLDI 2015. ACM, New York (2015). doi.acm.org/10.1145/2737924.2737964
26. Tarjan, R.: Depth first search and linear graph algorithms. SIAM J. Comput. 1, 146–160 (1972)
27. Théry, L.: Formally-proven Kosaraju's algorithm (2015). Inria report, Hal-01095533
28. Wengener, I.: A simplified correctness proof for a well-known algorithm computing strongly connected components. Inf. Process. Lett. 83(1), 17–19 (2002)
29. Why3 Development Team: Why3 gallery of programs. Technical report, CNRS and Inria (2016). toccata.lri.fr/gallery

Verifying Branch-Free Assembly Code in Why3

Marc Schoolderman$^{(\boxtimes)}$

Radboud University, Nijmegen, The Netherlands
m.schoolderman@science.ru.nl

Abstract. This paper discusses an approach to verification of assembly code using the Why3 platform. As a case study, we prove the functional correctness of hand-optimized routines for multiplying multiprecision integers on 8-bit microcontrollers which use an efficient version of Karatsuba's algorithm. We find that by carefully constructing an underspecified model of an instruction set architecture in Why3, and specifying a few simple lemmas, verification can succeed using a high degree of automation in a short amount of time. Furthermore, our approach is sensitive to subtle memory aliasing issues, demonstrating that formal verification of security-critical assembly code is not only feasible, but also effective.

Keywords: Why3 · Assembly language · Karatsuba multiplication

1 Introduction

Hand-optimized assembly code is usually hard to read and reason about. However, in application areas such as cryptographic engineering, the level of control over the code generation process it offers makes it a common means of implementing primitive operations. At the same time, the correctness of such implementations is critical for their security.

Formal verification often concerns itself with programs written in a higher level programming language. In these environments, the structured nature of programs aids reasoning about their properties, for example by allowing the formulation of loop invariants. In contrast, programs written in assembly language are more unstructured in nature. In these cases, the code itself does not facilitate structural reasoning, and so the structure of a correctness proof must be inferred from the code explicitly. Second, the semantics of assembly languages are more fine-grained, requiring more primitive operations to achieve a certain result, and consequently many more steps are needed in an accompanying deductive proof of its correctness.

This paper presents an approach to verifying optimized assembly code using the Why3 verification framework [8]. We show that this framework provides the tools to tackle both challenges, by allowing us to *logically partition* unstructured code to facilitate proofs, and enabling automation to take care of most intermediate steps needed in these proofs. We discovered that stepwise refinement of proofs — aimed at minimizing the need for user-supplied assertions, thus maximizing the utility of automated provers — allows this approach to scale.

© Springer International Publishing AG 2017
A. Paskevich and T. Wies (Eds.): VSTTE 2017, LNCS 10712, pp. 66–83, 2017.
https://doi.org/10.1007/978-3-319-72308-2_5

Using this approach, we have verified the multiprecision multiplication routines for the 8-bit AVR microarchitecture presented in [9], up to a 96 × 96-bit multiplication routine that employs Karatsuba's algorithm. We have also found that formal verification exposes a potential issue in some of the larger routines that is not likely to be detected by testing alone.

Organization of this paper. The remainder of this section will provide an overview of Why3, and the selected case study. In Sect. 2, we will discuss the general approach we propose for the verification of assembly programs using Why3. Section 3 shows how this approach has been applied in constructing a model for the AVR instruction set architecture, with Sect. 4 describing how we have subsequently used this model to verify the assembly programs we selected. Sections 5 and 6 conclude the paper by discussing related and future work.

1.1   The Why3 Verification Platform

Why3 [8] consists of two parts: a logical specification language, with libraries for reasoning about mathematical objects (such as integers, maps and sets) and a programming language in the form of WhyML. A verification condition generator extracts proof obligations from annotated WhyML programs; these are then discharged by either automated or interactive theorem provers. This process is illustrated in Fig. 1.

WhyML's primary use is as an intermediate language for verification of structured programs. However, it also has features that are useful in the context of unstructured code. In particular, its support for *abstract blocks*, *type invariants* and *bit-vector theories* turn out to be highly useful.

Using Why3 provides two major benefits. First, its verification condition generator and support for automated theorem provers allows the manual effort to focus more on *what* we need to prove, instead of *how* to prove it. Second, it allows using multiple theorem provers at no additional cost; allowing us to apply the state of the art in the field of automated (and interactive) theorem proving, and preventing a verification effort from getting hampered by the limitations of any single theorem prover.

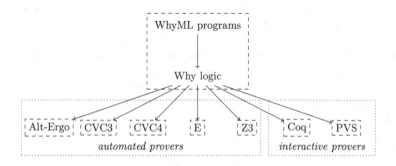

Fig. 1. Graphical representation of Why3 workflow

1.2 Multiprecision Multiplication

Optimization of multiprecision arithmetic for the AVR ATmega family of 8-bit microcontrollers is an active research area, with many possible implementation strategies [12]. As a case study for this paper, we selected the hand-optimized multiplication routines developed by Hutter and Schwabe [9]. These routines currently hold the speed records for multiplication on this architecture, and are written in the context of cryptographic engineering, to serve as a primitive for efficiently implementing elliptic curve computations. This makes it an interesting target for formal verification for two reasons:

1. These routines are used as primitives in other cryptographic code [6], and so their correctness is security-critical. Bug attacks have been demonstrated to lead to practical exploits [4]. Exhaustive testing of a multiplication routine is not feasible — testing a routine which multiplies two 32-bit numbers would already mean we have to check 2^{64} cases, and random testing is known to fail to catch bugs that are triggered with low probability [5].
2. Hand-optimized assembly code is difficult to analyse; as it will contain various tricks that would not suggest themselves at a higher level, such as direct manipulation of the carry flag, and bit manipulations aimed at eliminating conditional jumps.

In fact, the programs we selected for our case study are examples of *branch-free* code. In cryptographic engineering, branch-free code is preferred to avoid side-channel attacks [11,13]. This has the effect of eliminating control flow structure from assembly programs entirely, making verification potentially even harder. In essence, branch-free code is a sequential flow program, and a correctness proof of such code is a long sequence of symbolic rewriting steps. Note that when verifying assembly code that *does* contain jumps, the first step is also to split a program into a set of branch-free fragments [14], which then need to be verified in turn. Therefore, in this paper we focus purely on this type of code.

2 Verification Approach

To verify assembly code, we need a model of the underlying instruction set architecture. Such a model consists of a representation of the machine memory (i.e., the organization of the register file, condition flags, and memory), and a set of WhyML functions corresponding to the necessary instructions. Such a model can employ underspecification, as we can safely ignore features of a microarchitecture that are not used. The usefulness of a model can be increased by building a richer logical infrastructure on top of it. For example, to allow reasoning about multiprecision integers, we introduce the function uint in Sect. 3.1.

By modelling each instruction as a single WhyML function, expressing an assembly fragment as a WhyML program conforming to our model is a simple transformation which does not require special tools.

2.1   Validation of the Formal Model

The trustworthiness of formally verified software is only as good as the tools used for verification. This paper tries to address that issue by enforcing *internal consistency* of our model. That is, we carefully avoid introducing any logical axioms in our Why3 formalization that are not present in its standard library (or supporting theorem provers).

Furthermore, since all instructions are modelled using WhyML functions, we can simply provide full implementations of these functions (in terms of WhyML primitives). This will ensure that Why3 actually checks that the postconditions are possible to satisfy, and that they are consistent with respect to any type invariants specified, which is not the case had we modelled instructions using abstract function prototypes.

This approach also allows the model to act as a bridge between the official specification of an instruction set architecture, and a Why3 specification that is most suited for reasoning about the correctness of a particular piece of code. Since we use Why3 to verify the function body of a modelled instruction with respect to its specification, this specification can be tailored to fit a certain problem domain. At the same time, the function body can be created to adhere closely to an official reference document. This can increase the confidence in the correctness of a machine model without exposing automated provers to unnecessary complexity when using this model to verify programs.

2.2   Logical Partitioning

In principle the WhyML code obtained by translating an assembly program can be verified as any other — for example, we can insert `assert` statements anywhere to indicate conditions that are needed to achieve a particular result. However, for the scalability of our approach, it is important that the demands placed on automated provers can be kept under control for larger programs.

Using Why3's `abstract` mechanism, it is possible to group any number of instructions together in an *abstract block* and specify the effect that they collectively have on the program. This will hide all computations inside the block from being seen by theorem provers. The usefulness of this strategy rests on two observations:

1. Automated provers find proofs more efficiently when presented with as little irrelevant information as necessary.
2. By grouping related operations together, their collective result can be effectively summarized (by the user) as a formula that brings us closer to the result we are trying to prove.

The benefits of logically partitioning a program in this way are maximized if we are able to verify large groups of instructions fully automatically. To achieve this, a model should be optimized (using stepwise refinement) by trying it out on small program fragments, with the aim of reducing the number of user-inserted `assert` statements needed.

3   Modelling the AVR Instruction Set

The AVR architecture is a RISC architecture, containing 32 general purpose 8-bit registers. Most instructions take two operands; with the first operand functioning both as a source and destination for the operation. Memory is only accessed via dedicated load (LD, LDD) and store (ST, STD) instructions, which require a memory address to be stored (as a 16-bit value) in one of three dedicated register pairs, denoted in mnemonic form as X for the register pair (R26, R27), Y for the pair (R28, R29) and Z for the pair (R30, R31). The register file itself is also accessible, residing at memory address 0. The instructions that are most important in our case study are instructions for adding and subtracting with and without carry (ADD, ADC, SUB, SBC) and multiplication (MUL). The MUL instruction deviates from the two-operand convention by always producing its result in the register pair (R0, R1). In Karatsuba multiplication, bitwise exclusive or (EOR) and arithmetic right shift (ASR) also play an important role, as well as the BST and BLD instructions, which transfer a single bit between a general purpose register and the T flag in the CPU status register.

We model the AVR address space in Why3 as a map of addresses to integers, where we restrict the allowed values in the range of this map to conform to those representable as an unsigned 8-bit value by adding a *type invariant*:

```
type address_space = { mutable data: map int int }
  invariant { forall i. 0 <= self.data[i] < 256 }
```

This type is embellished with some syntactic sugar for accessing elements of an address space, allowing us to write a succinct specification of the MOV instruction, which copies a value from one register to another:

```
type register = int
val reg: address_space
val mov (dst src: register): unit
  writes { reg }
  ensures { reg = old (reg[dst<-reg[src]]) }
```

Here, the notation m[*addr<-value*] means the address space m obtained by assigning *value* to the address *addr*, and leaving all other values unaltered.

The AVR also contains eight 1-bit status flags, of which only the carry flag and 'transfer bit' (T flag) are relevant to our case study. We model these flags as a boolean value, and provide a conversion operator to interpret them as integers:

```
type cpu_flag = { mutable value: bool }
function (?) (x: cpu_flag): int = if x.value then 1 else 0
val cf: cpu_flag
```

Reasoning about the carry flag as an integer allows for the specification of the ADD instruction as follows:

```
val add (dst src: register): unit
```

```
writes { cf, reg }
ensures { reg = old (reg[dst <- mod (reg[dst]+reg[src]) 256]) }
ensures { ?cf = old (div (reg[dst]+reg[src]) 256) }
```

By specifying the result in terms of the mod and div operations, automated provers are easily able to use arithmetical theories to deduce that ?cf*256 + reg[dst] is exactly equal to the sum of the input values.

As an alternative approach, we have also attempted to model the register file using Why3's *bit-vector theories*; as a practical benefit, this would allow us to get rid of the type invariant mentioned above. However, it appears that the additional conversion function needed to convert a register to an integer value (similar to the one needed for the 1-bit status flags) hampered the efficacy of SMT solvers.

The largest Karatsuba routine we verified also required the AVR stack to store values; we have similarly modelled this as an address_space:

```
val stack_pointer: ref int
val stack: address_space

let push (src: register): unit
  writes { stack, stack_pointer }
  reads { reg }
  ensures { stack = old(stack[!stack_pointer <- reg[src]]) }
  ensures { !stack_pointer = old !stack_pointer - 1 }
```

This implicitly assumes that the stack and the space for registers and memory does not overlap. In our case study (as in most code), that is something that can be easily statically verified, and so we have not focused on this property.

3.1   Representing Multiprecision Integers

Integers that are too large to be represented as a single 8-bit value are represented by multiple bytes stored consecutively in memory (or the register file), with the least significant byte occupying the lowest address. To enable reasoning about this, we define a function uint n A b, taken to mean the integer formed by examining the n bytes stored in address space A, starting at position b. We can define this function in Why3 as uint n A $b = \sum_{0 \leq i < n} 2^{8i} \cdot A[i + b]$.

Automated provers, however, work much better when given an explicit first-order expression of a multiprecision integer for a concrete value of n, for instance by fully expanding uint 2 A b using the rule uint 2 A $b = A[b] + 256 \cdot A[b + 1]$. We can achieve this by adding these explicit rewrite rules as auxiliary lemmas, together with a set of meta directives instructing Why3 to expand matching occurrences of the uint function accordingly before handing a formula off to an SMT solver. This functionality is crucial, as it allows us to easily state properties about multiprecision integers in our model, while at the same time presenting them in a format that SMT solvers are able to cope with.

3.2   Using Ghost Code to Reduce Annotations

A drawback of modelling the AVR registers in combination with logical partitioning is that updates to individual registers will be hidden by the `abstract`
block: even if only a single register was altered, the only thing known outside
the `abstract` block is that the register file changed. This necessitates the specification of extra user-supplied annotations stating what part of the register file
remained constant.

Modelling each register individually (as a `ref int`) would solve this problem, as Why3 will in this case keep of track of which registers changed inside
the `abstract block`. However, this approach involves other drawbacks. For
instance, Why3's type system does not allow creating an array of `ref int`,
precluding the simple specification of the `uint` function of the previous section.

We solve this issue by combining both approaches, using *ghost code* [7]. In
addition to modelling the register file as specified in Sect. 3, we also model it a
second time using individual `ref int`'s, which are marked as `ghost` to prevent
them from affecting the semantics of the code under verification. We can then
specify as postcondition for each abstract block that the individual *ghost registers*
must be equal to those in the actual register file. Ensuring that this postcondition
holds is then simply done by updating only the registers that have actually been
modified — information that can be obtained by a simple static analysis — in
the *ghost register file*. We find that by using this trick Why3 is able to provide
SMT solvers with enough information so that unnecessary annotations can be
eliminated, reducing the total assertions needed by half.

3.3   Model Validation

As mentioned in Sect. 2.1, we are also interested in demonstrating the consistency
and validity of our model. As an example of this, consider the ADD instruction,
whose specification (as an abstract function prototype) was given in Sect. 3. The
reference manual [1] defines the effects of the ADD *Rd*, Rr instruction in terms of
operations on 8-bit registers, instead of the language of arithmetic:

$$Rd' \leftarrow Rd +_8 Rs$$
$$CF \leftarrow (Rd_7 \wedge Rr_7) \vee (Rr_7 \wedge \neg Rd_7') \vee (\neg Rd_7' \wedge Rd_7)$$

Where $+_8$ means 8-bit addition, and $R w_7$ denotes the most significant bit of $R w$.

We can let the *implementation* of our model of the ADD instruction follow this
specification closely by using Why3's *bit-vector theories*, which allow reasoning
about both arithmetical and bitwise operations on bit-vectors of various sizes,
and map onto the bit-vector theories of SMT solvers that support this reasoning
(CVC4 and Z3). In this case, the BV8 theory, which deals with 8-bit operations,
allows the above specification to be followed closely. The function BV8.add can
be used for performing the 8-bit addition, and the function BV8.nth for accessing
individual bits:

```
let add (dst src: register): unit
  writes { reg, cf }
  ensures { reg = old (reg[dst <- mod (reg[dst]+reg[src]) 256]) }
  ensures { ?cf = old (div (reg[dst]+reg[src]) 256) }
= let rd  = BV8.of_int (Map.get reg.data dst) in
  let rr  = BV8.of_int (Map.get reg.data src) in
  let rd' = BV8.add rd rr in
  reg.data <- Map.set reg.data dst (BV8.to_uint rd');
  if BV8.nth rd 7 && BV8.nth rr 7 ||
     BV8.nth rd 7 && not BV8.nth rd' 7 ||
     not BV8.nth rd' 7 && BV8.nth rr 7
  then
    cf.value <- 1
  else
    cf.value <- 0
```

Using this definition, Why3 will generate proof obligations to show that the postconditions and the type invariant of the register file hold. The proof of the type invariant is immediately discharged by the prover ALT-ERGO, and the first postcondition is easily solved by CVC3. The second postcondition is more complex, but is discharged by CVC4 in less then a minute.

By constructing the model in this manner, we can be confident that our model is as internally sound as the Why3 platform itself. Furthermore, by keeping the model readable we can get a high degree of confidence that our model captures the relevant parts of the AVR instruction set architecture correctly.

It should in theory also be possible to *externally validate* the model by using Why3's code extraction feature to turn it into an executable AVR simulator, and testing that against a reference implementation. However, code extraction of programs involving bit-vectors turned out to not be possible with the version of Why3 we used. Furthermore, since AVR devices can only be re-programmed a limited number of times, such validation could be costly if we were to use actual hardware as a reference.

3.4   Underspecification

Since our case study only required a small subset of the entire AVR microarchitecture, we have used underspecification in our model in the following areas:

– We only model instructions that are actually needed in the case study.
– We have only modelled the flags that are actually needed; since none of the other flags are ever used as inputs during any of the computations.
– We have modelled the register file and memory contents as two separate address spaces, and disallow accessing the register file in the LD and ST instructions, since the code we verify does not use this feature.
– We assume that there is enough room on the stack for the PUSH and POP instructions to work safely.

To properly handle loads and stores to and from memory, it is also necessary to know what constitutes a valid address for accessing SRAM. However, the allowed range of addresses is specific to each type of AVR microcontroller, and so we cannot verify this in general. A possible approach would be two specify two abstract constants in our model, ram_begin and ram_end, and add as a precondition to the LD and ST instructions that addresses must fall inside the interval [ram_begin, ram_end).

However, in our case study, memory is only accessed using addresses supplied by the caller, and so we have no choice but to assume that these addresses are correct anyway. Therefore we have not added an address sanity check in the current model.

4   Verifying AVR Assembly Code

The target of our verification effort was the *branch-free* multiplication routines presented by Hutter and Schwabe [9]. These consist of routines using a quadratic complexity "schoolbook" method called *operand-scanning* for integer sizes from 24 bits to 48 bits, as well as routines using the subquadratic Karatsuba method for multiplying integers of sizes from 48 bits to 256 bits.

For verification, we targeted all "schoolbook" routines for multiplying integers of 48 bits and less, as well as the routines using only one application of Karatsuba's method, which are all the routines for argument sizes of 96 bits and less. The routines for larger argument sizes require multiple (recursive) applications of Karatsuba's method. These do seem to be in reach of our approach, but we have not yet finished verification of these versions.

4.1   Operand-Scanning Multiplication

The operand-scanning multiplication can be summarized as follows. Let $A = \sum_{0 \leq i < n} 2^{8i} \cdot a_i$ and $B = \sum_{0 \leq i < n} 2^{8i} \cdot b_i$. Their product can be computed as:

$$A \cdot B = \sum_{0 \leq i,j < n} 2^{8(i+j)} \cdot a_i \cdot b_j$$

This can be implemented as an algorithm which iterates over the operands a_i and b_j, repeatedly multiplying and adding. This is exactly how the operand-scanning algorithms presented in [9] work. As an example, we show an AVR assembly version for multiplying two 16-bit values in Fig. 2, where A is stored in the register pair (R2,R3), and B is in the pair (R7,R8), with the result rendered in the registers (R12,R13,R14,R15). This algorithm first computes $2^{16} \cdot a_1 b_1 + a_0 b_0$, and then adds in $2^8 \cdot a_0 b_1$ and $2^8 \cdot a_1 b_0$ using two sequences consisting of ADD and ADC instructions.[1]

During verification, it appears the difficult part in the code of Fig. 2 is showing that after the last ADC in each such sequence, the carry flag is guaranteed to be

---

[1] As this version was not included in [9], we implemented it ourselves.

```
            CLR R23
            MUL R3, R8
            MOVW R14, R0
            MUL R2, R7
            MOVW R12, R0
            MUL R2, R8
            ADD R13, R0
            ADC R14, R1
            ADC R15, R23
            MUL R3, R7
            ADD R13, R0
            ADC R14, R1
            ADC R15, R23
```

```
let mul16()
ensures {
    uint 4 reg 12 = old(uint 2 reg 2*uint 2 reg 7)
}
= clr r23;
  mul r3 r8;
  movw r14  r0;
  mul r2 r7;
  movw r12 r0;
  mul r2 r8;
  add r13 r0;
  adc r14 r1;
  adc r15 r23;
  mul r3 r7;
  add r13 r0;
  adc r14 r1;
  adc r15 r23
```

Fig. 2. 16×16 bit multiplication in AVR assembly (left) and WhyML (right)

zero. At the end of the first sequence, this can still be easily manually asserted and automatically proven (by the prover z3), since the pair (R14,R15) contained at most the value $255 \cdot 255 = 254 \cdot 2^8 + 1$ before this sequence is executed, meaning that R15 contains at most the value 254. However, to prove that the second sequence does not result in a carry requires showing that a product of two 16-bit values fits in 32-bits. Manual attempts at showing this for larger routines with many sequences of ADD and ADC instructions resulted in a substantive amount of assertions, initially slowing down the verification effort. However, by iterative improvements of the proof for the small routine of Fig. 2, we discovered that adding a version of the aforementioned fact as a lemma in Why3 is beneficial:

Lemma. *Let m be a map from addresses to integers, where for each address i we have $0 \le m[i] < 256$. Then for all i, j we have $0 \le m[i] \cdot m[j] \le 255 \cdot 255$.*

Note that the condition in this lemma matches the type invariant in the definition of an **address_space** in Sect. 3 closely. Using this lemma, the prover CVC4 can automatically prove the code in Fig. 2 to be correct; that is, in the WhyML translation, the postcondition uint 4 reg 12 = old(uint 2 reg 2*uint 2 reg 7) is automatically verified in less than a second. The lemma itself is instantly proven by the prover ALT-ERGO.

More importantly, it turns out that this single lemma, together with the rewrite rules for the uint function mention in Sect. 3.1, are enough to prove the correctness of *all* other operand-scanning algorithms presented in [9] in a short amount of time, as shown in Table 1. This demonstrates that if we optimize proofs on small examples, automated provers can be successfully utilized to verify scaled-up versions without requiring further user intervention.

4.2   Karatsuba Multiplication

Starting at 48-bit multiplications, *subtractive Karatsuba multiplication* is found to be more efficient on the AVR than operand-scanning multiplication. In this case, the process for multiplying two n-bit integers A and B, looks as follows (slightly adapted from [9]):

- Write $A = 2^{n/2}A_h + A_l$, and $B = 2^{n/2}B_h + B_l$
- Let $L = A_l \cdot B_l$
- Let $H = A_h \cdot B_h$
- Let $M = |A_l - A_h| \cdot |B_l - B_h|$
- If $A_l \geq A_h \iff B_l \geq B_h$, obtain the result as

$$A \cdot B = L + 2^{n/2}(L + H - M) + 2^n H$$

- Otherwise, obtain the result as

$$A \cdot B = L + 2^{n/2}(L + H + M) + 2^n H$$

Note that to implement this algorithm as a strictly sequential program, some assembly tricks are needed. In particular, to obtain the result, and in the computation of M, a value needs to be conditionally negated. To achieve that without using a conditional branch, the assembly program uses the fact that, in two's complement representation, $-x$ is equal to $\overline{x} + 1 = (x \oplus \overline{0}) - \overline{0}$, where $\overline{v}$ denotes the bitwise complement of v, and $\oplus$ the bitwise exclusive or. Accordingly, when computing $A_l - A_h$ the program stores the resultant carry flag in a register using the SBC Rd, Rd instruction. This produces a value w in the register Rd, which will be $\overline{0}$ if the subtraction generated a carry, and 0 otherwise. And because a carry is only generated if $A_l < A_h$, we then have that for any value x, $(x \oplus w) - w$ is equal to $-x$ if $A_l < A_h$, and equal to x otherwise.

Partitioning. For verifying the Karatsuba implementations, we have used logical partitioning of the actual assembly program into *abstract blocks* by identifying (roughly) the following distinct computational steps in the implementation:

1. The computation of $L = A_l \cdot B_l$, using a *operand-scanning* multiplication.
2. The computation of $|A_l - A_h|$ and $|B_l - B_h|$.
3. A multiply-add step, which computes the product $H = A_h \cdot B_h$, and adds this to L to create $L + 2^{n/2}H$.
4. The computation of M by multiplying $|A_l - A_h|$ and $|B_l - B_h|$.
5. A processing step which prepares a bitmask $w = 0$ or $w = \overline{0}$ to control whether M will be negated in the next step, and which computes $(2^{n/2} + 1) \cdot (L + 2^{n/2}H) = L + 2^{n/2}(L + H) + 2^n H$.
6. Obtaining either M or $-M$ by computing $(M \oplus w) - w$.
7. Adding $2^{n/2}M$ or $-2^{n/2}M$ to the value from step 5 to obtain the desired result.

The steps mentioned are (in principle) documented in [9], which describes their design process, and they are also indicated by comments in the original source code. This structure is shared by all Karatsuba implementations (up to the 96×96-bit version). The main differences between these lie in the order in which data is loaded from memory into the available registers, and where the data is stored 'in flight'. For example, the 48×48-bit version does not use the 'T' flag, and only the 96×96-bit implementation used the CPU stack to store values. This did not alter the choice of partitioning. As an illustration, the WhyML code of the abstract block for step 2 for the 64×64-bit multiplication routine is shown in Fig. 3. The `modify_rN` statements at the end of this block indicate which registers are modified by the code inside it, and are used to update the *ghost registers*, as explained in Sect. 3.2.

In general, if assembly code is hand-written (or generated using a simple process), documentation is expected to be available for complicated routines, and should be sufficient to inform a partitioning of it into abstract blocks. If assembly code is written with verification in mind, it should also be possible to instruct programmers to indicate potential blocks, or even to employ verification already during the development process. On the other hand, it is probably much harder to find a useful partitioning in code emitted by an optimizing compiler.

Lemmas Needed. As in Sect. 4.1, some simple lemmas were needed to help along the automated verification of some of the resultant abstract blocks. In the case of Karatsuba's routine, these concerned themselves primarily with the bit manipulation involved in computing absolute values, as explained in the previous section. For instance, a lemma was needed for the fact that $w \oplus 0 = w$, and $w \oplus \overline{0} = 255 - w$, where w is an 8-bit vector.

Ordering of Load and Stores. As opposed to the operand-scanning routines, which multiply values already stored in the register file, the Karatsuba multiplication routine reads its input from SRAM (under control of the register pairs X and Y), and writes its result back to SRAM as well (under control of the register pair Z). In order to deal with register pressure, some of these loads and stores happen after some computation has already been performed. In particular, the lower three bytes of L are committed to memory before the values needed to compute H are loaded. In the 48-bit implementation, this happens in the following fragment:

```
abstract
ensures { synchronized shadow reg }
ensures { uint 4 reg 2 = old (abs (uint 4 reg 2 - uint 4 reg 18)) }
ensures { uint 4 reg 6 = old (abs (uint 4 reg 6 - uint 4 reg 22)) }
ensures { ?tf = 0 <-> old((uint 4 reg 2 < uint 4 reg 18) <->
                           (uint 4 reg 6 < uint 4 reg 22)) }
   sub r2 r18;
   sbc r3 r19;
   sbc r4 r20;
   sbc r5 r21;
   sbc r0 r0;

   sub r6 r22;
   sbc r7 r23;
   sbc r8 r24;
   sbc r9 r25;
   sbc r1 r1;

   eor r2 r0;
   eor r3 r0;
   eor r4 r0;
   eor r5 r0;
   eor r6 r1;
   eor r7 r1;
   eor r8 r1;
   eor r9 r1;

   sub r2 r0;
   sbc r3 r0;
   sbc r4 r0;
   sbc r5 r0;
   sub r6 r1;
   sbc r7 r1;
   sbc r8 r1;
   sbc r9 r1;

   eor r0 r1;
   bst r0 0;
modify_r0(); modify_r1(); modify_r2(); modify_r3(); modify_r4();
modify_r5(); modify_r6(); modify_r7(); modify_r8(); modify_r9();
end;
```

Fig. 3. Abstract block for computing $|A_l - A_h|$ and $|B_l - B_h|$, where A_l is stored in the registers R2,R3,R4,R5, A_h is stored in the registers R18,R19,R20,R21; B_l is stored in the registers R6,R7,R8,R9 and B_h is stored in the registers R22,R23,R24,R25.

```
STD Z+0, R8
STD Z+1, R9
STD Z+2, R10
LD R14, X+
LD R15, X+
LD R16, X+
LDD R17, Y+3
LDD R18, Y+4
LDD R19, Y+5
```

This code fragment caused several of the assertions relating the original memory contents to the contents of the register file to fail — the reason for this is that it cannot be proven that the memory contents read by the load instructions (LD and LDD) is not altered by the store (STD) instructions. This would indeed cause an invalid computation in the unlikely case where the memory pointed to by Z overlaps with the upper three bytes of either of the input values.

To prohibit this situations and allow the entire Karatsuba routine to be verified, preconditions are necessary to ensure the memory separation of the input and outputs, which take the form:

uint 2 reg Z $+ m \leq$ uint 2 reg X $\lor$ uint 2 reg Z $\geq$ uint 2 reg X $+ n$

uint 2 reg Z $+ m \leq$ uint 2 reg Y $\lor$ uint 2 reg Z $\geq$ uint 2 reg Y $+ n$

However, in the case of the 48-bit and 64-bit implementations, it was straightforward to rearrange the code fragment so that the STD instructions happen after the LD instructions, removing the problem (and the need for any special precondition) altogether. In the 80-bit implementation, improving the implementation in this manner is not possible due to the increased register pressure, and so the preconditions (with $m = 0$ and $n = 10$) were necessary. For the 96-bit implementation, this separation precondition was even more restrictive ($m = 6$ and $n = 12$), prohibiting most forms of aliasing input and output memory locations.

This leads to the observation that these routines are not perfect drop-in replacement for each-other: whereas the 80-bit (or smaller) implementations can safely be called if the output overlaps with either of the inputs, the 96-bit cannot. This could be a problem if the implementations are not used properly. While we do not consider this to be a bug in the original code, it does show that formal verification using our technique is indeed able to catch subtle issues like these in real-world complex assembly code.

Discovery of this problem was guided by automated provers and Why3: when several assertions fail to verify within a reasonable time frame, one approach is to insert more assertions in order to find the exact step that automated provers have difficulties with, and see what can be done to address this. In this case, this led to the discovery that the code did not satisfy the assertion.

Verification Results. Using the partitioned and annotated WhyML program as input, we can use Why3 to generate verification conditions. All proof obligations that were generated, as well as the lemmas we needed, could be proven

Table 1. Statistics of verifying optimized AVR multiplication routines

	Program size	Annotations	Verification time	Provers used
Operand scanning				
16×16	13 lines	1	0 s	CVC4
24×24	33 lines	1	1 s	CVC4
32×32	59 lines	1	4 s	CVC4
40×40	93 lines	1	10 s	CVC4
48×48	136 lines	1	33 s	CVC4
Karatsuba				
48×48	169 lines	23	52 s	CVC4, CVC3, E
64×64	286 lines	21	96 s	CVC4, CVC3, E
80×80	411 lines	31	215 s	CVC4, CVC3, E
96×96	611 lines	39	906 s	CVC4, CVC3, E

by a combination of the SMT solvers CVC3 and CVC4. In a handful of cases the automated E theorem prover was needed. As shown in Table 1, many of the smaller routines could be verified in less than a minute. We have also listed the number of annotations that had to be supplied by the user, in the form of `assert` statement or `ensures`-clauses for the abstract blocks described in Sect. 4.2. This count also includes the desired post-condition for the entire function, and any possible `requires`-clauses needed as described in Sect. 4.2.

Due to the growing complexity of the verification conditions, the total verification time does grow dramatically, especially for the 96×96 multiplication routine. On the other hand, the number of required annotations required per line of code actually decreases. It should be noted that we have also found that the verification time of the 96×96-bit routine can be brought down by adding extra annotations — however, we prefer to minimize the number of user-annotations required, since we have found these to be the largest bottleneck in verification.

5   Related Work

An early work on verifying machine code using an automated prover is given by Yu [16], who used the Nqthm theorem prover to produce formal proofs about object code generated for the Motorola 68020 microprocessor.

Pereira and Sousa [14] have used WhyML as an intermediate language for the verification of ARM code. Their work focuses on handling the unstructured control flow of assembly language: they have written the ARMY tool that splits an assembly language program containing jumps into a series of purely sequential basic blocks, where the user specifies pre- and postconditions for each block, and then hands these off to Why3. They also provide a cost model to enable complexity analysis. This work is therefore complementary to ours, since we focus on the effective verification of large purely sequential programs that are supposed to run in constant time. In essence we show that for verification, assembly programs can benefit from being split into more basic blocks than strictly necessary in their approach.

Chen et al. [5] have verified a *Montgomery ladder step* of an elliptic curve computation for the X86-64. architecture. The most complex step of this computation is a 256×256-bit multiplication, which is verified by translating (using a special-purpose converter) annotated QHASM [3] code to input for the SMT solver BOOLECTOR. Their approach appears to require more user intervention (in the form of annotations) to perform the actual proofs, as well as more computational resources — requiring more than an hour of computational effort. On a 64-bit machine, a 256×256-bit multiplication is equivalent (in terms of instruction complexity) to a 32×32-bit multiplication on the 8-bit AVR, which we are able to verify using modest resources and without annotations. On the other hand, the code they verify is more extensive and diverse, as they also verify that their code performs other operations (such as an efficient reduction modulo $2^{255} - 19$), making the results hard to compare directly.

Schwabe and Schmaltz [15] first attempted to verify the 48-bit multiplication routines examined in this paper using ACL2 in combination with external SAT solvers. However, their approach focused on proving functional equivalence between two implementations, instead of proving correctness with respect to a simple specification, and required much more CPU time than the approach presented in this paper.

Branch-free assembly code provides many more opportunities for formal verification. For instance, Barthe et al. [2] present a type system to mark certain data as confidential, and provide an analysis that can be used to show that the control flow and sequences of memory accesses of programs does not depend on this confidential data. They also prove that x86 programs that are constant-time in this sense are safe from cache-based attacks, using the Coq interactive theorem prover.

6   Conclusion

The main contribution of this paper is the fact that by finding the right balance between manual verification and proof automation, verification of large and optimized assembly code is feasible. The Why platform offers the machinery for striking this balance. In particular, the key to using automated provers to prove large and complex properties efficiently is the ability to not only *summarize*, but also *prune* the proof context. Why3's `abstract` blocks provides a significant degree of control over this context.

Another advantage of using an off-the-shelf verification platform such as Why3 is that we have a higher confidence in the correctness of our result, as it can be proven to be internally consistent, assuming that Why3 itself is consistent. The validity of our model is also more easily examined than in the approach taken in [5].

The manual effort involved in our approach concerns itself with imposing a structure on an assembly language program by partitioning it into blocks, controlling the information that will be presented to an automated prover. This requires knowledge that is not necessarily easily deduced from the source code of an assembly program. The best way to reduce this manual effort would be to have programmers annotate assembly programs while writing them, indicating which groups of instructions form a block and specifying the pre- and postconditions of such a block.

6.1 Future Work

We would like to try our approach on even larger examples; the larger multiple-level Karatsuba routines presented in [9], up to 256 bits, are an obvious first choice. To verify assembly programs that contain control flow, combining our approach with the sequentialization technique of [14] seems an obvious next step, and should not pose much difficulties.

We are also interested in trying out the approach for other forms of unstructured code, such as the portable assembly language implemented in QHASM [3] or the Instruction List language used in programmable logic controllers. In these latter two cases, we expect the challenge to mainly consists of constructing a model that can be both validated, and has the right expressivity so that it is suitable for many different applications.

Finally, an interesting research question remains with the respect of identifying an appropriate *logical partitioning*. We expect that determining the point at which some proof context becomes irrelevant should be detectable by some automatic means. Why3 already has some support for automatically pruning a proof context in the poorly documented *bisect* feature [10], but this is computationally expensive and needs to be repeated for every individual verification condition.

Availability of Code. The Why3 code used in this paper can be obtained in full at https://gitlab.science.ru.nl/sovereign/why3-avr.

Acknowledgement. This work is part of the research programme 'Sovereign' with project number 14319 which is (partly) financed by the Netherlands Organisation for Scientific Research (NWO).

References

1. Atmel Corporation: AVR Instruction Set Manual, revision 0856L (2016)
2. Barthe, G., Betarte, G., Campo, J., Luna, C., Pichardie, D.: System-level non-interference for constant-time cryptography. In: Proceedings of the 2014 ACM SIGSAC Conference on Computer and Communications Security, CCS 2014, pp. 1267–1279. ACM, New York (2014)
3. Bernstein, D.J.: qhasm: tools to help write high-speed software. http://cr.yp.to/qhasm.html. Accessed 01 Dec 2016
4. Brumley, B.B., Barbosa, M., Page, D., Vercauteren, F.: Practical realisation and elimination of an ECC-related software bug attack. In: Dunkelman, O. (ed.) CT-RSA 2012. LNCS, vol. 7178, pp. 171–186. Springer, Heidelberg (2012). https://doi.org/10.1007/978-3-642-27954-6_11
5. Chen, Y.F., Hsu, C.H., Lin, H.H., Schwabe, P., Tsai, M.H., Wang, B.Y., Yang, B.Y., Yang, S.Y.: Verifying Curve25519 software. In: Proceedings of the 2014 ACM SIGSAC Conference on Computer and Communications Security, CCS 2014, pp. 299–309. ACM (2014)
6. Düll, M., Haase, B., Hinterwälder, G., Hutter, M., Paar, C., Sánchez, A.H., Schwabe, P.: High-speed Curve25519 on 8-bit, 16-bit, and 32-bit microcontrollers. Des. Codes Crypt. **77**(2–3), 493–514 (2015)
7. Filliâtre, J.-C., Gondelman, L., Paskevich, A.: The spirit of ghost code. In: Biere, A., Bloem, R. (eds.) CAV 2014. LNCS, vol. 8559, pp. 1–16. Springer, Cham (2014). https://doi.org/10.1007/978-3-319-08867-9_1
8. Filliâtre, J.-C., Paskevich, A.: Why3 — Where programs meet provers. In: Felleisen, M., Gardner, P. (eds.) ESOP 2013. LNCS, vol. 7792, pp. 125–128. Springer, Heidelberg (2013). https://doi.org/10.1007/978-3-642-37036-6_8
9. Hutter, M., Schwabe, P.: Multiprecision multiplication on AVR revisited. J. Cryptographic Eng. **5**(3), 201–214 (2015)
10. Jackson, P., Schanda, F., Wallenburg, A.: Auditing user-provided axioms in software verification conditions. In: Pecheur, C., Dierkes, M. (eds.) FMICS 2013. LNCS, vol. 8187, pp. 154–168. Springer, Heidelberg (2013). https://doi.org/10.1007/978-3-642-41010-9_11
11. Kocher, P., Jaffe, J., Jun, B.: Differential power analysis. In: Wiener, M. (ed.) CRYPTO 1999. LNCS, vol. 1666, pp. 388–397. Springer, Heidelberg (1999). https://doi.org/10.1007/3-540-48405-1_25
12. Liu, Z., Seo, H., Großschädl, J., Kim, H.: Reverse product-scanning multiplication and squaring on 8-bit AVR processors. In: Hui, L.C.K., Qing, S.H., Shi, E., Yiu, S.M. (eds.) ICICS 2014. LNCS, vol. 8958, pp. 158–175. Springer, Cham (2015). https://doi.org/10.1007/978-3-319-21966-0_12
13. Molnar, D., Piotrowski, M., Schultz, D., Wagner, D.: The program counter security model: automatic detection and removal of control-flow side channel attacks. In: Won, D.H., Kim, S. (eds.) ICISC 2005. LNCS, vol. 3935, pp. 156–168. Springer, Heidelberg (2006). https://doi.org/10.1007/11734727_14
14. Pereira, M., de Sousa, S.M.: Complexity checking of ARM programs, by deduction. In: Proceedings of the 29th Annual ACM Symposium on Applied Computing, SAC 2014, pp. 1309–1314. ACM, New York (2014)
15. Schwabe, P., Schmaltz, J.: Verification of optimised 48-bit multiplications on AVR. Radboud University, Technical report (2015)
16. Yu, Y.: Automated proofs of object code for a widely used microprocessor. University of Texas at Austin, Austin, TX, USA, Technical report (1993)

How to Get an Efficient yet Verified Arbitrary-Precision Integer Library

Raphaël Rieu-Helft[1,2,3], Claude Marché[2,3(✉)], and Guillaume Melquiond[2,3]

[1] École Normale Supérieure, 75230 Paris, France
[2] Inria, Université Paris-Saclay, 91120 Palaiseau, France
Claude.Marche@inria.fr
[3] LRI (CNRS & Univ. Paris-Sud), Université Paris-Saclay, 91405 Orsay, France

Abstract. The GNU Multi-Precision library is a widely used, safety-critical, library for arbitrary-precision arithmetic. Its source code is written in C and assembly, and includes intricate state-of-the-art algorithms for the sake of high performance. Formally verifying the functional behavior of such highly optimized code, not designed with verification in mind, is challenging. We present a fully verified library designed using the Why3 program verifier. The use of a dedicated memory model makes it possible to have the Why3 code be very similar to the original GMP code. This library is extracted to C and is compatible and performance-competitive with GMP.

Keywords: Arbitrary-precision arithmetic
Deductive program verification · C language · Why3 program verifier

1 Introduction

The GNU Multi-Precision library,[1] GMP for short, is a widely used library for arithmetic on integers and rational numbers of arbitrary size. Its applications range from academic research (e.g. research on computational algebra) to concrete applications of our daily life (e.g. security of Internet applications). Some of these applications make GMP safety-critical. In this paper, we focus on the mpn component of GMP, which is dedicated to non-negative integers and is used as a basis in all others components. For maximal performance, GMP uses numerous state-of-the-art algorithms for basic operations like addition, multiplication, and division; these algorithms are selected depending on size of the numbers involved. Moreover, the implementation is written in low-level C code, and depending on the target computer architecture, some parts are even rewritten in assembly.

Being highly optimized for run-time efficiency, the code of GMP is intricate and thus error-prone. It is extensively tested but it is hard to reach a satisfactory coverage in practice: the number of possible inputs is very large, the different branches of the algorithms are numerous, and some of them are taken with a very low probability (some branches are taken with probability 2^{-64} or less).

---

[1] http://gmplib.org/.

© Springer International Publishing AG 2017
A. Paskevich and T. Wies (Eds.): VSTTE 2017, LNCS 10712, pp. 84–101, 2017.
https://doi.org/10.1007/978-3-319-72308-2_6

Bugs in the division, occurring with very low probability, were discovered in the past.[2] Verifying the code for all inputs using static program verification is thus desirable. Such a verification, however, is difficult, not only because of the intrinsic complexity of the algorithms, but also because the code is written in a low-level language with performance in mind, but not verification. In this paper we present an approach to address this latter challenge.

The main idea of our approach is to first write the code in some higher-level language, namely the programming language WhyML supported by the Why3 verification environment. This language is designed for static verification with respect to some functional behavior specified using an expressive formal specification language. The main issue is then to convert such a high-level code into an efficient executable code. Our approach is to first design a dedicated *memory model* in Why3, on top of which we then implement our functions. This memory model is designed to permit a direct compilation from WhyML to C. As a result, we obtain the first fully verified library, compatible with GMP (function signatures are the same), and almost as efficient as GMP on medium-sized integers (up to around 20 words of 64 bits). The full development is available from http://toccata.lri.fr/gallery/multiprecision.en.html.

The paper is organized as follows. In Sect. 2, we present the design of our dedicated memory model and explain how it is suitable for compilation to C. In Sect. 3, we present the specifications and the algorithms we implemented for arithmetic operations. In Sect. 4, we present an extensive evaluation of the efficiency of the generated code, comparing it with GMP. We discuss related work in Sect. 5 and we conclude in Sect. 6.

2   From WhyML to C

Why3 is an environment for deductive program verification, providing a rich language for specification and programming, called WhyML. WhyML is used as an intermediate language for verification of C, Java, and Ada programs [12,18], and is also intended to be comfortable as a primary programming language [13]. WhyML function definitions are annotated with pre- and postconditions both for normal and exceptional termination, and loops are annotated with invariants.

The specification component of WhyML [5,9], used to write program annotations and background theories, is an extension of first-order logic. It features ML-style polymorphic types (prenex polymorphism), algebraic data types, inductive and co-inductive predicates, and recursive definitions over algebraic types. Constructions like pattern matching, let-binding, and conditionals, can be used directly inside formulas and terms. Why3 comes with a rich standard library providing general-purpose theories useful for specifying programs, including integer and real arithmetic. From programs annotated with specifications, Why3 generates proof obligations and dispatches them to multiple provers, including SMT solvers Alt-Ergo, CVC4, Z3, TPTP first-order provers E, SPASS, Vampire, and interactive theorem provers Coq, Isabelle, and PVS. As most of the provers do

---

[2] Look for 'division' at https://gmplib.org/gmp5.0.html.

```
type int32
val function to_int (n:int32) : int
meta coercion function to_int
predicate in_bounds (n:int) = - 0x8000_0000 ≤ n ≤ 0x7fff_ffff
axiom to_int_in_bounds: forall n:int32. in_bounds (to_int n)
val mul (x y:int32) : int32
  requires { in_bounds (to_int x * to_int y)  }
  ensures  { to_int result = to_int x * to_int y }
```

Fig. 1. Excerpt from the specification of 32-bit machine words in Why3.

not support some of the language features, typically pattern matching, polymorphic types, or recursion, Why3 applies a series of encoding transformations to eliminate unsupported constructions before dispatching a proof obligation.

The programming part of WhyML is a dialect of ML with a number of restrictions to make automated proving easier. The major restriction concerns the potential aliasing of mutable data structures. The language and its typing system are designed so that all aliases are statically known. Technically, the typing system computes *read* and *write effects* on *singleton regions* for each sub-expression [10]. These effects allow the design of a weakest precondition calculus that is as simple as for the *while* languages usually considered in classical Hoare logic. Verification of complex code with Why3 and automatic provers typically expects user guidance through addition of intermediate assertions [19] and verification-only code (*ghost code*) [11]. See Why3's Web site[3] for an extensive tutorial and a large collection of examples [6].

The *extraction* mechanism of Why3 amounts to compiling WhyML code into a regular programming language while forgetting verification-only annotations. Why3 natively supports extraction to OCaml. For our work we had to implement extraction to C code. To obtain C code that includes low-level memory access through pointers, it was mandatory to start by designing a Why3 model of the C memory heap and pointers, where potential pointer aliasing is controlled in a way that accommodates WhyML typing system. The description of this memory model and the extraction to C is the purpose of the rest of this section.

2.1 Machine Words and Arithmetic Primitives

In WhyML, only the type int of unbounded mathematical integers is a built-in data type. Machine integers are defined instead in Why3's standard library, specified either in terms of intervals of mathematical integers or with bitvectors [15]. We use the first option here, which is roughly described in Fig. 1 for signed 32-bits words. The type int32 is abstract, equipped with a projection to_int mapping words to their mathematical value. Predicate in_bounds together with axiom to_int_in_bounds specify their possible range. Arithmetic operators like

---

[3] http://why3.lri.fr/.

```
let constant max = 0xffff_ffff_ffff_ffff
val mul_mod (x y:uint64) : uint64
   ensures { to_int result = mod (x * y) (max+1) }
val mul_double (x y:uint64) : (uint64,uint64)
   returns { (l,h) → l + (max+1) * h = x * y }
```

Fig. 2. Multiplication operations on `uint64`.

multiplication are then specified in terms of a pre-condition preventing overflows, and a post-condition giving the expected value of the result. Notice the special `meta` declaration which is a recent addition in Why3. It indicates that `int32` words should be implicitly cast to their integer values in specifications. For example, in the contract of function `mul`, we could omit all occurrences of `to_int`, which we do in the rest of the paper.

To implement arbitrary-precision arithmetic, we have added primitive operations that allow overflows. This is shown in Fig. 2 for unsigned 64-bit words. The function `mul_mod` has a wrap-around semantics (result is taken modulo 2^{64}), while the function `mul_double` returns the full product as a pair of words. Similarly, addition and subtraction come in different flavors (defensive against overflow, 2-complement, with carry in/out). Logical shifts also have both a defensive version and a version with a two-word output. Finally, there is only one division primitive, which takes a two-word numerator and a one-word denominator, and computes a quotient and a remainder.

Regarding extraction, all these data types for machine words are translated into their relevant C types (e.g. `uint64_t`). The axiomatized operations are replaced by their equivalent native C functions when possible. For example, both operations `mul` and `mul_mod` are extracted to C multiplication, since C operators on unsigned integer types are guaranteed to have the expected semantics for overflows. The `mul_double` operation, however, does not map to any C operator, so we import the corresponding operation from GMP's `longlong.h` file. Reusing GMP's primitives does not only make our library portable to numerous architectures, but it also makes for fairer benchmarks, allowing us to compare the efficiency of big integer algorithms independently of the primitives.

2.2 A Simple Model for C Pointers and Heap Memory

Arbitrary-precision integers are represented in C as buffers of unsigned machine words. The functions manipulate pointers, make use of aliasing, and sometimes operate in place. To implement these functions in WhyML, we design a model where the needed pointer operations are axiomatized, as shown in Fig. 3. At extraction, these operations are then directly replaced by their C equivalents, indicated as comments in Fig. 3. Our model only specifies the C features we need. For pointer arithmetic, we only model incrementation of a pointer by an integer, as we have no use for pointer comparisons or subtractions. We do not need pointer cast either, nor do we need the C address-of operator &. Generally

```
1   type ptr 'a = { mutable data : array 'a ; offset : int }
2
3   function plength (p:ptr 'a) : int = p.data.length
4
5   function pelts (p:ptr 'a) : (int → 'a) = p.data.elts
6
7   val malloc (sz:uint32) : ptr 'a    (*    malloc(sz * sizeof('a))   *)
8     requires { sz > 0 }
9     ensures  { plength result = sz ∨ plength result = 0 }
10    ensures  { result.offset = 0 }
11
12  val free (p:ptr 'a) : unit                           (*    free(p)   *)
13    requires { p.offset = 0 }
14    writes   { p.data }
15    ensures  { plength p = 0 }
16
17  predicate valid (p:ptr 'a) (sz:int) =
18    0 ≤ sz ∧ 0 ≤ p.offset ∧ p.offset + sz ≤ plength p
19
20  val get (p:ptr 'a) : 'a                              (*      *p    *)
21    requires { 0 ≤ p.offset < plength p }
22    ensures  { result = p.data[p.offset] }
23
24  val set (p:ptr 'a) (v:'a) : unit                     (*    *p = v  *)
25    requires { 0 ≤ p.offset < plength p }
26    writes   { p.data.elts }
27    ensures  { pelts p = Map.set (pelts (old p)) p.offset v }
28
29  val incr (p:ptr 'a) (ofs:int32) : ptr 'a             (*    p+ofs   *)
30    requires { p.offset + ofs ≤ plength p }
31    alias    { p.data ~ result.data }
32    ensures  { result.offset = p.offset + ofs }
33    ensures  { result.data = p.data }
34
35  val get_ofs (p:ptr 'a) (ofs:int32) : 'a              (*    *(p+ofs)  *)
36    requires { 0 ≤ p.offset + ofs < plength p }
37    ensures  { result = p.data[p.offset + ofs] }
```

Fig. 3. A Why3 memory model for C pointers and heap memory.

speaking, we do not use a model that would cover all features of C, because we want to benefit from the non-aliasing properties provided by Why3's static typing system. The benefit is that both the specifications and the proofs are simpler. With a general model of C heap memory, we would need to state a lot of non-aliasing hypotheses among the pointers, these properties would generate extra VCs to be established by back-end provers, moreover the other VCs will be more difficult to discharge.

The C heap memory is seen as a set of memory blocks called *objects* in the C99 standard. The WhyML polymorphic type `ptr` `'a` (Fig. 3, line 1) represents pointers to blocks storing data of type `'a`. The field `data` of a pointer is an array containing the block content, while the field `offset` indicates which array cell it points to. This construction supports pointer aliasing: several pointers may reference the same array (and thus point inside the same memory block). Thanks to WhyML's region-based type system, an assignment through one pointer is propagated to other pointers.

Pointers are allocated by the `malloc` function. In case of failure it returns an *invalid* pointer, represented by a block of length 0. As such, we forbid passing 0 to `malloc`. The `free` function invalidates its parameter by setting the length of its block to 0. A pointer is considered *valid for a size s* (Fig. 3, line 17) if its offset plus s does not exceed the size of its block. The function `get` (line 20) represents pointer dereferencing for reading. The function `set` represents memory assignment; the `writes` clause specifies the expected write effect on the block.

The `incr` function (line 29) returns the sum of a pointer and an integer. Just as in the C standard [16, Sect. 6.5.6, "Additive Operators"], one may only compute a pointer that points inside a valid block or to the element just past it. The Why3 keyword `alias` in the signature of `incr` declares the aliasing of the returned pointer with the pointer parameter. Behind the scenes, it unifies the regions of `p.data` and `result.data` [10]. This aliasing is correct not only with respect to setting the contents of the pointed block, but also with respect to `free`. This makes it possible to write a particularly short specification for `free`: the `writes` effect on `p.data` induces a so-called *reset* on it [10], meaning that the region formerly pointed by `p` can no longer be accessed by any of its aliases, which are invalidated.

2.3   Extracting to Idiomatic C Code

The main objective of our extraction is to produce code that is correct and as efficient as possible for our arbitrary-precision library. Some WhyML language features, such as algebraic types and higher-order functions, are hard to translate into C because they would require introducing complex constructions like closures and automatic memory allocation and deallocation. Therefore, we decided to support only a small fragment of the WhyML language in our extraction. The goal is not so much to extract arbitrary WhyML code to C as to extract imperative, almost C-like WhyML code to a simple and efficient C program. The supported features of WhyML are those that can be translated straightforwardly to C, such as loops or references. What we gain by giving up on so many language features is that the extraction process is extremely straightforward, and the extracted code resembles the WhyML code line-to-line, with very little added complexity. This makes it easier to obtain efficient C code, as the WhyML programmer can have a good idea of what the extracted code will be like. The straightforwardness of the extraction also gives a measure of additional trust in the extracted code and in the extraction process, which is not formally verified.

We now present in more details a few language features that we need to design our library, for which the translation to C is not direct.

Compilation of Exceptions into break or return Statements. WhyML does not support certain standard imperative constructs natively. For example, it provides neither **break** nor **return**, which are used by some GMP algorithms, e.g. big integer comparison (Sect. 3.2). So, we encode these constructs using WhyML's exception mechanism. Our extraction recognizes when exceptions can be turned into **break** or **return** statements. For **break**, we essentially detect the following pattern and extract all instances of **raise B** in the body of the loop (but not inside potential inner nested loops) as **break**.

```
try while ... do ... raise B ... done with B → () end
```

For **return**, we similarly detect the following pattern of function definitions and extract all instances of **raise (R e)** as **return e**.

```
let f (args) = ... ; try ... raise (R e) ... with R v → v end
```

Note that the **try with** construct must be in tail position of the function body. Our extraction recognizes these patterns independently of the names of the exceptions being used. Any **try with** or **raise** construct that does not fit in any of these patterns causes the program to be rejected by our extraction.

Multiple Return Values. Many of our WhyML functions, particularly arithmetic primitives, return multiple values in a tuple, as can be seen with the mul_double primitive (Fig. 2). This has no native equivalent in C. We choose to extract each function returning a tuple as a C function returning void, taking as extra parameters a pointer per component of the tuple. We detect the call pattern

```
let f (a:int32) : (int32,int32) =
  let b = a+a in
  (a,b)


let g () : int32 =
  let x = Int32.of_int 42 in
  let (y,z) = f x in
  z - y
```

```
void f(int32_t * result,
       int32_t * result1,
       int32_t a) {
  int32_t b;
  b = (a + a);
  (*result) = a;
  (*result1) = b;
  return;
}

int32_t g() {
  int32_t y, z;
  f(&y, &z, 42);
  return (z - y);
}
```

Fig. 4. WhyML function returning a tuple (on the left) and its C extraction.

```
let (x1, x2, ...) = f(args) in ...
```

and extract it as

```
f(&x1, &x2, ..., args); ...
```

Figure 4 shows the C program extracted from a WhyML code that defines and calls a function that returns a tuple.

3   Computing with Arbitrary-Precision Integers

3.1   Algorithm Specifications

Just as in GMP, we represent natural integers as buffers of unsigned integers called *limbs*. We set a radix β (generally $\beta = 2^{32}$ or 2^{64}, but the proofs only require it to be a power of 2). Any natural number N has a unique radix-β decomposition $\sum_{k=0}^{n-1} a_k \beta^k$, which is represented as the buffer $a_0 a_1 \ldots a_{n-1}$ (with the least significant limb first).

For efficiency, there is no memory management in the low-level functions, so the caller code has to keep track of number sizes. Operands are specified by a pointer to their least significant limb and a limb count of type `int32`.

```
type limb = uint64
type t = ptr limb
```

If a pointer a is valid over a size n, we denote:

$$\mathtt{value}(a, n) = \overline{a_0 \ldots a_{n-1}} = \sum_{k=0}^{n-1} a_k \beta^k.$$

In our Why3 development, `value` is defined recursively

```
let rec ghost function value_sub (x:map int limb) (n:int) (m:int) : int
    variant {m - n}
= if n < m then x[n] + radix * value_sub x (n+1) m else 0

function value (x:t) (sz:int) : int =
    value_sub (pelts x) x.offset (x.offset + sz)
```

While the functions of our library use only machine types (pointers, limbs, etc.), their specifications are expressed in terms of mathematical integers through extensive use of the function `value`. As an example, Fig. 5 shows the specification of the addition function. Note that the region-based type system forbids aliasing `r` with `x` or `y`. Notice also that the specification is well-typed because the conversion functions from `int32` and `limb` to `int` are coercions: otherwise many applications of `to_int` would be required.

```
(** [wmpn_add r x sx y sy] adds [(x, sx)] to [(y,sy)] and writes the
result in [(r, sx)]. [sx] must be greater than or equal to [sy].
Returns carry, either 0 or 1. Corresponds to [mpn_add]. *)
let wmpn_add (r:t) (x:t) (sx:int32) (y:t) (sy:int32) : limb
  requires { 0 ≤ sy ≤ sx }
  requires { valid x sx }
  requires { valid y sy }
  requires { valid r sx }
  writes   { r.data.elts }
  ensures  { 0 ≤ result ≤ 1 }
  returns  { carry → value r sx + (power radix sx) * carry
                   = value x sx + value y sy }
```

Fig. 5. Specification of `wmpn_add`.

3.2   Example of Proved Algorithm: Comparison

Let us look at the Why3 implementation of GMP's `mpn_cmp` function, shown in
Fig. 6. Just like GMP, this is the only comparison function on natural integers
provided by our library. The `mpn_cmp` function takes two pointers to the integers
as arguments, as well as the size of the pointed buffers. It returns -1, 0, 1,
depending on the way the numbers are ordered. Our implementation has the
same interface and the same behavior. The algorithm is very straightforward:
it simply iterates both operands until it finds a difference, starting at the most
significant limb. Once a difference is found, we can conclude immediately. If no
difference is found, then the integers are equal.

The most important part of the proof is the loop invariant at line 10: both
source operands are identical from offsets $i+1$ to n. The following lemma is used
to prove the postcondition. It simply states that two big integers have the same
value if their limbs are equal.

Lemma 1 *(value_sub_frame). Let* $a_0, \ldots, a_{n-1}, b_0, \ldots, b_{n-1}$ *such that for all* i,
$a_i = b_i$. *Then* $\overline{a_0 \ldots a_{n-1}} = \overline{b_0 \ldots b_{n-1}}$.

The proof is a straightforward induction, which translates well into a Why3
lemma function where the recursive call provides the induction hypothesis.

```
let rec lemma value_sub_frame (x y:map int limb) (n m:int)
  requires { MapEq.map_eq_sub x y n m }
  variant  { m - n }
  ensures  { value_sub x n m = value_sub y n m }
= if n < m then value_sub_frame x y (n+1) m else ()
```

This lemma makes it possible to conclude that the numbers are equal if no
difference was found by the end of the loop. Notice that the loop body raises an
exception as soon as a difference is found. This emulates the return-inside-a-loop
pattern found in imperative languages. At extraction, this pattern is detected
and the extracted code simply has a **return** inside the main loop (Sect. 2.3).
Figure 7 shows the extracted code for the `wmpn_cmp` function.

```
1  let wmpn_cmp (x y:t) (sz:int32) : int32
2    requires { valid x sz }
3    requires { valid y sz }
4    ensures  { result = compare_int (value x sz) (value y sz) }
5  = let i = ref sz in
6    try
7      while Int32.(≥) !i (Int32.of_int 1) do
8        variant { to_int !i }
9        invariant { 0 ≤ !i ≤ sz }
10       invariant { forall j. !i ≤ j < sz →
11                    (pelts x)[x.offset+j] = (pelts y)[y.offset+j] }
12       i := Int32.(-) !i (Int32.of_int 1);
13       let lx = get_ofs x !i in let ly = get_ofs y !i in
14       if (Limb.ne lx ly) then
15         if Limb.(>) lx ly
16         then raise (Return32 (Int32.of_int 1))
17         else raise (Return32 (Int32.of_int (-1)))
18       end
19     done;
20     Int32.of_int 0
21   with Return32 r → r
22   end
```

Fig. 6. Why3 implementation of mpn_cmp.

```
int32_t wmpn_cmp(uint64_t * x, uint64_t * y, int32_t sz) {
  int32_t i, o;
  uint64_t lx, ly;
  i = (sz);
  while (i >= 1) {
    o = (i - 1); i = o;
    lx = (*(x+(i)));
    ly = (*(y+(i)));
    if (lx != ly) {
      if (lx > ly) return (1);
      else return (-(1));
    }
  }
  return (0);
}
```

Fig. 7. Extracted C code for wmpn_cmp.

3.3 Trickier Example: Long Division

Let us now showcase one of the many algorithmic tricks from GMP that we ported in our implementation. Long division consists in computing the quotient q and remainder of the division of a big integer a of size m by a big integer d of

---

Algorithm 1. General case long division (abridged).

1: **function** DIVMOD_GEN(q, a, d, m, n)
2:     ...   ▷ Initialize
3:     **while** $i > 0$ **do**
4:         $i \leftarrow i - 1$
5:         **if** $x = d_{n-1}$ **and** $a_{n+i-1} = d_{n-2}$ **then**
6:             ...   ▷ Unlikely special case
7:         **else**
8:             $(\hat{q}, x, l) \leftarrow$ DIV_3BY2($x, a_{n+i-1}, a_{n+i-2}, d_{n-1}, d_{n-2}, v$)
9:             $b \leftarrow$ SUBMUL_LIMB($a + i, d, n - 2, \hat{q}$)
10:             $b_1 \leftarrow (l < b)$ ▷ Last two steps of the subtraction are inlined
11:             $a_{n+i-2} \leftarrow (l - b \bmod \beta)$
12:             $b_2 \leftarrow (x < b_1)$
13:             $x \leftarrow (x - b_1 \bmod \beta)$ ▷ Finish subtraction
14:             ...   ▷ Adjust
15:         $q_i \leftarrow \hat{q}$
16:     ...   ▷ Finish and return

---

size n. It is a significantly more complex problem than long addition or multiplication. Algorithm 1 is an excerpt of the general case algorithm for long division in GMP (file `mpn/generic/sbpi1_div_qr.c`).

The algorithm consists in computing the limbs of the quotient one by one, starting with the most significant one. The numerator a is overwritten at each step to contain the partial remainder. At each iteration of the loop (with i decreasing from $m - n$), we compute a quotient limb $\hat{q}$ by dividing the three most significant limbs of the current remainder a (of size $n + i$) by the two most significant limbs from the denominator d. We then subtract from the high part of the current remainder the product of that quotient limb by the denominator. Note that the most significant limb of the current remainder is never stored back to a_{n+i}. It is kept in the local variable x as an optimization.

Let us take a closer look at lines 9 to 13 in Algorithm 1, which expose another optimization of GMP meant to shave a few more processor cycles. The candidate quotient limb $\hat{q}$ is computed at line 8, and we need to subtract the product of this quotient limb and the denominator from the current remainder. This could be done with only the function call at line 9 by passing n instead of $n - 2$ (or rather $n - 1$ and inlining the last step on x), but we can do better and optimize the last two steps by making use of the remainder that was computed at line 8. Indeed, we can show that the last two steps simply consist in propagating the borrow from the previous subtraction, as the result of the 3 most significant limbs of subtraction is known to be $\overline{\ell x 0} = \ell + \beta x$ in the absence of borrow-in (the postcondition of the division is exactly that $\overline{a_{n+i-2} a_{n+i-1} x} = \hat{q} \times \overline{d_{n-2} d_{n-1}} + \overline{\ell x}$). Therefore, all that is left to do is propagate the borrow on $\overline{\ell x 0}$. Hence, lines 11 to 15 are equivalent to computing the subtraction

$$\overline{a_i \dots a_{n+i-1} x} - \hat{q} \times \overline{d_0 \dots d_{n-1}}$$

```
let a' = C.incr a !i in
let a'' = C.incr a' (Int32.(-) n two) in
label L in
let qu,l,h = div3by2_inv !x (C.get_ofs a'' one) (C.get a'') dh dl v in
let b = submul_limb a' y qu (Int32.(-) n two) in
let b1 = if (Limb.(<) l b) then uone else uzero in
C.set a'' (sub_mod l b);
let b2 = if (Limb.(<) h b1) then uone else uzero in
x := sub_mod h b1;
assert { value a' (n - 1) + power beta (n - 1) * !x
                       - power beta n * b2
       = value (a' at L) n + power beta n * (!x at L)
         - qu * (value d n) };
```

Fig. 8. Transcription (modified for readability) of Algorithm 1, lines 8 to 13.

returning b_2 as borrow and writing the result in $\overline{a_i \ldots a_{n+i-2}x}$ (one limb fewer). This is exactly the last assertion of Fig. 8, which shows an abridged version of our proof for this part of the algorithm.

All in all, this algorithmic trick saves several arithmetic operations: two multiplications, as the two most significant limbs of d are not multiplied by $\hat{q}$, and two subtractions, as in the last two steps, only a carry is propagated instead of doing a subtraction and then propagating a carry. This is far from irrelevant: this loop is the performance-critical one for long integer division, and almost all the cost of the loop is in the submul_limb call (it is the only operation with a cost that scales with the size of the input that is run with non-negligible probability). This trick, which makes the cost of the loop similar to what it would be if the denominator was two limbs shorter, illustrates the kind of GMP implementation details that we have to preserve in order to keep up in terms of performance.

3.4 Statistics on the Proof Effort

We have implemented and verified functions for performing addition, subtraction, multiplication, division, comparison, and logical shifts on arbitrary-precision integers. In many cases, we also provide lower-level functions for the cases when one of the inputs is a single limb or when the two inputs have the same length (equivalent to the functions suffixed by _1 and _n in GMP[4]).

This totals 6000 lines of Why3, which break down into 1350 lines of code and 4650 lines of specifications and proofs, most of which are assertions. The theorem provers Alt-Ergo, CVC3, CVC4, Eprover, and Z3 are used. All of these provers are necessary for at least some subgoals. It is hard to precisely characterize which subgoals are discharged by each prover, but we can provide some heuristics. Typically, CVC3 is the best of these provers at discharging non-linear arithmetic subgoals, with Z3 second. Z3 is also good at proving upper bounds

---

[4] http://gmplib.org/manual/Low_002dlevel-Functions.html.

and absence of overflows. CVC4 tends to be the best at proving preconditions such as pointer validity. The E prover is the best at instantiating hypotheses modulo associativity and commutativity. Finally, Alt-Ergo is the best at instantiating complex lemmas and tends to require fewer cut indications. The total proof time is around 20 min. For a more detailed breakdown, refer to http://toccata.lri.fr/gallery/multiprecision.en.html. The proof effort is about 5 person-months, most of it being for the division, for a neophyte in computer arithmetic and automated program verification.

4 Benchmarks

We have compared the execution time of our extracted code against GMP on randomly generated medium-sized integers, up to 1280 bits. For bigger inputs, the comparison becomes increasingly meaningless since GMP switches to divide-and-conquer algorithms which have a better asymptotic complexity. To prevent GMP from using too many architecture-specific optimizations, we have configured GMP with the `--disable-assembly` flag, so that GMP uses only generic C code. This is true both for the arithmetic primitives (which we share with GMP to focus the benchmarks on the algorithms rather than the primitives) but also for the operations on big numbers. Indeed, on many architectures, GMP uses handwritten assembly functions for most of the performance-critical big number algorithms, with performances out of reach of even very efficient C code.

We compare the execution times of GMP (without assembly) and our library on three different functions: addition, multiplication, and division. We do separate measures for all valid combinations of lengths of the input operands between 1 and 20. For each of these, we generate a few thousand random inputs and call each function a hundred times on each input, and record the total time.

For multiplication, our library is between 5 and 10% slower than GMP across all sizes (Fig. 9a). One possible cause for the discrepancy is the use of a different basic block for addition: while we use a primitive that adds two one-limb integers and a carry, GMP uses a primitive that adds two two-limb integers. We intend to switch to GMP's primitive in the near future.

n \ m	5	7	10	13	15	20
5	0%	7%	8%	6%	8%	12%
7	—	5%	7%	8%	9%	14%
10	—	—	9%	7%	7%	13%
13	—	—	—	9%	7%	14%
15	—	—	—	—	6%	15%
20	—	—	—	—	—	13%

(a) multiplication

n \ m	5	7	10	13	15	20
5	130%	8%	25%	18%	17%	16%
7	—	67%	3%	14%	19%	14%
10	—	—	61%	2%	4%	12%
13	—	—	—	33%	7%	3%
15	—	—	—	—	54%	5%
20	—	—	—	—	—	40%

(b) division

Fig. 9. Overhead for m-by-n operations.

For division, the difference in execution times is much more dependent on the length of the inputs, particularly in the difference in length between numerator and denominator (Fig. 9b). When the length of the denominator is less than half the length of the numerator, our algorithm is quite similar to GMP's and runs in about 20% more time.

The situation changes when the length n of the denominator is more than half the length m of the numerator, that is, more than the length of the quotient. Indeed, GMP no longer applies Algorithm 1 directly on the operands. Instead, the algorithm is called on the $2q$ most significant limbs of the numerator and q most significant limbs of the denominator, where q is the length of the quotient. This gives an estimated quotient, and a rather involved adjustment step follows. This alternative algorithm is not yet implemented in our library, which simply applies the general algorithm in all cases.

Note that GMP's adjustment step is somewhat expensive in that it requires the allocation of a long integer. Thus, for the small sizes we are considering, the adjustment step seems to dominate the complexity in such a way that the algorithm switch is only worth it when the denominator is almost as long as the numerator. Thus, for $m/2 \leq n < m-1$, the overhead of our library is below 10%. It then increases drastically when the sizes of the numerator and denominator get very close: for $n = m - 1$, our library is around 25% slower than GMP; for $n = m$, our library is sometimes twice as slow.

We also compared our library with mini-gmp, a minimalistic implementation of the GMP interface in a single C file that can be found in the main GMP repository. The mini-gmp division does not implement the alternative algorithm either, which makes our division 10 to 20% slower than it across the board.

5   Related Work

In this work, we have obtained our library in three steps: we first write some WhyML code and specification, we then verify that the code satisfies the specification, finally we extract the C code from the WhyML code. There are numerous other approaches to obtain some verified C code; let us mention three examples. In the case of the B method, an abstract specification is progressively refined until it is detailed enough so that some C code can be extracted from it [1]. In the case of the Frama-C environment, the C code is written by hand and it is specified using the behavioral specification language ACSL; the verification is then directly performed at the level of the C code [8]. Finally, in the case of the seL4 microkernel, the C code is again written by hand, but so is some Haskell code that models it; the verification process then consists of formally proving that this Haskell code both models the C code and satisfies a specification written in Isabelle/HOL [17].

Let us focus a bit more on the topic of verifying an arbitrary-precision integer library. Bertot et al. verified the GMP's divide-and-conquer algorithm for square root [4]. It was performed using the Correctness tool which translates a program and its specification into verification conditions for Coq. In that work, the memory is seen as a large array of machine integers, so function specifications have to tell which zones of memory are left unchanged. Other than that, the way the authors implement and specify their algorithm is quite close to the way we do ours; thus, had they wished to, they could easily have extracted it to C.

Myreen and Curello verified a library with a scope similar to the one presented in this paper, although their division algorithm is simpler than GMP's [21]. The implementation, specification, and verification were done using HOL4. An interesting aspect of this work is that the implementation language is some kind of x86-64 pseudo-assembly, so as to effectively produce a low-level verified library. Another interesting point is that it is not the assembly code that is verified but the Hoare triples obtained by decompiling the corresponding machine code. These triples are formally proved to be compatible with the specification of correct algorithms. The memory model is based on separation logic, and the compiler and decompiler are specifically instrumented to preserve the corresponding assertions about integer separation in the generated triples. The library also supports signed integers but their encoding does not match GMP's.

Affeldt verified a binary GCD algorithm and the functions it depends on [2]. Neither multiplications nor divisions are present. The implementation, specification, and verification were done using Coq. This time, the implementation language is a variant of MIPS assembly. An interesting aspect of this work is that, even if the verified algorithm is not GMP's binary GCD, the numbers are encoded using GMP's layout for signed integers, which incurs a pointer indirection. To account for this complexity, the memory model is again based on separation logic.

Further away from GMP, Berghofer verified an Ada library for performing modular exponentiation [3]. It was written and specified using the SPARK subset of Ada and the verification conditions were then proved using Isabelle/HOL. The use of Montgomery multiplication makes it slightly more complicated than the binary GCD example from an algorithmic point of view. There is no need for a memory model, since arbitrary-precision integers are represented using plain Ada arrays and SPARK prevents them from being aliased.

Fischer designed a modular exponentiation library developed for C and verified using Isabelle/HOL [14]. Multiplication and division algorithms are naive and use arbitrary-precision integers represented using garbage-collected doubly-linked lists of machine integers. Thus, this library is certainly not meant to be efficient. Aliasing issues are solved by using both a Bornat-like memory model [7], so as to automatically distinguish integer words from pointer words, and frame predicates in specifications, so as to declare which heap positions are possibly modified by a function.

Finally, there have also been various efforts to verify specific cryptography primitives and their underlying arithmetic. Zinzindohoué et al. verified an elliptic curve library written in F* and meant to be extracted to C [22]. A peculiarity is that integers are no longer of arbitrary precision; they are represented by fixed-size arrays. Moreover, only part of a machine word is used to store a limb; for instance, a 448-bit integer is stored using 8 limbs of 56 bits (out of 64). As a consequence, arithmetic operations on limbs do not have to be modular (which makes them simpler for SMT solvers to reason about) and carry bits do not have to be propagated. Regarding the memory model, function specifications explicitly tell which parts of the heap are modified.

6   Conclusions

Our work aims at devising a formally verified C library that provides the same arbitrary-precision arithmetic primitives as GMP. At the time of this paper, we have implemented and verified the following algorithms from GMP: comparison, addition, subtraction, multiplication, and division. For multiplication and division, those are only the algorithms meant to be used with integers of size less than 20 limbs, that is, the so-called *schoolbook* algorithms. Moreover, in the case of the division, we are lacking an optimized algorithm when the final quotient is short, which means that the version for computing long quotients is always being called (unless the divisor is one or two limbs long).

Thanks to our memory model and the notion of pointer it provides, we were able to write the functions the same way GMP developers did. It also made it easy to implement an extraction mechanism to C for Why3. Moreover, since this memory model piggybacks on the region mechanism of Why3, we did not have to bother with pointer aliasing, so the specification of the functions is just about their arithmetic properties, contrarily to most of the other verified libraries.

Despite the terminology, the algorithms we have considered are far more intricate than the algorithms one finds in a schoolbook and are still the topic of active research [20]. For instance, the division operator is designed to correctly compute the remainder after a single pass with probability almost 1, and thus does not incur a correction step. Our code implements all the algorithmic tricks that can be found in the corresponding functions of GMP, which makes our library competitive with GMP's non-assembly implementation. In fact, the extracted C code is so close to GMP's own code that the formal verification of our library increases the confidence in the correctness of GMP as a by-product.

As it stands, the proof effort for getting a verified GMP-like library is way too costly. Indeed, while the algorithms are highly intricate, the effort required is compounded by the nonlinear nature of the integer properties submitted to the automated solvers. SMT solvers are especially unhelpful there, so the user has to split proofs at a deeper level of detail than what an interactive theorem prover with support for algebraic reasoning would require. Thus, before tackling the implementation and verification of other GMP functions, we intend to work on designing decision procedures dedicated to verifying these arithmetic properties. While the class of nonlinear integer problems is undecidable, the properties that occur when verifying a GMP-like library are sufficiently specific that we have good hope for success.

Once the issue of proof automation has been tackled, we intend to implement and verify divide-and-conquer algorithms for multiplication (e.g. Toom-Cook algorithms) and division, so as to stay competitive with GMP even for larger integers. We also intend to provide the same high-level interface as GMP for abstract signed arbitrary-precision integers. This comes as a new challenge for the memory model, since most `mpz` functions allow for aliasing between their arguments. For instance, one can pass the same arbitrary-precision integer as both input and output, so operators have to properly resolve any aliasing issue (e.g. by allocating temporary buffers) before calling into the `mpn` functions.

Another future work is to extract not only the Why3 code to C, but also the specifications. The C code could then be verified using an existing C verification framework, e.g. Frama-C, so that our code extractor no longer needs to be part of the trusted code base. It would be quite costly, however, to translate all the annotations to the ACSL specification language of Frama-C and to perform once again the whole verification, especially since ACSL is not as expressive as Why3. The goal is rather to improve the interaction between Frama-C and Why3 (which Frama-C already uses as a back-end), so as to minimize the proof effort when verifying a C function whose algorithm has already been proved using Why3.

Acknowledgments. We gratefully thank Pascal Cuoq, Jean-Christophe Filliâtre and Mário Pereira for their comments on preliminary versions of this article.

References

1. Abrial, J.R.: The B-Book, Assigning Programs to Meaning. Cambridge University Press, Cambridge (1996)
2. Affeldt, R.: On construction of a library of formally verified low-level arithmetic functions. Innov. Syst. Softw. Eng. **9**(2), 59–77 (2013)
3. Berghofer, S.: Verification of dependable software using SPARK and Isabelle. In: Brauer, J., Roveri, M., Tews, H. (eds.) 6th International Workshop on Systems Software Verification. OpenAccess Series in Informatics (OASIcs), Dagstuhl, Germany, vol. 24, pp. 15–31 (2012)
4. Bertot, Y., Magaud, N., Zimmermann, P.: A proof of GMP square root. J. Autom. Reason. **29**(3–4), 225–252 (2002)
5. Bobot, F., Filliâtre, J.-C., Marché, C., Paskevich, A.: Why3: Shepherd your herd of provers. In: Boogie 2011: First International Workshop on Intermediate Verification Languages, Wrocław, Poland, pp. 53–64, August 2011. https://hal.inria.fr/hal-00790310
6. Bobot, F., Filliâtre, J.-C., Marché, C., Paskevich, A.: Let's verify this with Why3. Int. J. Softw. Tools Technol. Transf. (STTT) **17**(6), 709–727 (2015). See also http://toccata.lri.fr/gallery/fm2012comp.en.html
7. Bornat, R.: Proving pointer programs in Hoare logic. In: Backhouse, R., Oliveira, J.N. (eds.) MPC 2000. LNCS, vol. 1837, pp. 102–126. Springer, Heidelberg (2000). https://doi.org/10.1007/10722010_8
8. Cuoq, P., Kirchner, F., Kosmatov, N., Prevosto, V., Signoles, J., Yakobowski, B.: Frama-C: a software analysis perspective. In: Eleftherakis, G., Hinchey, M., Holcombe, M. (eds.) SEFM 2012. LNCS, vol. 7504, pp. 233–247. Springer, Heidelberg (2012). https://doi.org/10.1007/978-3-642-33826-7_16
9. Filliâtre, J.-C.: One logic to use them all. In: Bonacina, M.P. (ed.) CADE 2013. LNCS (LNAI), vol. 7898, pp. 1–20. Springer, Heidelberg (2013). https://doi.org/10.1007/978-3-642-38574-2_1

10. Filliâtre, J.-C., Gondelman, L., Paskevich, A.: A pragmatic type system for deductive verification. Research report, Université Paris Sud (2016). https://hal.archives-ouvertes.fr/hal-01256434v3

11. Filliâtre, J.-C., Gondelman, L., Paskevich, A.: The spirit of ghost code. Formal Methods Syst. Des. **48**(3), 152–174 (2016)

12. Filliâtre, J.-C., Marché, C.: The Why/Krakatoa/Caduceus platform for deductive program verification. In: Damm, W., Hermanns, H. (eds.) CAV 2007. LNCS, vol. 4590, pp. 173–177. Springer, Heidelberg (2007). https://doi.org/10.1007/978-3-540-73368-3_21

13. Filliâtre, J.-C., Paskevich, A.: Why3 — where programs meet provers. In: Felleisen, M., Gardner, P. (eds.) ESOP 2013. LNCS, vol. 7792, pp. 125–128. Springer, Heidelberg (2013). https://doi.org/10.1007/978-3-642-37036-6_8

14. Fischer, S.: Formal verification of a big integer library. In: DATE Workshop on Dependable Software Systems (2008). http://www-wjp.cs.uni-sb.de/publikationen/Fi08DATE.pdf

15. Fumex, C., Dross, C., Gerlach, J., Marché, C.: Specification and proof of high-level functional properties of bit-level programs. In: Rayadurgam, S., Tkachuk, O. (eds.) NFM 2016. LNCS, vol. 9690, pp. 291–306. Springer, Cham (2016). https://doi.org/10.1007/978-3-319-40648-0_22

16. International Organization for Standardization: ISO/IEC 9899:1999: Programming Languages - C (2000)

17. Klein, G., Andronick, J., Elphinstone, K., Heiser, G., Cock, D., Derrin, P., Elkaduwe, D., Engelhardt, K., Kolanski, R., Norrish, M., Sewell, T., Tuch, H., Winwood, S.: seL4: formal verification of an OS kernel. Commun. ACM **53**(6), 107–115 (2010)

18. Kosmatov, N., Marché, C., Moy, Y., Signoles, J.: Static versus dynamic verification in Why3, Frama-C and SPARK 2014. In: Margaria, T., Steffen, B. (eds.) ISoLA 2016. LNCS, vol. 9952, pp. 461–478. Springer, Cham (2016). https://doi.org/10.1007/978-3-319-47166-2_32

19. Leino, K.R.M., Moskal, M.: Usable auto-active verification. In: Usable Verification Workshop, Redmond, WA, USA, November 2010. http://fm.csl.sri.com/UV10/

20. Moller, N., Granlund, T.: Improved division by invariant integers. IEEE Trans. Comput. **60**(2), 165–175 (2011)

21. Myreen, M.O., Curello, G.: Proof pearl: a verified bignum implementation in x86-64 machine code. In: Gonthier, G., Norrish, M. (eds.) CPP 2013. LNCS, vol. 8307, pp. 66–81. Springer, Cham (2013). https://doi.org/10.1007/978-3-319-03545-1_5

22. Zinzindohoué, J.K., Bartzia, E.I., Bhargavan, K.: A verified extensible library of elliptic curves. In: Hicks, M., Köpf, B. (eds.) 29th IEEE Computer Security Foundations Symposium (CSF), Lisbon, Portugal, pp. 296–309, June 2016

Automating the Verification
of Floating-Point Programs

Clément Fumex[1,2,3(✉)], Claude Marché[1,2], and Yannick Moy[3]

[1] Inria, Université Paris-Saclay, 91120 Palaiseau, France
[2] LRI, CNRS & Univ. Paris-Sud, 91405 Orsay, France
[3] AdaCore, 75009 Paris, France
fumex@adacore.com

Abstract. In the context of deductive program verification, handling floating-point computations is challenging. The level of proof success and proof automation highly depends on the way the floating-point operations are interpreted in the logic supported by back-end provers. We address this challenge by combining multiple techniques to separately prove different parts of the desired properties. We use abstract interpretation to compute numerical bounds of expressions, and we use multiple automated provers, relying on different strategies for representing floating-point computations. One of these strategies is based on the native support for floating-point arithmetic recently added in the SMT-LIB standard. Our approach is implemented in the Why3 environment and its front-end SPARK 2014 for the development of safety-critical Ada programs. It is validated experimentally on several examples originating from industrial use of SPARK 2014.

1 Introduction

Numerical programs appear in many critical software systems, for example to compute trajectories, to control movements, to detect objects. As most processors are now equipped with a floating-point (FP for short) unit, many numerical programs are implemented in FP arithmetic, to benefit from the additional precision of FP numbers around the origin compared to fixed-point numbers, and from the speed of FP computations performed in hardware.

Safety conditions for critical software systems require strong guarantees on the functional behavior of the computations performed. Automatically verifying that these guarantees are fulfilled is desirable. Among other verification approaches, deductive program verification is the one that offers the largest expressive power for the properties to verify: complex functional specification can be stated using expressive formal specification languages. Verification then relies on the abilities of automated theorem provers to check that a code satisfies a given formal specification.

Work partly supported by the Joint Laboratory ProofInUse (ANR-13-LAB3-0007, http://www.spark-2014.org/proofinuse) and by the SOPRANO project (ANR-14-CE28-0020, http://soprano-project.fr/) of the French national research organization.

© Springer International Publishing AG 2017
A. Paskevich and T. Wies (Eds.): VSTTE 2017, LNCS 10712, pp. 102–119, 2017.
https://doi.org/10.1007/978-3-319-72308-2_7

For some time, FP arithmetic was not well-supported by automated provers and thus deductive verification of FP programs was relying on interactive proof assistants, requiring a lot of expertise [6]. In recent years, FP arithmetic started to be supported natively by the automated solvers of the SMT (*Satisfiability Modulo Theory*) family. A theory reflecting the IEEE-754 standard for FP arithmetic [24] was added in the SMT-LIB standard in 2010 [33]. This theory is now supported by at least the solvers Z3 [32] and MathSAT5 [8].

Our initial goal is to build upon the recent support for FP arithmetic in SMT-LIB to propose an environment for deductive verification of numerical programs with a higher level of automation. We implemented this approach in the program verifier Why3 and in its front-end SPARK for verifying Ada programs. Indeed a support for FP arithmetic in Why3 already existed before [1,6], but it was based on an axiomatization of FP operations in terms of their interpretations into operations on real numbers. It was suitable for using as back provers either the Gappa solver dedicated to reason about FP rounding [14], for the simplest verification conditions, or the Coq proof assistant for the rest. To achieve a higher level of automation, in particular on the examples we considered coming from users of SPARK, we identified the need for combining several theorem provers, and even more, a need for combining deductive verification with an abstract interpretation based analysis (namely the CodePeer tool for Ada). The main goal of the new support we designed is thus to exploit the SMT solvers with native support for FP arithmetic (Z3), while maintaining the ability to use solvers that do not offer native support (CVC4, Alt-Ergo, Gappa, Coq). Our new approach can prove automatically FP properties that were beyond the reach of the previous approach. For example, we were previously unable to prove automatically the assertion in the following toy Ada code, because the rounding error on X + 2.0 was over-approximated.

```
procedure Range_Add (X : Float_32; Res : out Float_32) is
begin
   pragma Assume (X in 10.0 .. 1000.0);
   Res := X + 2.0;
   pragma Assert (Res >= 12.0);
end Range_Add;
```

We first give a quick introduction to auto-active verification with the environments SPARK and Why3 in Sect. 2. In Sect. 3, we present a new Why3 theory used in the verification condition generation process so as to exploit the support of FP arithmetic in SMT-LIB, while still keeping use of other provers, thanks to an axiomatization. We evaluate experimentally our approach in Sect. 4, showing our results on 22 examples extracted from industrial programs. We also present a case study for the computation of safe bounds for the trajectory of a device from an embedded safety-critical software, where the combination of techniques is achieved through the insertion of ghost code. We refer to our extended research report [19] for more details on our approach, including the full axiomatization and the complete source code of our examples. Section 5 draws conclusions and discusses some related work and future work.

2   Quick Introduction to SPARK and Why3

Why3 is an environment for deductive program verification, providing a rich language for specification and programming, called WhyML. WhyML is used as an intermediate language for verification of C, Java or Ada programs [17,25], and is also intended to be comfortable as a primary programming language. Why3 generates proof obligations, called verification conditions (VCs for short), from program annotations using a weakest-precondition calculus. It relies on external provers, both automated and interactive, in order to discharge the auxiliary lemmas and VCs. As most of the provers do not support some of the language features (typically pattern matching, polymorphic types, or recursion), Why3 applies a series of encoding transformations to eliminate unsupported constructions before dispatching a VC. Why3 comes with a rich standard library providing general-purpose theories useful for specifying programs [3]. This naturally includes integer and real arithmetic. In this work, we added a new theory of floating-point arithmetic, that we present in Sect. 3. Why3 provides a mechanism called *realization* that allows a user to construct a model for her axiomatizations, using a proof assistant. This feature can be used to guarantee that an axiomatization is consistent, or even that it is a faithful abstraction of an existing model. In Sect. 3.6, we use this feature to ensure that our own axiomatization of FP arithmetic is faithful to the IEEE-754 standard [24].

SPARK is an environment for the verification of Ada programs used in critical software development [10,29]. The SPARK language subset and toolset for static verification has been applied for many years in on-board aircraft systems, control systems, cryptographic systems, and rail systems. As displayed in Fig. 1, to formally prove a SPARK program, the tool GNATprove uses WhyML as an intermediate language. The SPARK program is translated into an equivalent WhyML program which can then be verified using the Why3 tool. Since version SPARK 17, GNATprove also includes the static analyzer CodePeer as prover. CodePeer [2] is a tool developed at AdaCore to detect errors in Ada programs, based on modular abstract interpretation. The benefit of this integration for our work is that CodePeer computes precise bounds on FP computations.

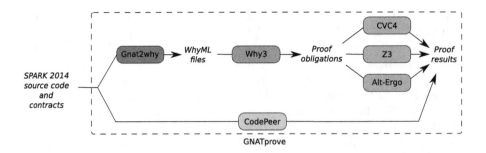

Fig. 1. Deductive verification in SPARK 2014

Automatic verification in both Why3 and GNATprove relies on the ability to interact with users through assertions, and more generally verification-only code also called *ghost code* [25]. This type of verification is called *auto-active verification*, to characterise *tools where user input is supplied before VC generation [and] therefore lie between automatic and interactive verification* (hence the name auto-active) [26]. We use ghost code in Sect. 4.2 to prove a case study involving FP computations.

3   VC Generation for Floating-Point Computations

We now describe what we designed for the support for FP types in Why3 and then how we use this support to enhance SPARK's already existing support for FP types. In Sect. 3.1 we present the signature, in other words the user interface, of our Why3 formalization of the IEEE-754 standard. That signature is generic, parameterized by the size of FP numbers. In Sect. 3.2 we show how we build specific instances for 32 and 64 bits formats, and how we can write literal constants in these formats. Then in Sect. 3.3 we show how the FP computations in Ada programs are translated by GNATprove into Why3 intermediate code based on our formalization, thus producing verification conditions involving the symbols of our signature. Section 3.4 explains how we map our signature to the SMT-LIB FP theory, so as to exploit SMT solvers with native support for that theory. Section 3.5 presents an axiomatization for our Why3 theory of FP, to be used by provers that do not support FP natively. Finally Sect. 3.6 explains how we ensure that our theory and axiomatization is conformant to the IEEE standard.

The IEEE-754 standard [24] defines an expected behavior of FP computations. In any binary formats, an interpretation of a bit sequence under the form of a sign, a mantissa and an exponent is given, so that the set of FP numbers denotes a finite subset of real numbers.

sign s	biased exponent e	mantissa m

The number of bits of e is denoted eb. The *significand* is the mantissa plus a *hidden bit* which is 1 for the so-called *normal* numbers and 0 for *subnormal* ones. The number of bits of the significand, that is also the number of bits of the mantissa plus 1, is denoted sb. The numbers eb and sb characterize the format, for the standard binary format on 32 bits and 64 bits we respectively have $eb = 8, sb = 24$ and $eb = 11, sb = 53$. Let us call *bias* the number $2^{eb-1} - 1$. The interpretation of the sequence of bits above is then as follows.

- if $0 < e < 2^{eb} - 1$, it represents the real number $(-1)^s \cdot \overline{1.m} \cdot 2^{e-bias}$ (normal numbers)
- if $e = 0$, it represents ± 0 if $m = 0$ (positive and negative zeros), $(-1)^s \cdot \overline{0.m} \cdot 2^{-bias+1}$ otherwise (subnormal numbers)
- if $e = 2^{eb} - 1$, $\pm\infty$ if $m = 0$ (positive and negative infinities) *Not-a-Number* otherwise, abbreviated as NaN.

For each of the basic arithmetic operations (add, sub, mul, div, and also sqrt, fused-multiply-add, etc.) the standard requires that it acts as if it first computes a true real number, and then *rounds* it to a number representable in the chosen format, according to some *rounding mode*. The standard defines five rounding modes: if a real number x lies between two consecutive representable FP numbers x_1 and x_2, then the rounding of x is as follows. With directed modes toward $+\infty$ (resp. $-\infty$) it is x_2 (resp. x_1). With directed mode toward 0, it is x_1 if $x > 0$ and x_2 if $x < 0$. With directed modes to nearest, it is the closest to x among x_1 and x_2, and if x is exactly the middle of $[x_1, x_2]$ then in the case 'ties to away' it is x_2 if $x > 0$ and x_1 if $x < 0$; whereas in the case 'ties to even' the one with even mantissa is chosen.

As seen above, the standard defines three special values: $-\infty, +\infty$ and NaN. It also distinguishes between positive zero ($+0$) and negative zero (-0). These numbers should be treated both in the input and the output of the arithmetic operations as usual, e.g. $(+\infty) + (+\infty) = (+\infty)$, $(+\infty) + (-\infty) = \text{NaN}$, $1/(-\infty) = -0$, $\pm 0/\pm 0 = \text{NaN}$, etc.

3.1   Signature for a Generic Theory of IEEE FP Arithmetic

We first present the signature of our theory. Such a signature presents the elements that some user should use: type names, constants, logic symbols for functions and predicates. These elements are only declared with their proper profiles, but no definition nor axiomatization are given.

One of our goals was to make this signature as close as possible to the SMT-LIB theory. One of the difficulty is that one wants to describe a generic signature, in the sense that it should be parameterized by the number of bits eb and sb. In SMT-LIB, this is done using the ad-hoc built-in construct with underscore character to handle parametric sorts, e.g. (_FloatingPoint 8 24) denotes the sort of IEEE 32-bits binary floating-point numbers. In Why3 there is no such ad-hoc construct, but instead it is possible to define a parametric theory that can be *cloned* later on, for particular instances of the parameters.

Our generic signature for floats thus starts as follows.

```
theory GenericFloat
   constant eb : int   (* number of bits of the exponent *)
   constant sb : int   (* number of bits of the significand *)
   axiom eb_gt_1: 1 < eb
   axiom sb_gt_1: 1 < sb
   type t     (* abstract type of floats *)
```

The abstract type t denotes the sort of FP numbers for the given eb and sb, both assumed greater than 1.

The next part of the signature provides the rounding modes and the arithmetic operations.

```
type mode = RNE | RNA | RTP | RTN | RTZ
function add mode t t : t     (* add *)
function sub mode t t : t     (* sub *)
```

```
function mul mode t t : t     (* mul *)
function div mode t t : t     (* div *)
```

It continues with the comparison operators

```
predicate le t t
predicate lt t t
predicate ge (x:t) (y:t) = le y x
predicate gt (x:t) (y:t) = lt y x
predicate eq t t                         (* different from = *)
```

It includes predicates for classification of numbers.

```
predicate is_infinite  t
predicate is_nan       t
predicate is_finite    t
```

Finally, it includes rounding and conversion functions.

```
function roundToIntegral mode t : t     (* rounding to an integer *)
function to_real    t       : real  (* conversion to a real number *)
function of_int mode int : t        (* conversion from an integer *)
function to_int mode t   : int      (* conversion to an integer *)
```

Conversions from and to integers need a rounding mode in both ways, since not all integers are representable. `of_int` may even return an infinite value. The results of `to_int` and `to_real` are unspecified if the argument is infinite or NaN. See [19] for additional elements in the signature.

3.2   Theory Clones and FP Literals

The theory above is generic. So far, it does not allow the construction of FP literals. Indeed it is possible only on *clones* of our theory for the binary formats of standard sizes 32 and 64 bits. For the purpose of allowing literal constants, we implemented a new feature in Why3 itself: the possibility to declare a type denoting FP values. Cloning the generic theory for 32-bit format is then done by the Why3 code below.

```
theory Float32

  type t = < float 8 24 >

  clone export GenericFloat with
    type t = t, constant eb = t'eb, constant sb = t'sb,
    function to_real = t'real, predicate is_finite = t'isFinite

end
```

The new declaration feature is the line of the form type t = < float *eb* *sb* > above. It introduces a new type identifier *t* that represents the FP values for the given sizes for *eb* and *sb*. It also introduces the functions t'eb, t'sb, t'isFinite and t'real, that are used in the cloning substitution above. The main purpose this new built-in Why3's declaration is the handling of literals: what is normally a real literal in Why3 can be cast to the type t, so that one may write float literals in decimal (e.g. (1.0:t), (17.25:t)), possibly with exponent (e.g. (6.0e23:t)), possibly also in hexadecimal[1] (e.g. (0x1.8p-4:t) that represents $\frac{3}{32}$). A very important design choice is that only the real numbers that are representable in the target type can be cast. Casting a literal constant that is not representable is *rejected* by Why3's typing engine, e.g. (0.1:t) will raise a typing error[2]. See below for implications of this choice.

Finally, each clone contains declarations of conversions with bitvectors of the appropriate sizes. We reuse here existing Why3 theories for bitvectors [18].

```
function to_bv mode t : BV32.t
function of_bv mode BV32.t : t
```

3.3   Interpreting FP Computations in Ada

The Ada standard does not impose the rounding mode used for FP computations, except for conversions from floats to integers where it is nearest, ties to away, and from integers to floats where it is nearest, ties to even. To avoid non-determinism, the SPARK fragment of Ada imposes the rounding mode nearest, ties to even, for arithmetic operations. Moreover, in SPARK, overflow is forbidden, so special values for infinities and NaN are not allowed to appear. Thus encoding an FP operation from an Ada program amounts to generating the corresponding operation in Why3 with the proper rounding mode, and to insert a check for the absence of overflow. Roughly speaking, a piece of Ada code like:

```
procedure P (X : in out Float_32) is
begin
   X := X + 2.0;
end P;
```

is translated into WhyML intermediate code as follows:

```
let p (x : ref Float32.t) : unit
   requires { is_finite x }
= let tmp = Float32.add RNE x (2.0:Float32.t) in
   assert { is_finite tmp };
   x := tmp
```

The additional assertion will lead to a VC to check the absence of overflow.

All operations are handled in a similar way. Signed integers in Ada are interpreted as integers in Why3, and Ada unsigned integers are interpreted as bitvectors [18]. The conversions are translated using the functions to_int, to_bv and of_int, of_bv with the modes RNA and RNE respectively.

---

[1] C99 notation for hexadecimal FP literals: 0xhh.hhpdd, where h are hexadecimal digits and dd is in decimal, denotes number $hh.hh \times 2^{dd}$.

[2] For that purpose, we had to implement in the typing engine a specific code that checks that a literal is representable and compute its mantissa and exponent. It is worth to note that implementing such a code is significantly easier than a code that would compute a correct rounding for any literals.

A remark about literals: in the translation from SPARK to Why3, the FP literals of the Ada source are first interpreted by the GNAT compiler. For example, if one uses the constant 0.1 in Ada for a 32-bit float, it is rounded to the closest representable value `0x1.99999Ap-4`. Thus the rounded value that may be used for such constants to produce a binary code is the very same value that is passed to Why3. Thus, not only are we sure that the generated Why3 literals are representable, but we are also sure that we use the same value as the executable.

3.4   Proving VCs Using Native Support for SMT-LIB FP

To attempt to discharge generated VCs using an SMT solver like Z3 that provides native support for floats, we simply have to map the symbols of our theory to the ones of SMT-LIB. The mapping is quite straightforward since most symbols have an SMT counterpart, with the same name, prefixed by 'fp.'. An exception is the predicate `is_finite` which does not exists in SMT-LIB, we encode it as (not (or (fp.isInfinite x) (fp.isNaN x))). Other notable exceptions are the conversions with integers, of_int and to_int, which do not exist in SMT-LIB. The two functions are left uninterpreted, and such conversions are dealt with the axiomatization below.

Regarding the literals, we use the mechanism that we implemented in Why3 together with our extension of float type declarations, that allows Why3 to print literals under the SMT-LIB bitvector form (fp s e m), for example the constant `0x1.99999Ap-4` in 32 bits is written as

(fp #b0 #b01111011 #b10011001100110011001101)

3.5   Axiomatization for Provers Without Native Support

Because the VCs generated from Ada programs mix FP computations with other data-types (integers, bitvectors, arrays. . .) but also quantified hypotheses, we cannot hope the solver to be complete. With an axiomatization, we can hope that a prover may discharge goals including elements outside the SMT-LIB FP theory (such as conversions with integers) and we can even call a prover without native support of FP arithmetic. We provide an axiomatization for the operators introduced in our theory, thus we rely on the generic handling of first-order axioms the prover may have. Our axiomatization is naturally incomplete: our intent is to provide the axioms that are useful in practice to discharge VCs. Notice that when using a solver with native FP support, the driver mechanism of Why3 removes all these axioms, so as to avoid the prover getting lost with the extra logic context.

Handling of Literals. We need a mechanism to interpret our built-in Why3 support for literals for provers without native support. This is done using a Why3 transformation that replaces each literal of the proof task by an extra constant with an axiom that specifies its value. That is, if some FP literal $(v : t)$ appears in the proof task, it is replaced by a fresh constant l of type t, declared with the axiom (t'isFinite l) $\wedge$ (t'real $l = v$).

Overflow Checks. We start by introducing a few useful constants derived from eb and sb:

```
constant pow2sb    : int = pow2 sb         (* 2^{sb} *)
constant emax      : int = pow2 (eb - 1)    (* 2^{eb-1} *)
constant max_int   : int = pow2 emax - pow2 (emax - sb)
constant max_real  : real = FromInt.from_int max_int
```

The constants `max_real` and `max_int` both represent the exact value of the biggest finite float, as a real and an integer respectively. In order to speak about overflows and finiteness, we introduce the following predicates.

```
predicate in_range (x:real) = - max_real <= x <= max_real
predicate no_overflow (m:mode) (x:real) = in_range (round m x)
axiom is_finite: forall x:t. is_finite x → in_range (to_real x)
axiom Bounded_real_no_overflow :
  forall m:mode, x:real. in_range x → no_overflow m x
```

The predicate `in_range` specifies the range of floats. The predicate `no_overflow` composes `round` and `in_range` to check for overflows. We stress that the two axioms specify that to be finite implies that the projection is in the float range, which in turns implies that there is no overflow. However we do not specify that no overflows implies finiteness in order to force the provers to reason on reals as well as avoid circularity in their proof attempts.

Rounding and Arithmetic. The rounding function, that is used to specify the FP operations, plays a central role in our axiomatization. This rounding function operates on real numbers, as defined in IEEE-754. It takes a rounding mode m, a real value x and returns the value of the FP number nearest to x up to m.

```
function round mode real : real
axiom Round_monotonic :
  forall m:mode, x y:real. x <= y → round m x <= round m y
axiom Round_idempotent :
  forall m1 m2:mode, x:real. round m1 (round m2 x) = round m2 x
axiom Round_to_real :
  forall m:mode, x:t. is_finite x → round m (to_real x) = to_real x
```

Those axioms are completed with axioms in the clones for 32 and 64 bits, giving quite precise bounds on the error made by rounding [31]. Here are the ones for 32 bits:

```
lemma round_bound_ne :
  forall x:real [round RNE x]. no_overflow RNE x →
    x - 0x1p-24 * Abs.abs(x) - 0x1p-150 <= round RNE x
      <= x + 0x1p-24 * Abs.abs(x) + 0x1p-150
lemma round_bound :
  forall m:mode, x:real [round m x]. no_overflow m x →
    x - 0x1p-23 * Abs.abs(x) - 0x1p-149 <= round m x
      <= x + 0x1p-23 * Abs.abs(x) + 0x1p-149
```

For 64 bits, the constants `0x1p-24`, `0x1p-150`, `0x1p-23`, `0x1p-149` are replaced by `0x1p-53`, `0x1p-1075`, `0x1p-52` and `0x1p-1074`.

Of course the axioms are not completely specifying the rounding function but only give bounds. A complete specification is not an objective. Indeed, giving a complete semantic with axioms would only lose the provers, the function `round` is too complex for that. Furthermore we don't want solvers to "reason" about the function `round` itself but rather up to it. Hence we only provide some properties to help provers move the predicate around. This is at the cost of losing precision in computations, in particular proof of equality and proofs dealing with precise ranges are hard, or even impossible.

The axiomatization of arithmetic operators derives from the rounding function. We only present the float addition, the other arithmetic operators are in the same line. It is axiomatized through the projection to reals. The main axiom `add_finite` specifies the non overflowing addition of two finite floats.

```
axiom add_finite: forall m:mode, x y:t [add m x y].
  is_finite x → is_finite y →
  no_overflow m (to_real x + to_real y) →
  is_finite (add m x y) ∧
  to_real (add m x y) = round m (to_real x + to_real y)
lemma add_finite_rev: forall m:mode, x y:t [add m x y].
  is_finite (add m x y) → is_finite x ∧ is_finite y
lemma add_finite_rev_n: forall m:mode, x y:t [add m x y].
  (m = RNE ∨ m = RNA) → is_finite (add m x y) →
  no_overflow m (to_real x + to_real y) ∧
  to_real (add m x y) = round m (to_real x + to_real y)
```

The two lemmas specify what we can deduce from the finiteness of an addition, `add_finite_rev` for the general case and `add_finite_rev_n` for the rounding modes RNE and RNA. The two lemmas are important when the finiteness of an addition appears in the context of a VC without any other fact about how it was proven (e.g. it was proven in another VC, or provided as an hypothesis). As mentioned, a second axiom is provided in the theory to specify all other cases dealing with special values (overflows, addition with a NaN, etc.). All other arithmetic operators, namely subtraction, multiplication, division, negation as well as absolute value, square root and fused multiply-add are specified in the same way. See [19] for all the axioms.

Conversions with Integers. Since these conversions are not supported by SMT-LIB, we handle them specially with a set of axioms that are useful to discharge goals coming from our Ada examples. Here is an excerpt of these axioms concerning the addition of FP numbers that come from integer conversions.

```
predicate in_safe_int_range (i: int) = - pow2sb <= i <= pow2sb
axiom of_int_add_exact: forall m n, i j.
  in_safe_int_range i → in_safe_int_range j →
    in_safe_int_range (i + j) →
      eq (of_int m (i + j)) (add n (of_int m i) (of_int m j))
```

The predicate `in_safe_int_range`, building on `pow2sb`, specifies the range in which every integer is representable in the float format. The axiom then expresses the necessary conditions to deduce that some addition is indeed exact. We have similar axioms for other operations. See [19] for a more detailed description of this part of the axiomatization.

3.6   Consistency and Faithfulness

Our FP theory, with all its axioms, is proven conformant to the IEEE standard by realizing a model of it in Coq, using the existing library Flocq [7]. While part of the realization was simply to reuse results already proved in Flocq, we did provide significant proof efforts, in particular to deal with the relation between integers and floats which is absent from this library (and might end up contribute to it). The faithfulness of the axiomatization with regard to IEEE standard is then enforced by modeling the theory's operators with Flocq's corresponding IEEE operators.

For SMT solvers with native support, we need to ensure that the axiomatization is coherent with the SMT-LIB theory of floats. This is the case if the implementation of SMT-LIB FP in a given solver is itself consistent with the IEEE standard, which is supposed to be the case.

4   Experiments

The tables from Figs. 2 and 4 summarize the proof results with provers from the current SPARK toolset: SMT solvers CVC4, Alt-Ergo, Z3 and static analyzer CodePeer. We add in these figures two provers: *AE_fpa*, the prototype of Alt-Ergo with FP support [12], and *COLIBRI*, a prover based on constraint solving techniques [11,28]. Gray cells correspond to unproved VCs. White cells correspond to proved VCs with the running time of the prover given in seconds (round to nearest, away from zero).

4.1   Small Representative Examples

We start with 22 simple examples representative of the problems encountered with proof of industrial programs using FP arithmetic. Each example consists in a few lines of code with a final assertion. Although each assertion should be provable, none of the assertions were provable with the version of SPARK released in 2014, when we established this list. These examples show a variety of FP computations that occur in practice, combining linear and non-linear arithmetic, conversions between integers and FP, conversions between single and double precision FP. The first 11 examples correspond to reduced examples from actual programs. The last 11 examples correspond to so-called *user rules*, i.e. axioms that were manually added to the proof context in the SPARK technology prior to SPARK 2014. Out of 22 examples, 20 directly come from industrial needs. See [19] for the complete Ada source code for these small examples. Figure 2 summarizes the proof results. It can be noted that all examples are now proved by the combination of provers.

Example	CVC4	Alt-Ergo	Z3	CodePeer	AE_fpa	COLIBRI
Range_Add			0	1	0	0
Range_Mult			0			0
Range_Add_Mult						0
Int_To_Float_Simple	25	0	0	1	0	
Float_To_Long_Float	0	0	0	1	0	0
Incr_By_Const			12			
Polynomial			2		0	
Float_Different			0	1	0	
Float_Greater			0	1	0	
Diffs			1			
Half_Bound		7	0	1	4	0

Example	CVC4	Alt-Ergo	Z3	CodePeer	AE_fpa	COLIBRI
User_Rule_2			0	1	1	0
User_Rule_3		2			0	0
User_Rule_4		2			0	0
User_Rule_6		2	1		2	0
User_Rule_7					1	0
User_Rule_9						0
User_Rule_10						0
User_Rule_11	1	1			2	0
User_Rule_13		20				0
User_Rule_14		1				0
User_Rule_15						0

Fig. 2. Proof times in seconds for the reduced examples (timeout = 30 s)

4.2 A Case Study

We now present a simple case study representative of production code from an embedded safety-critical software, on which we have applied the combination of techniques presented previously. The complete Ada source code for this case study is available online at http://toccata.lri.fr/gallery/trajectory_computation. en.html. This program computes the speed of a device submitted to gravitational acceleration and drag from the atmosphere around it. The formula to compute the new speed $S(N+1)$ from the speed $S(N)$ at the previous step, after a given increment of time is:

$$S(N+1) = S(N) + \delta \tag{1}$$

where $\delta = drag + factor \times G \times framelength$, where $factor$ is a value between -1 and 1 reflecting the importance of Archimedes' principle on the system, G is the gravitational acceleration constant, and $framelength$ is a constant that defines the time in seconds between two steps in the computations.

Because of the types and the values of constants involved, both CodePeer and Z3 can prove that there is no possible overflow. To go beyond absence of overflows, we aim at proving safe bounds for the speed computed by the program at each step, based on the extreme values allowed for $drag$ and the initial speed. Reasoning in real numbers, we'd like to state that (showing only the upper bound here, the lower bound is similar):

$$\delta \leq maxdrag + G \times framelength$$

and, starting from an initial speed $S(0)$ of value zero, by summation over N steps, that

$$S(N) \leq N \times (maxdrag + G \times framelength)$$

Naturally, these bounds in real numbers do not necessarily hold for the FP computations in the program. But they do hold when considering the ceiling

```
Bound : constant Float64 :=
   Drag_T'Last + Float64'Ceiling (G * Frame_Length)
with Ghost;

function Low_Bound (N : Frame) return Float64 is
   (Float64 (N) * (- Bound))
with Ghost;

function High_Bound (N : Frame) return Float64 is
   (Float64 (N) * Bound)
with Ghost;

function Invariant (N : Frame; Speed : Float64) return
      Boolean is
   (Speed in Low_Bound (N) .. High_Bound (N))
with Ghost;

procedure Compute_Speed (N           : Frame;
                         Factor      : Ratio_T;
                         Drag        : Drag_T;
                         Old_Speed   : Float64;
                         New_Speed   : out Float64)
with Global => null,
     Pre     => N < Frame'Last
                 and then Invariant (N, Old_Speed),
     Post    => Invariant (N + 1, New_Speed);
```

Fig. 3. Formal specification of `Compute_Speed`

value of the FP computations above, using $\oplus$ for FP addition and $\otimes$ for FP multiplication:

$$\delta \leq \lceil maxdrag \oplus G \otimes framelength \rceil \tag{2}$$

$$S(N) \leq N \otimes \lceil maxdrag \oplus G \otimes framelength \rceil \tag{3}$$

Indeed, given the magnitude of the integers involved (both operands and results of arithmetic operations), they are in a safe range where all integers are represented exactly as FP numbers, and arithmetic operations like additions and multiplications are thus exact as well on such integers. This is expressed in axioms such as `of_int_add_exact` of our axiomatization relating floats and integers, as presented in Sect. 3.5. Hence, for the integer value Q of ceiling in the equation above, we have that $(N \otimes Q) \oplus Q = (N \oplus 1) \otimes Q$ which allows to prove the bounds on $S(N)$ by induction on N, from Eqs. (1), (2) and (3). We follow this strategy in proving a corresponding contract on procedure `Compute_Speed` which computes the value of $S(N)$, shown in Fig. 3. The ghost function `Invariant` expresses a bound on the Nth term of the series $S(N)$.

The automatic proof of `Compute_Speed`in GNATprove requires the collaboration of static analyzer CodePeer and SMT solvers Alt-Ergo, CVC4 and Z3.

VC	CVC4	Alt-Ergo	Z3	CodePeer	AE_fpa	COLIBRI
Delta_Speed in -Bound .. Bound				1	3	0
In_Bounds (High_Bound(N))				1	1	
In_Bounds (Low_Bound(N))			0	1	2	
Float64(N_Bv) * Bound + Bound = (Float64(N_Bv) + 1.0) * Bound			_42_			0
Float64(N) * Bound + Bound = (Float64(N) + 1.0) * Bound			44	1	25	0
Float64(N) * (-Bound) - Bound = (Float64(N) + 1.0) * (-Bound)				1		0
T(1) = 1.0	0	0		_1_	0	0
Float64(N) + 1.0 = Float64(N + 1)	_0_	1			1	0
New_Speed >= Float64 (N) * (-Bound) Bound	_27_					0
New_Speed >= Float64 (N + 1) * (-Bound)			_1_			0
New_Speed <= Float64 (N) * Bound + Bound	_26_					0
New_Speed <= Float64 (N + 1) * Bound			_1_			0
Postcondition	_20_	0			1	

Fig. 4. Proof times in seconds for the case study (timeout = 60 s). Underlined cells correspond to provers actually used by GNATprove when using switches `--codepeer=on --level=2`

The way that we make this collaboration work is that we state intermediate assertions that are proved by either CodePeer or an SMT solver, and which are used by all to prove subsequent properties. Figure 4 gives the list of intermediate assertions that we wrote to fully prove the case study, and summarizes the proof results. It can be noted that all VCs in the case study are proved by the combination of provers.

We start by bounding all quantities involved using a ghost function In_Bounds. CodePeer is used to prove automatically three assertions bounding the values of Delta_Speed, High_Bound(N) and Low_Bound(N). Then, Z3 is used to prove the distribution of addition over multiplication that is required to prove Invariant(N+1) from Invariant(N), using a value N_BV which is the conversion of N into a modular type. As modular types are converted into bitvectors for Z3, the assertion mixing integers and floats can be interpreted fully in bitvectors by Z3, which allows to prove it. Then, CodePeer is used to prove equivalent assertions on signed integers. CodePeer is also used to prove that the conversion of integer 1 into float is 1.0, using an expression function T returning its input, which prevents the analyzer frontend from simplifying this assertion to True. Then, CVC4 is used to prove that adding 1 to N can be done with the same result in integers and in floats, using the previously proved assertion and the axiom of_int_add_exact presented in Sect. 3.5. Finally, a combination of

CVC4 and Z3 is used to prove bounds on the value of New_Speed. With these assertions, the postcondition of Compute_Speed is proved by CVC4.

5   Conclusions and Perspectives

Our approach for automated verification of floating-point programs relies on a generic theory, written in Why3's specification language, to model FP arithmetic. This theory is faithful to the IEEE standard. Its genericity allows to map it both to the Flocq library of Coq and to the FP theory of SMT-LIB. This theory is used to encode FP computations in the VC generation process performed by Why3. The resulting VCs can be dispatched either to the CodePeer analyzer that performs interval analysis, or to SMT solvers, with or without a native support for FP theory. The versatility of the different targets for discharging VCs permit a high degree of automation of the verification process.

Related Work. Since the mid 1990s, FP arithmetic has been formalized in interactive deductive verification systems: in PVS [9], in ACL2 [34], in HOL-light [22], and in Coq [15]. These formalizations allowed one to represent abstraction of hardware components or algorithms, and prove soundness properties. Representative case studies were the formal verification of FP multiplication, division and square root instructions of the AMD-K7 microprocessor in ACL2 [34], and the development of certified algorithms for computing elementary functions in HOL-light [21,22]. See also [23] for a survey of these approaches.

In 2007, Boldo and Filliâtre proposed an approach for proving properties related to FP computations in concrete C, using the Caduceus tool and Coq for the proofs [5]. The support for FP in Caduceus was somehow ported to the Frama-C environment [13] and its Jessie plug-in, aiming at using automated solvers instead of Coq, for a higher degree of automation [1]. Several case studies using Frama-C/Jessie, with various degree of complexity were designed by different authors [4,6,20,27]. In these various case studies, proofs using Coq or PVS were still needed to discharge the most complex VCs. Yet, a significant improvement in the degree of automation was obtain thanks to the use of the automated solver Gappa dedicated to reasoning on FP rounding [14].

Regarding the use of abstract interpretation to verifying FP programs, this indeed obtained very good successes in industrial contexts. In 2004, Minéused relational abstract domains to detect FP run-time errors [30], an approach that was implemented in the Astrée tool and successfully applied to the verification of absence of run-time errors in the control-command software of the Airbus A380. Another tool based on abstract interpretation is Fluctuat [16], which is not limited to the verification of absence of runtime errors, but is also able to compare between executions of the same code in finite precision and in infinite precision, giving some bounds on the difference between the two.

Previous support for floats in GNATprove translated every FP value in SPARK into a real value in Why3 and relied on the support for real arithmetic in provers, plus explicit use of rounding after each arithmetic operation.

A limitation (documented in previous versions of SPARK) was that the mapping from FP values to the real line, even when excluding infinities and NaN, is not injective: both FP values $+0$ and -0 are translated into the real number zero. Thus, the translation was not sound when programs in the input language may distinguish values -0 and $+0$, as the representation in real numbers cannot distinguish them anymore. Contrary to the axiomatization presented in Sect. 3, the previous axiomatization of rounding was not realized. Consistency and conformance of the set of axioms was ensured by review only.

In our own approach, we combine different techniques from abstract interpretation (interval analysis) and theorem proving (recent support of FP in SMT solvers), to achieve verification not only of runtime errors but also functional properties given by the user, with a high degree of automation. Our approach indeed follows the same path we followed for improving the support for bit-level computations [18], where in that case we tried to exploit native support for bitvectors in SMT solvers.

Future Work. The new combined approach we designed is successful on the typical examples with FP computations coming from current industrial use of SPARK. Yet, we noticed that this new technique is not as good as the former one used in Frama-C and Why3 [6] for proving very advanced functional behaviors of programs, relating the concrete computations with some purely mathematical computations on real numbers [4,6,27]. A short term perspective is to better unify the two approaches. Notice that the authors of the CVC4 SMT solver are currently working on a native support for FP arithmetic, it will be worth to experiment our approach with this new prover when it is available. As shown by our case study, handling conversion between integers and FP numbers remains quite challenging, a better support by back-end provers is desirable.

These future work, together with further improvements in the prototype back-end experimental solvers *COLIBRI* and *AE_fpa* we mentioned quickly in the experimental results of Sect. 4.2, are central in the on-going project SOPRANO.

Acknowledgements. We would like to thank Guillaume Melquiond for his help with the design of the new Why3 theory for FP arithmetic and with the realization in Coq using Flocq. We also thank Florian Schanda for providing the case study used in this article, Mohamed Iguernlala and Bruno Marre for fruitful exchanges on the use of *AE_fpa* and *COLIBRI* as well as the anonymous reviewers for their comments.

References

1. Ayad, A., Marché, C.: Multi-prover verification of floating-point programs. In: Giesl, J., Hähnle, R. (eds.) IJCAR 2010. LNCS (LNAI), vol. 6173, pp. 127–141. Springer, Heidelberg (2010). https://doi.org/10.1007/978-3-642-14203-1_11
2. Baird, S., Charlet, A., Moy, Y., Taft, T.S.: CodePeer - beyond bug-finding with static analysis. In: Boulanger, J.-L. (ed.) Static Analysis of Software: The Abstract Interpretation. Wiley, Hoboken (2013)

3. Bobot, F., Filliâtre, J.C., Marché, C., Paskevich, A.: Let's verify this with Why3. Int. J. Softw. Tools Technol. Transfer (STTT) **17**(6), 709–727 (2015). http://toccata.lri.fr/gallery/fm2012comp.en.html

4. Boldo, S., Clément, F., Filliâtre, J.C., Mayero, M., Melquiond, G., Weis, P.: Wave equation numerical resolution: a comprehensive mechanized proof of a C program. J. Autom. Reason. **50**(4), 423–456 (2013)

5. Boldo, S., Filliâtre, J.C.: Formal verification of floating-point programs. In: IEEE International Symposium on Computer Arithmetic, pp. 187–194 (2007)

6. Boldo, S., Marché, C.: Formal verification of numerical programs: from C annotated programs to mechanical proofs. Math. Comput. Sci. **5**, 377–393 (2011)

7. Boldo, S., Melquiond, G.: Flocq: A unified library for proving floating-point algorithms in Coq. In: 20th IEEE Symposium on Computer Arithmetic, pp. 243–252 (2011)

8. Brain, M., D'silva, V., Griggio, A., Haller, L., Kroening, D.: Deciding floating-point logic with abstract conflict driven clause learning. Form. Methods Syst. Des. **45**(2), 213–245 (2014)

9. Carreño, V., Miner, P.S.: Specification of the IEEE-854 floating-point standard in HOL and PVS. In: International Workshop on Higher-Order Logic Theorem Proving and Its Applications (1995)

10. Chapman, R., Schanda, F.: Are we there yet? 20 years of industrial theorem proving with SPARK. In: Klein, G., Gamboa, R. (eds.) ITP 2014. LNCS, vol. 8558, pp. 17–26. Springer, Cham (2014). https://doi.org/10.1007/978-3-319-08970-6_2

11. Chihani, Z., Marre, B., Bobot, F., Bardin, S.: Sharpening constraint programming approaches for bit-vector theory. In: Salvagnin, D., Lombardi, M. (eds.) CPAIOR 2017. LNCS, vol. 10335, pp. 3–20. Springer, Cham (2017). https://doi.org/10.1007/978-3-319-59776-8_1

12. Conchon, S., Iguernlala, M., Ji, K., Melquiond, G., Fumex, C.: A three-tier strategy for reasoning about floating-point numbers in SMT. In: Majumdar, R., Kunčak, V. (eds.) CAV 2017. LNCS, vol. 10427, pp. 419–435. Springer, Cham (2017). https://doi.org/10.1007/978-3-319-63390-9_22

13. Cuoq, P., Kirchner, F., Kosmatov, N., Prevosto, V., Signoles, J., Yakobowski, B.: Frama-C. In: Eleftherakis, G., Hinchey, M., Holcombe, M. (eds.) SEFM 2012. LNCS, vol. 7504, pp. 233–247. Springer, Heidelberg (2012). https://doi.org/10.1007/978-3-642-33826-7_16

14. Daumas, M., Melquiond, G.: Certification of bounds on expressions involving rounded operators. Trans. Math. Softw. **37**(1), 1–20 (2010)

15. Daumas, M., Rideau, L., Théry, L.: A generic library for floating-point numbers and its application to exact computing. In: Boulton, R.J., Jackson, P.B. (eds.) TPHOLs 2001. LNCS, vol. 2152, pp. 169–184. Springer, Heidelberg (2001). https://doi.org/10.1007/3-540-44755-5_13

16. Delmas, D., Goubault, E., Putot, S., Souyris, J., Tekkal, K., Védrine, F.: Towards an industrial use of FLUCTUAT on safety-critical avionics software. In: Alpuente, M., Cook, B., Joubert, C. (eds.) FMICS 2009. LNCS, vol. 5825, pp. 53–69. Springer, Heidelberg (2009). https://doi.org/10.1007/978-3-642-04570-7_6

17. Filliâtre, J.-C., Marché, C.: The Why/Krakatoa/Caduceus platform for deductive program verification. In: Damm, W., Hermanns, H. (eds.) CAV 2007. LNCS, vol. 4590, pp. 173–177. Springer, Heidelberg (2007). https://doi.org/10.1007/978-3-540-73368-3_21

18. Fumex, C., Dross, C., Gerlach, J., Marché, C.: Specification and proof of high-level functional properties of bit-level programs. In: Rayadurgam, S., Tkachuk, O. (eds.) NFM 2016. LNCS, vol. 9690, pp. 291–306. Springer, Cham (2016). https://doi.org/10.1007/978-3-319-40648-0_22

19. Fumex, C., Marché, C., Moy, Y.: Automated verification of floating-point computations in ADA programs. Research report RR-9060, Inria (2017)

20. Goodloe, A.E., Muñoz, C., Kirchner, F., Correnson, L.: Verification of numerical programs: from real numbers to floating point numbers. In: Brat, G., Rungta, N., Venet, A. (eds.) NFM 2013. LNCS, vol. 7871, pp. 441–446. Springer, Heidelberg (2013). https://doi.org/10.1007/978-3-642-38088-4_31

21. Harrison, J.: Floating point verification in HOL light: the exponential function. Form. Methods Syst. Des. **16**(3), 271–305 (2000)

22. Harrison, J.: Formal verification of floating point trigonometric functions. In: Hunt, W.A., Johnson, S.D. (eds.) FMCAD 2000. LNCS, vol. 1954, pp. 254–270. Springer, Heidelberg (2000). https://doi.org/10.1007/3-540-40922-X_14

23. Harrison, J.: Floating-point verification. In: Fitzgerald, J., Hayes, I.J., Tarlecki, A. (eds.) FM 2005. LNCS, vol. 3582, pp. 529–532. Springer, Heidelberg (2005). https://doi.org/10.1007/11526841_35

24. IEEE standard for floating-point arithmetic (2008). https://dx.doi.org/10.1109/IEEESTD.2008.4610935

25. Kosmatov, N., Marché, C., Moy, Y., Signoles, J.: Static versus dynamic verification in Why3, Frama-C and SPARK 2014. In: Margaria, T., Steffen, B. (eds.) ISoLA 2016. LNCS, vol. 9952, pp. 461–478. Springer, Cham (2016). https://doi.org/10.1007/978-3-319-47166-2_32

26. Leino, K.R.M., Moskal, M.: Usable auto-active verification. In: Usable Verification Workshop (2010)

27. Marché, C.: Verification of the functional behavior of a floating-point program: an industrial case study. Sci. Comput. Program. **96**(3), 279–296 (2014)

28. Marre, B., Michel, C.: Improving the floating point addition and subtraction constraints. In: Cohen, D. (ed.) CP 2010. LNCS, vol. 6308, pp. 360–367. Springer, Heidelberg (2010). https://doi.org/10.1007/978-3-642-15396-9_30

29. McCormick, J.W., Chapin, P.C.: Building High Integrity Applications with SPARK. Cambridge University Press, Cambridge (2015)

30. Miné, A.: Relational abstract domains for the detection of floating-point run-time errors. In: Schmidt, D. (ed.) ESOP 2004. LNCS, vol. 2986, pp. 3–17. Springer, Heidelberg (2004). https://doi.org/10.1007/978-3-540-24725-8_2

31. Monniaux, D.: The pitfalls of verifying floating-point computations. ACM Trans. Programm. Lang. Syst. **30**(3), 12 (2008)

32. de Moura, L., Bjørner, N.: Z3: an efficient SMT solver. In: Ramakrishnan, C.R., Rehof, J. (eds.) TACAS 2008. LNCS, vol. 4963, pp. 337–340. Springer, Heidelberg (2008). https://doi.org/10.1007/978-3-540-78800-3_24

33. Rümmer, P., Wahl, T.: An SMT-LIB theory of binary floating-point arithmetic. In: International Workshop on Satisfiability Modulo Theories (2010)

34. Russino, D.M.: A mechanically checked proof of IEEE compliance of the floating point multiplication, division and square root algorithms of the AMD-K7 processor. LMS J. Comput. Math. **1**, 148–200 (1998)

Adaptive Restart and CEGAR-Based Solver for Inverting Cryptographic Hash Functions

Saeed Nejati[(✉)], Jia Hui Liang, Catherine Gebotys, Krzysztof Czarnecki, and Vijay Ganesh

University of Waterloo, Waterloo, ON, Canada
{snejati,jliang,cgebotys,czarnecki,vganesh}@uwaterloo.ca

Abstract. SAT solvers are increasingly being used for cryptanalysis of hash functions and symmetric encryption schemes. Inspired by this trend, we present MAPLECRYPT which is a SAT solver-based cryptanalysis tool for inverting hash functions. We reduce the *hash function inversion problem for fixed targets* into the satisfiability problem for Boolean logic, and use MAPLECRYPT to construct preimages for these targets. MAPLECRYPT has two key features, namely, a multi-armed bandit based adaptive restart (MABR) policy and a counterexample-guided abstraction refinement (CEGAR) technique. The MABR technique uses reinforcement learning to adaptively choose between different restart policies during the run of the solver. The CEGAR technique abstracts away certain steps of the input hash function, replacing them with the identity function, and verifies whether the solution constructed by MAPLECRYPT indeed hashes to the previously fixed targets. If it is determined that the solution produced is spurious, the abstraction is refined until a correct inversion to the input hash target is produced. We show that the resultant system is faster for inverting the SHA-1 hash function than state-of-the-art inversion tools.

1 Introduction

Over the last 15 years we have seen a dramatic improvement in the efficiency of conflict-driven clause-learning (CDCL) SAT solvers [2,7,35,43] over industrial instances generated from a large variety of applications such as verification, testing, security, and AI [9,11,46]. Inspired by this success many researchers have proposed the use of SAT solvers for cryptanalysis of hash functions and symmetric encryption schemes [41]. The use of SAT solvers in this context holds great promise as can be seen based on their success to-date in automating many aspects of analysis of cryptographic primitives [51]. SAT solvers are an increasingly important tool in the toolbox of the practical cryptanalyst and designer of hash functions and encryption schemes. Examples of the use of SAT solvers in cryptanalysis include tools aimed at the search for cryptographic keys in 1999 [36], logical cryptanalysis as a SAT problem in 2000 [37], encoding modular root finding as a SAT problem in 2003 [21] and logical analysis of hash functions in 2005 [26]. Most of these approaches used a direct encoding of the said problems into a satisfiability problem and used SAT solvers as a blackbox.

© Springer International Publishing AG 2017
A. Paskevich and T. Wies (Eds.): VSTTE 2017, LNCS 10712, pp. 120–131, 2017.
https://doi.org/10.1007/978-3-319-72308-2_8

In this paper, we propose a set of techniques and an implementation, we call MAPLECRYPT, that dramatically improve upon the state-of-the-art in solving the *cryptographic hash function inversion problem*. The problem of inverting a hash function is of great importance to cryptographers and security researchers, given that many security protocols and primitives rely on these functions being *hard-to-invert*. Informally, the problem is "given a specific hash value (or target) H find an input to the hash function that hashes to H". We focus on the inversion problem, as opposed to the more well-studied collision problem. The value of this research is not only the fact that cryptanalysis is an increasingly important area of application for SAT solvers, but also that instances generated from cryptographic applications tend to be significantly harder for solvers than typical industrial instances, and hence are a very good benchmark for solver research.

Summary of Contributions. We focus on the SHA-1 cryptographic hash function in this paper, and make the following contributions:

1. We present a counter-example guided abstraction-refinement [13] (CEGAR) based technique, wherein certain steps of the hash function under analysis are abstracted away and replaced by the identity function. The inversion problem for the resultant abstracted hash function is often much easier for solvers, and we find that we do not have to do too many steps of refinement. An insight from this experiment is that certain steps of the SHA-1 hash function do not have sufficient levels of diffusion, a key property of hash functions that makes them difficult to invert.
2. In addition to the above-mentioned CEGAR technique, we present a multi-armed bandit [50] based adaptive restart policy. The idea is that a reinforcement learning technique is used to select among a set of restart policies in an online fashion during the run of the solver. This method is of general value, beyond cryptanalysis. The result of combining these two techniques is a tool, we call MAPLECRYPT, that is around two times faster on the hash function inversion problem than most state-of-the-art SAT solvers. More importantly, with a time limit of 72 h, MAPLECRYPT can invert a 23-step reduced version of SHA-1 consistently, whereas other tools we compared against can do so only occasionally.
3. We perform extensive evaluation of MAPLECRYPT on the SHA-1 inversion problem, and compare against CryptoMiniSat, Lingeling, MiniSAT, Minisat-BLBD. In particular, MAPLECRYPT is competitive against the best tools out there for inverting SHA-1.

2 Background on Cryptographic Hash Functions

In this section we provide a brief background on cryptographic hash functions, esp. SHA-1. We refer the reader to [22] for a more detailed overview of hash functions. A hash function maps an arbitrary length input string to a fixed length output string (e.g., 160 bits in the case of SHA-1). There are three main properties that are desired for a cryptographic hash function [30]. Informally, they are:

- *Preimage Resistance*: Given a hash value H, it should be computationally infeasible to find a message M, where $H = hash(M)$.
- *Second Preimage Resistance*: Given a message M_1, it should be computationally infeasible to find another message M_2, where $hash(M_1) = hash(M_2)$ and $M_1 \neq M_2$.
- *Collision Resistance*: It should be computationally infeasible to find a pair of messages M_1 and M_2, where $hash(M_1) = hash(M_2)$ and $M_1 \neq M_2$. (There is a subtle difference between second pre-image resistance and collision resistance, in that the message M_1 is not fixed in the case of collision resistance.)

Preimage resistance implies that the hash function should be hard to invert. The terms preimage attack and inversion attack are used interchangeably. Standard cryptographic hash functions at their core have a compression function, which can essentially be seen as repeated application of a step function on its input bits for a fixed number of steps. The compression function takes as input a fixed length input and outputs a fixed length (with smaller length) output. For making a collision resistant compression function, one method is to use a block cipher and apply the Davis-Meyer method. Feistel ladder which is widely used in hash functions like MD5 and SHA-1 (and also block ciphers like DES), is an implementation of this method, where the key is a message word. If the key is known, each step is easily reversible. For making a hash function able to accept arbitrary long messages as input, one can use Merkle-Damgard structure [40], where it is shown that if one block is collision resistant, the whole structure would be collision resistant.

2.1   SHA-1

SHA-1 (Secure Hash Algorithm), was designed by NSA, and adopted as a standard in 1995 [22], and is still widely used in many applications. SHA-1 consists of iterative application of a so-called compression function which takes a 160-bit chaining value and transforms it into the next chaining value using a 512-bit message block. The current chaining value would be added to the output of compression function to make the next chaining value: $CV_{i+1} = Comp(CV_i, M_i) + CV_i$, and the CV_0 is set to a fixed initialization vector. The input message will be padded to make the input message length a multiple of 512. A single bit '1' followed by a set of '0's and the original message length (as a 64-bit value) will be appended to the message. The message is broken down to blocks of 512 bits. Each compression function breaks down the input message block into sixteen 32-bit words. Then it will go through a message expansion phase, which extends sixteen words to eighty words, using the following formulation (consider that W_i for $0 \leq i \leq 15$ refers to input message words):

$$W_i = (W_{i-3} \oplus W_{i-8} \oplus W_{i-14} \oplus W_{i-16}) \lll 1 \quad (16 \leq i \leq 79) \qquad (1)$$

where '$\lll 1$' is left rotation by one position.

There are five 32-bit words (namely, a, b, c, d, e) as the intermediate variables. In each step a function F_t is applied to three of these words, and it changes every 20 steps:

$$F_t(b, c, d) = \begin{cases} Ch(b,c,d) = (b \wedge c) \oplus (\neg b \wedge d) & 0 \leq t \leq 19 \\ Parity(b,c,d) = b \oplus c \oplus d & 20 \leq t \leq 39 \\ Maj(b,c,d) = (b \wedge c) \oplus (b \wedge d) \oplus (c \wedge d) & 40 \leq t \leq 59 \\ Parity(b,c,d) = b \oplus c \oplus d & 60 \leq t \leq 79 \end{cases} \quad (2)$$

The step process would be like:

$$(a_{t+1}, b_{t+1}, c_{t+1}, d_{t+1}, e_{t+1}) \leftarrow$$
$$(F_t(b_t, c_t, d_t) \boxplus e_t \boxplus (a_t \lll 5) \boxplus W_t \boxplus K_t, a_t, b_t \lll 30, c_t, d_t) (3)$$

where $\lll$ is left rotation, $\boxplus$ is modulo-2^{32} addition and K_t is the round constant. This is repeated for next 512-bit message block in the Merkel-Damagard chain.

Step-Reduced Version: Usually inverting or finding collision for full version of a hash function is very hard. Thus, cryptanalysts work on a relaxed version of those functions like step-reduced versions, which means the function under attack is the same, except that the number of steps is reduced.

3 Architecture of MapleCrypt

We seek to perform a preimage or inversion attack on a step-reduced version of SHA-1, with one block input (512 bits). Although the current work is focused on SHA-1, our approach is applicable to other iterative hash functions. The two main contributions in our design are adaptive restart and a CEGAR-based approach. The adaptive restart is not directly dealing with the structure of the function and therefore could be used in solving other SAT instances. The CEGAR approach is abstracting and refining step functions. Thus it could be used for the other hash functions that have a repeated use of a step function (e.g. MD4, MD5, SHA-2).

3.1 SAT Encoding

The encoding we use in this paper is based on the one in [44]. Most of the operations are encoded using Tseitin transformation, but some operations are described using high level relations. There is a 5-operand addition in each step of SHA-1 (refer to Eq. (3)). The main contribution of the encoding in [44] is the encoding of this multi-operand addition (instead of encoding of multiple two-operand additions). Current SHA-1 instances in SAT competition are generated using this tool [45]. We have made minor modifications, namely to the encoding of round-dependent logical function (F_t in Eq. (2)), replacing XOR operations with inclusive-OR to simplify the corresponding clauses.

3.2 CEGAR Loop Design

The SHA-1 SAT instances of up to 20 steps are very easy to solve (less than a second using most modern solvers), but the level of difficulty rapidly rises from 20 steps to 23 steps (needs 2 to 3 days to solve). To the best of our knowledge, preimage for more than 23 steps cannot be constructed in a reasonable amount of time even with the latest techniques and hardware [31, 32, 44].

For the instances of more than 20 steps (e.g. 22 steps), we abstract away initial step functions and keep the last 20 steps intact (abstracting first 2 steps), but we do not abstract away the message words and the message expansion relations. We solve the simplified instance, and find a solution for the message words. However, the resultant solution may be spurious, i.e., may not actually hold for the specific hash target. In order to verify the solution, we run the hash function in the forward direction and check the result with the target, and record values of intermediate variables throughout the hashing. If the computed hash does not match the target (i.e., the solution produced by the solver is spurious), we refine back those parts of abstracted steps of the hash function that are unsatisfiable under the spurious solution. Finally we also add a subset (all except last 8 steps) of intermediate values (computed during the forward run of the hash function on spurious solutions) as blocking clauses.

The intuition behind this procedure is that, first of all, 20 steps are very easy to solve, and it is the highest number of steps that we are better off solving directly, rather than using an abstraction. Secondly, the first few intermediate variables have the most degree of freedom when searching for a preimage or collision. Lastly, blocking a subset of intermediate values, although might block some legitimate solutions, but also blocks many spurious solutions. We can divide our main procedure into two main functions, listed in Algorithm 1.

In the listing of Algorithm 1, *interValues* refers to the collection of intermediate variables across working steps that will be negated and added as a conflict clause to a CCDB (conflict clause database). The *Refine* function evaluates the clauses of the original formula with the found solution and checks which variables are in the UNSAT clauses and add them back to the current abstracted instance.

3.3 Multi-armed Bandit Restart

Many restart policies have been proposed in the SAT literature [4–6, 34], in particular we focus on the uniform, linear, Luby, and geometric restart policies [10]. For a given preimage attack instance, we can not know a priori which of the 4 restart policies will perform the best. To compensate for this, we use multi-armed bandits (MAB) [50], a special case of reinforcement learning, to switch between the 4 policies dynamically during the run of the solver. We chose to use discounted UCB algorithm [24] from MAB literature, as it accounts for the nonstationary environment of the CDCL solver, in particular changes in the learnt clause database over time. Discounted UCB has 4 actions to choose from corresponding to the uniform, linear, Luby, and geometric restart policies.

Algorithm 1. Finding Preimage using a CEGAR loop

Require: W: 512-bit found preimage, H: Hash target, *nsteps*: number of hash steps
Ensure: *true* if W is a valid preimage, *false* otherwise
1: **function** CHECK($W, H, nsteps$)
2:    (H', interValues) ← SHA-1(W, nsteps)
3:    **if** $H = H'$ **then**
4:        **return** true
5:    **else**
6:        CCDB.add(interValues)
7:        **return** false
8:

Require: H: Hash target, *nsteps*: number of hash steps
Ensure: W: 512-bit preimage of H
9: **function** FINDPREIMAGE($H, nsteps$)
10:    InstanceSteps ← AbsInstGen(nsteps)   ▷ Abstracted set of step functions
11:    InstanceW ← MsgInstGen(nsteps) ▷ All of input and expanded message words
12:    **while** true **do**
13:        $W[0..15]$ ← SATSolver(InstanceSteps, InstanceW, CCDB)
14:        **if** Check(W, H, nsteps) = true **then**
15:            **return** W
16:        InstanceSteps ← Refine(InstanceSteps, W, nsteps)

Once the action is selected, the solver will proceed to perform the CDCL backtracking search until the chosen restart policy decides to restart. The algorithm computes the average LBD (Literals Block Distance [3]) of the learnt clauses generated since the action was selected, and the reciprocal of the average is the reward given to the selected action. Intuitively, a restart policy which generates small LBDs will receive larger rewards and UCB will increase the probability of selecting that restart policy in the future. Over time, this will bias UCB towards restart policies that generate small LBDs.

4 Experimental Results

4.1 Experimental Setup

Our baseline benchmark consists of instances of preimage of step-reduced SHA-1, from 21 to 23 steps. Instances for less than 21 steps were trivial for every solver we tried. For each step we generated 25 random targets and encoded them as fixed value for the hash output. All jobs were run on AMD opteron CPUs at 2.2 GHz and 8 GB RAM. The timeout for solving a single instance was 72 h, with 4 GB of memory allocated for each process. We used 5 SAT solvers, CryptoMiniSat-4.5.3 [47], Minisat_BLBD [12], Lingeling-ayv [8], Minisat-2.2 [18] and MAPLESAT [33]. We also tried 4 SMT solvers to take advantage of their BitVector theory solvers. We used, STP-2.0/CryptoMinisat4, Boolector-2.0.7/Lingeling, CVC4-1.5, Z3-4.4. However, all of these SMT solvers performed surprisingly poorly (marginally better than the worst performing SAT solver in our solver set). Hence, we did not include them in our comparisons.

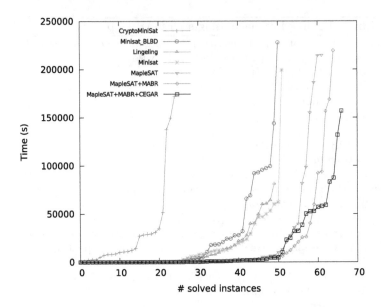

Fig. 1. The performance of various SAT solvers against MAPLESAT with adaptive MAB-restart and CEGAR.

4.2   CEGAR and MABR

State-of-the-art results for automated and practical preimage of SHA-1 that construct a result rather than presenting an upper bound for attack complexity, propose a SAT encoding of the preimage attack and solve it using modern SAT solvers. Therefore we picked the best existing encoding method for SHA-1 [44] and applied our solving techniques on them. We are comparing our runtimes with other SAT solvers, given the same instances. Figure 1 shows the cactus plot of solving times where each data point shows how many instances could be solved in the corresponding time. Curves more toward bottom are faster and more toward right are solving more instances. It can be seen that MAPLESAT with MAB restart dominates in terms of runtime and number of instances solved, and after employing the CEGAR technique, we are able to solve faster and more instances. MapleCrypt is the CEGAR architecture that uses MapleSAT+MABR as backend solver.

4.3   Partial Preimage

This is the kind of attack where the attacker knows some bits of the input message and wants to find out the rest. Our experiments on SHA-1 show that knowing parts of the message does not necessarily make the problem easier, as it might force the solver to find a specific input that matches those bits and reduces the possibilities. Our results mostly confirm the observations on hardness of partial preimage of SHA-1 in [45]. We could invert up to 27 steps of SHA-1 when having 40 bits of the input message unknown, which matches the best results known in this setting for SHA-1 [42].

5   Related Work

We review the related work on inversion attacks, and touch upon collision attacks as appropriate. Note that for inversion attacks, every additional round of a hash function inverted is considered significant improvement over previous work.

SAT-Based Constructive Methods. Since 2005, several hash functions have been shown to be prone to collision attacks [52,53]. In 2006, Mironov et al. [41] automated parts of collision attack of Wang et al. [52] using SAT solvers. Not many of the collision attack methods use SAT solvers, as the collision finding problem is studied very well and most cryptanalysts use direct implementation of mathematical analyses (e.g., differential cryptanalysis) for this problem.

Given that the focus of our paper is on inversion attacks, we provide a thorough overview of the related work for the same. In 2007, De et al. [14] used a SAT solver for an inversion attack on MD4 and enhanced number of steps inverted, up to 2 rounds and 7 steps, by encoding Dobbertin's attack model [17] into SAT constraints. In 2008, Srebrny et al. [48] formulated inversion of SHA-1 as a SAT instance and could solve for restricted message size up to 22 steps. Several later works could solve up to 23 rounds of SHA-1 [31,32,44]. Lafitte et al. [29] presented a generic way to encode basic cryptographic operations which was an improvement over operator overloading model in [26] and used it in a preimage test on MD4 and finding weak keys in IDEA and MESH ciphers, although other than finding weak keys, preimage results were not better than the best previously published attack. In 2013, Morawiecki et al. [42] used the idea of minimization of SAT instances generated via analysis of cryptographic primitives. They applied their tool CryptLogVer on some hash functions like SHA-1 and Keccak to analyze their preimage resistance. Although they did not increase the number of inverted steps, they showed improvement in solving time. Nossum [45], also presents an encoding for preimage attack of SHA-1 which targets the 5-operand addition operation that is performed in each step of SHA-1 and the generated instances have fewer variables than the work of Srebrny et al. [48] and Morwiecki et al. [42], and in general are easier to solve by modern SAT solvers. It is used to generate SHA-1 instances of SAT competition [45]. The work presented in this paper is using Nossum's instance generator with small tweaks. All of the mentioned techniques use SAT solvers as a black box tool. By contrast our design leverages CEGAR and modifies the restart policies of SAT solvers. Additionally, our method is faster for finding preimages and can solve more hash targets in the given time limit than previous work.

Non SAT Solver Based Constructive Attacks. These methods are almost exclusively aimed at collision attacks. In 2006, De Cannière et al. [15] built a non SAT solver based tool for SHA-1 collision attack leveraging the breakthrough of Wang et al. [53]. In 2011, Mendel et al. [38] extended it for SHA-256 which was further improved in their work in 2013 [39]. Eichlseder et al. [19] improved upon the branching heuristics of this tool and applied it to SHA-512. Recently Stevens et al. [49] presented a parallelized search implementation and found free-start collision on full SHA-1.

Non-constructive Theoretical Bounds. Here we review known theoretical bounds on preimage attack on various hash functions. One of the first preimage results on SHA-1 was achieved by using techniques like reversing the inversion problem and mathematical structures like P^3 graphs [16], which could invert 34 and 44 steps with complexity of 2^{80} and 2^{157} respectively. Aoki and Sasaki [1] used meet-in-the-middle to attack SHA-1 (and also MD4 and MD5) and improved the number of steps to 48 with the solving complexity of $2^{159.3}$. Knellwolf et al. [28] improved it in 2012 by providing a differential formulation of MITM model and raised the bar up to 57 steps. Espiatu et al. [20] extended this work further to higher order differentials for preimage attack on SHA-1 and BLAKE2 and went up to 62 steps for SHA-1. Mathematical structure like Biclique [27], allowed extending coverage of MITM over larger number of steps.

Adaptive Restarts. Armin Biere proposed monitoring variable assignment flips in PicoSAT, and delayed restarts when the weighted average of flips is below a predetermined threshold [5]. Audemard and Simon proposed monitoring the LBD of learnt clauses, and a restart is triggered if the short term LBDs exceeds the long term LBDs by a constant factor [4]. Haim and Walsh used machine learning to train a classifier to select from a portfolio of restart policies [25]. Gagliolo and Schmidhuber used bandits to select between Luby and uniform restart heuristic [23].

6   Conclusion and Future Work

We presented a tool called MAPLECRYPT for preimage attack on SHA-1 hash functions, which uses CEGAR and adaptive restart techniques. Our tool is faster than other automated search tools in the literature for the constructive preimage attack. Our results show that SAT solvers and SAT-based techniques are a promising approach for handling the laborious parts of cryptanalysis, and identifying weaknesses in hash function designs. This design can be extended to work on other hash functions like SHA-2 family.

References

1. Aoki, K., Sasaki, Y.: Preimage attacks on one-block MD4, 63-step MD5 and more. In: Avanzi, R.M., Keliher, L., Sica, F. (eds.) SAC 2008. LNCS, vol. 5381, pp. 103–119. Springer, Heidelberg (2009). https://doi.org/10.1007/978-3-642-04159-4_7
2. Audemard, G., Simon, L.: GLUCOSE: a solver that predicts learnt clauses quality. SAT Compet. 7–8 (2009)
3. Audemard, G., Simon, L.: Predicting learnt clauses quality in modern SAT solvers. IJCAI **9**, 399–404 (2009)

4. Audemard, G., Simon, L.: Refining restarts strategies for SAT and UNSAT. In: Milano, M. (ed.) CP 2012. LNCS, pp. 118–126. Springer, Heidelberg (2012). https://doi.org/10.1007/978-3-642-33558-7_11

5. Biere, A.: Adaptive restart strategies for conflict driven SAT solvers. In: Kleine Büning, H., Zhao, X. (eds.) SAT 2008. LNCS, vol. 4996, pp. 28–33. Springer, Heidelberg (2008). https://doi.org/10.1007/978-3-540-79719-7_4

6. Biere, A.: PicoSAT essentials. J. Satisf. Boolean Model. Comput. **4**, 75–97 (2008)

7. Biere, A.: Lingeling, Plingeling, Picosat and Precosat at SAT Race 2010. FMV Report Series Technical report, 10/1 (2010)

8. Biere, A.: Lingeling ayv (2015). http://fmv.jku.at/lingeling/

9. Biere, A., Cimatti, A., Clarke, E.M., Strichman, O., Zhu, Y.: Bounded model checking. Adv. Comput. **58**, 117–148 (2003)

10. Biere, A., Fröhlich, A.: Evaluating CDCL restart schemes. In: Pragmatics of SAT (2015)

11. Cadar, C., Ganesh, V., Pawlowski, P.M., Dill, D.L., Engler, D.R.: EXE: automatically generating inputs of death. ACM Trans. Inf. Syst. Secur. (TISSEC) **12**(2), 10 (2008)

12. Chen, J.: A bit-encoding phase selection strategy for satisfiability solvers. In: Gopal, T.V., Agrawal, M., Li, A., Cooper, S.B. (eds.) TAMC 2014. LNCS, vol. 8402, pp. 158–167. Springer, Cham (2014). https://doi.org/10.1007/978-3-319-06089-7_11

13. Clarke, E., Grumberg, O., Jha, S., Lu, Y., Veith, H.: Counterexample-guided abstraction refinement. In: Emerson, E.A., Sistla, A.P. (eds.) CAV 2000. LNCS, vol. 1855, pp. 154–169. Springer, Heidelberg (2000). https://doi.org/10.1007/10722167_15

14. De, D., Kumarasubramanian, A., Venkatesan, R.: Inversion attacks on secure hash functions using SAT solvers. In: Marques-Silva, J., Sakallah, K.A. (eds.) SAT 2007. LNCS, vol. 4501, pp. 377–382. Springer, Heidelberg (2007). https://doi.org/10.1007/978-3-540-72788-0_36

15. De Cannière, C., Rechberger, C.: Finding SHA-1 characteristics: general results and applications. In: Lai, X., Chen, K. (eds.) ASIACRYPT 2006. LNCS, vol. 4284, pp. 1–20. Springer, Heidelberg (2006). https://doi.org/10.1007/11935230_1

16. De Cannière, C., Rechberger, C.: Preimages for reduced SHA-0 and SHA-1. In: Wagner, D. (ed.) CRYPTO 2008. LNCS, vol. 5157, pp. 179–202. Springer, Heidelberg (2008). https://doi.org/10.1007/978-3-540-85174-5_11

17. Dobbertin, H.: Cryptanalysis of MD4. In: Gollmann, D. (ed.) FSE 1996. LNCS, vol. 1039, pp. 53–69. Springer, Heidelberg (1996). https://doi.org/10.1007/3-540-60865-6_43

18. Eén, N., Sörensson, N.: Minisat 2.2. http://minisat.se/

19. Eichlseder, M., Mendel, F., Schläffer, M.: Branching heuristics in differential collision search with applications to SHA-512. IACR Cryptology ePrint Archive 2014:302 (2014)

20. Espitau, T., Fouque, P.-A., Karpman, P.: Higher-order differential meet-in-the-middle preimage attacks on SHA-1 and BLAKE. In: Gennaro, R., Robshaw, M. (eds.) CRYPTO 2015. LNCS, vol. 9215, pp. 683–701. Springer, Heidelberg (2015). https://doi.org/10.1007/978-3-662-47989-6_33

21. Fiorini, C., Martinelli, E., Massacci, F.: How to fake an RSA signature by encoding modular root finding as a SAT problem. Discrete Appl. Math. **130**(2), 101–127 (2003)

22. PUB FIPS: 180–4. Federal Information Processing Standards Publication, Secure Hash (2011)

23. Gagliolo, M., Schmidhuber, J.: Learning restart strategies. In: IJCAI, pp. 792–797 (2007)
24. Garivier, A., Moulines, E.: On upper-confidence bound policies for switching bandit problems. In: Kivinen, J., Szepesvári, C., Ukkonen, E., Zeugmann, T. (eds.) ALT 2011. LNCS (LNAI), vol. 6925, pp. 174–188. Springer, Heidelberg (2011). https://doi.org/10.1007/978-3-642-24412-4_16
25. Haim, S., Walsh, T.: Restart strategy selection using machine learning techniques. In: Kullmann, O. (ed.) SAT 2009. LNCS, vol. 5584, pp. 312–325. Springer, Heidelberg (2009). https://doi.org/10.1007/978-3-642-02777-2_30
26. Jovanović, D., Janičić, P.: Logical analysis of hash functions. In: Gramlich, B. (ed.) FroCoS 2005. LNCS (LNAI), vol. 3717, pp. 200–215. Springer, Heidelberg (2005). https://doi.org/10.1007/11559306_11
27. Khovratovich, D., Rechberger, C., Savelieva, A.: Bicliques for preimages: attacks on Skein-512 and the SHA-2 family. In: Canteaut, A. (ed.) FSE 2012. LNCS, vol. 7549, pp. 244–263. Springer, Heidelberg (2012). https://doi.org/10.1007/978-3-642-34047-5_15
28. Knellwolf, S., Khovratovich, D.: New preimage attacks against reduced SHA-1. In: Safavi-Naini, R., Canetti, R. (eds.) CRYPTO 2012. LNCS, vol. 7417, pp. 367–383. Springer, Heidelberg (2012). https://doi.org/10.1007/978-3-642-32009-5_22
29. Lafitte, F., Nakahara Jr., J., Van Heule, D.: Applications of SAT solvers in cryptanalysis: finding weak keys and preimages. J. Satisf. Boolean Model. Comput. **9**, 1–25 (2014)
30. Lai, X., Massey, J.L.: Hash functions based on block ciphers. In: Rueppel, R.A. (ed.) EUROCRYPT 1992. LNCS, vol. 658, pp. 55–70. Springer, Heidelberg (1993). https://doi.org/10.1007/3-540-47555-9_5
31. Legendre, F., Dequen, G., Krajecki, M.: Encoding hash functions as a SAT problem. In: 2012 IEEE 24th International Conference on Tools with Artificial Intelligence (ICTAI), vol. 1, pp. 916–921. IEEE (2012)
32. Legendre, F., Dequen, G., Krajecki, M.: Logical reasoning to detect weaknesses about SHA-1 and MD4/5. IACR Cryptology ePrint Archive 2014:239 (2014)
33. Liang, J.H., Ganesh, V., Poupart, P., Czarnecki, K.: Learning rate based branching heuristic for SAT solvers. In: Creignou, N., Le Berre, D. (eds.) SAT 2016. LNCS, vol. 9710, pp. 123–140. Springer, Cham (2016). https://doi.org/10.1007/978-3-319-40970-2_9
34. Luby, M., Sinclair, A., Zuckerman, D.: Optimal speedup of Las Vegas algorithms. In: Proceedings of the 2nd Israel Symposium on the Theory and Computing Systems, pp. 128–133. IEEE (1993)
35. Marques-Silva, J.P., Sakallah, K.A.: GRASP: a search algorithm for propositional satisfiability. IEEE Trans. Comput. **48**(5), 506–521 (1999)
36. Massacci, F.: Using walk-SAT and Rel-SAT for cryptographic key search. In: IJCAI 1999, pp. 290–295 (1999)
37. Massacci, F., Marraro, L.: Logical cryptanalysis as a SAT problem. J. Autom. Reasoning **24**(1–2), 165–203 (2000)
38. Mendel, F., Nad, T., Schläffer, M.: Finding SHA-2 characteristics: searching through a minefield of contradictions. In: Lee, D.H., Wang, X. (eds.) ASIACRYPT 2011. LNCS, vol. 7073, pp. 288–307. Springer, Heidelberg (2011). https://doi.org/10.1007/978-3-642-25385-0_16
39. Mendel, F., Nad, T., Schläffer, M.: Improving local collisions: new attacks on reduced SHA-256. In: Johansson, T., Nguyen, P.Q. (eds.) EUROCRYPT 2013. LNCS, vol. 7881, pp. 262–278. Springer, Heidelberg (2013). https://doi.org/10.1007/978-3-642-38348-9_16

40. Merkle, R.C.: One way hash functions and DES. In: Brassard, G. (ed.) CRYPTO 1989. LNCS, vol. 435, pp. 428–446. Springer, New York (1990). https://doi.org/10.1007/0-387-34805-0_40

41. Mironov, I., Zhang, L.: Applications of SAT solvers to cryptanalysis of hash functions. In: Biere, A., Gomes, C.P. (eds.) SAT 2006. LNCS, vol. 4121, pp. 102–115. Springer, Heidelberg (2006). https://doi.org/10.1007/11814948_13

42. Morawiecki, P., Srebrny, M.: A SAT-based preimage analysis of reduced KECCAK hash functions. Inf. Process. Lett. **113**(10), 392–397 (2013)

43. Moskewicz, M.W., Madigan, C.F., Zhao, Y., Zhang, L., Malik, S.: Chaff: engineering an efficient SAT solver. In: Proceedings of the 38th Annual Design Automation Conference, pp. 530–535. ACM (2001)

44. Nossum, V.: SAT-based preimage attacks on SHA-1 (2012)

45. Nossum, V.: Instance generator for encoding preimage, second-preimage, and collision attacks on SHA-1. In: Proceedings of the SAT Competition, pp. 119–120 (2013)

46. Rintanen, J.: Planning and SAT. Handbook of Satisfiability, vol. 185, pp. 483–504 (2009)

47. Soos, M.: CryptoMiniSat 4.5.3 (2015). http://www.msoos.org/cryptominisat4/

48. Srebrny, M., Srebrny, M., Stepien, L.: SAT as a programming environment for linear algebra and cryptanalysis. In: ISAIM (2008)

49. Stevens, M., Karpman, P., Peyrin, T.: Freestart collision for full SHA-1. Cryptology ePrint Archive (2015/967):1–21 (2015)

50. Sutton, R.S., Barto, A.G.: Introduction to Reinforcement Learning, vol. 135. MIT Press, Cambridge (1998)

51. Tomb, A.: Applying satisfiability to the analysis of cryptography (2015). https://github.com/GaloisInc/sat2015-crypto/blob/master/slides/talk.pdf

52. Wang, X., Yu, H.: How to break MD5 and other hash functions. In: Cramer, R. (ed.) EUROCRYPT 2005. LNCS, vol. 3494, pp. 19–35. Springer, Heidelberg (2005). https://doi.org/10.1007/11426639_2

53. Wang, X., Yu, H., Yin, Y.L.: Efficient collision search attacks on SHA-0. In: Shoup, V. (ed.) CRYPTO 2005. LNCS, vol. 3621, pp. 1–16. Springer, Heidelberg (2005). https://doi.org/10.1007/11535218_1

Practical Void Safety

Alexander Kogtenkov[✉] [iD]

Independent scientist, Podolsk, Russia
`kwaxer@mail.ru`

Abstract. Null pointer dereferencing remains one of the major issues in modern object-oriented languages. An obvious addition of keywords to distinguish between never null and possibly null references appears to be insufficient during object initialization when some fields declared as never null may be temporary null before the initialization completes. Unlike all previous publications on the subject, this work avoids explicit encoding of these intermediate states in programs in favor of statically checked validity rules that do not depend on special conditionally non-null types. I review all object initialization examples proposed earlier and I suggest new ones to compare applicability of different approaches. I demonstrate the usability of the proposed scheme on open-source libraries with a million lines of code that were converted to satisfy the rules.

Keywords: Null pointer dereferencing · Null safety · Void safety
Object initialization · Static analysis Library-level modularity

1 Introduction

In his talk at a conference in 2009 Hoare [8] called his invention of the null reference in 1965 a "billion-dollar mistake". The reason is simple: most object-oriented languages suffer from the problem of null pointer dereferencing. What does it mean in practice? Even in a type-safe language, if an expression is expected to reference an existing object, it can reference none, or be *null*. On the other hand, the core of object-oriented languages is in the ability to make calls on objects. If there is no object, the normal program execution is disrupted.

Because most popular languages do not prevent null pointer dereferencing at compile time, it remains one of the day-to-day issue discovered in open source and private software. My analysis of the public database of cybersecurity vulnerabilities known as Common Vulnerabilities and Exposures (CVE®)[1] reveals that in the past 10 years entries mentioning null pointer dereference bugs appear at a consistent rate of about 78 bugs a year. As the database lists only the issues affecting most widespread software on the planet, real economy losses are much higher.

---

[1] http://cve.mitre.org/ (visited on 2017-08-29).

© Springer International Publishing AG 2017
A. Paskevich and T. Wies (Eds.): VSTTE 2017, LNCS 10712, pp. 132–151, 2017.
https://doi.org/10.1007/978-3-319-72308-2_9

Possible solutions of the problem are not new, and either require special type annotations or are non-modular. The idea of distinguishing between different types of expressions, ones that always return existing objects and ones that may return null was discussed in the early days of Java in 1995 by Stata [18]. He proposed a notation T ? in the spirit of the Clanguage notation T * to denote that the value may be null. However, the idea was not adopted for the standard Java. Later authors of *Extended Static Checked for Java* (ESC/Java) [6] used @non_null annotations for declarations of non-null types. Today's developers of the Checkers Framework[2] mention that most static analyzers for Java use similar annotations: @Nullable and @NonNull, from different packages.

Fähndrich and Leino [4] used C# attributes [NotNull] and [MayBeNull] for non-null and maybe-null types respectively to construct a sound null-safe type system. In different forms, similar annotations are used in Spec# [2] (with type marks ! and ?), Eiffel [9] (with type marks **attached** and **detachable**), and Kotlin [10] (with a mark ? for maybe-null types). Such annotations would be sufficient to solve the problem if objects could be created in an atomic operation, so that all fields marked as [NotNull] were initialized with object references. Unfortunately, sequential initialization of the fields breaks the solution.

Most proposals solving the object initialization issue [4,5,16,20] suggest extending existing type systems to identify objects that are not completely initialized. In this work, I analyze public Eiffel libraries to see how much code could be converted to null-safe code without any new type marks. The portion of such code turns out to be extremely high.

Therefore, instead of tweaking the type system, I propose a static-analysis-based solution. This solution relies on the validity rules checked during compilation to cover the cases left by the type system checks. The approach has the following properties:

- all examples relevant to this problem [4,5,16,20] could be correctly compiled or rejected;
- it permits new scenarios, impossible with type-system-based solutions.

Combined with removal of annotations for local variables [11], based on typing rules similar to those establishing security data flow [21] and recently named *flow-sensitive typing* [15], the solution is very effective in practice for avoiding null dereferencing problems, whilst having low cost in compilation time: (i) it reduces the annotation overhead compared to previous solutions for the null-safe programming; (ii) it simplifies the conversion of legacy code to satisfy null safety rules; (iii) it makes the null-safe programming more accessible.

The paper is organized as follows. Section 2 presents a list of examples that reveal the difficulties and cases that my approach aims to solve. Section 3 provides an intuitive overview of the solution proposed. Section 4 compares my solution with the existing works. Section 5 formalizes validity predicates used for the program analysis. Section 6 discusses experimental results. Finally, Sect. 7 summarizes main advantages and drawbacks of the solution.

---

[2] The Checker Framework 2.1.10, (2017). https://checkerframework.org/ (visited on 2017-05-08).

2   Motivating Examples

I. Polymorphic call from a constructor. When a constructor of a superclass is invoked in C#, a call to a virtual method on `this` is considered a bad practice. At this moment, subclass fields of the object are not initialized yet and using them in the polymorphic call is unsafe. An example of this situation described by Fähndrich and Leino [4] is shown in Fig. 1. In class B, before the field `path` is set, the superclass constructor is called. The constructor invokes the virtual method m. The override of the method m in the class B causes `NullReferenceException`.

Qi and Myers [16] give a similar example where they consider a class `Point` and its subclass `CPoint` that adds a color attribute.

II. Polymorphic callback from a constructor. Figure 2 shows a class *DIALOG* that allows creating and displaying a window dialog to a user. Its creation procedure adds a reset button to put controls to a default state and creates an implementation communicating with the underlying window toolkit to initialize the dialog. On success, the creation procedure of *DIALOG_IMP* calls back the procedure *on_create*.

The class *CHILD* adds a text area that a user can fill in. The user can also press the button `Reset` available from the parent dialog to reset the text area value to the initial value saved in the attribute *default_text*. The child class creation procedure calls the parent creation procedure to initialize parent attributes, creates a text area and records the default text. The parent creation procedure invokes *implementation.make* that calls *on_create*. With the dynamic type of the current object *CHILD*, the creation procedure (indirectly) executes *text.put* (*default_text*). But at this point, the field *text* is not set yet that causes a null dereferencing problem.

III. Modification of existing structures. The ability to invoke regular procedures inside a creation procedure is convenient, e.g., for a mediator pattern [7]. This pattern decouples objects so that they do not know about each other, but still can communicate using an intermediate object, *mediator*. Concrete types of the

```
class A {                        class B : A {
  [NotNull] string name;           [NotNull] string path;
  public A([NotNull] string s)     public B([NotNull] string p,
  {                                    [NotNull] string s) :
    this.name = s; this.m(55);       base(s) { this.path = p; }
  }                                override void m(int x)
  virtual void m(int x) {...}       {... this.path ...}
}                                }
```

Fig. 1. Example of a polymorphic call from a constructor [4] (in C#)

```
class DIALOG create make              class CHILD inherit DIALOG
feature                                   rename make as make_parent
  make                                    redefine on_create end
    do                                 create make feature
      create reset_button                make (original_text: STRING)
          -- Calls back on_create.         do
      create implementation.make           make_parent
        (Current)                          create text
      reset_button.select_actions.         default_text := original_text
          extend (agent on_create)         end
    end                                  text: TEXT_AREA
  reset_button: BUTTON                   default_text: STRING
  on_create                              on_create
    do                                     do
    end                                      text.put (default_text)
  implementation: DIALOG_IMP             end
end                                    end
```

Fig. 2. Example of a polymorphic callback (in Eiffel)

communicating objects are unknown to the mediator, and, therefore, the mediator cannot create them. A mediator's client is responsible for creating necessary communicating objects instead.

Communicating objects know about the mediator and can register themselves in the mediator according to their role. If the registration is done in constructors of the communicating objects, the mediator's clients do not need to clutter the code with calls to a special feature *register* every time they create a new communicating object. An assignment like x = new Comm (mediator) should do both actions: the recording of the mediator object in the new communicating object, and the registration of the communicating object in the mediator. A chat room adapted from [13] and shown in Fig. 3 is an example implementing a mediator pattern.

When the feature *join* is called in the creation procedure *make* of a *USER* object, all fields of the object should be set. Approaches based on type declarations fail to capture that at some point the new object is completely initialized and can be safely used in the context that does not expect uninitialized objects.

IV. Circular references. An issue arises when two objects reference each other. If the corresponding fields have non-null types, access to them should be protected to avoid retrieving null by the code that relies on the field types and, therefore, expects non-null values. Fähndrich and Xia [5] demonstrate the problem on a linked list example with a sentinel (Fig. 4). When a new data is added to an existing list, insertAfter calls the constructor to obtain a new data node. This constructor initializes all fields using the supplied arguments that refer to completely initialized objects created earlier.

```
class ROOM create make feature          class USER create make feature
    users: ARRAYED_LIST [USER]               room: ROOM
    make                                     make (r: ROOM)
        do                                       do
            create users.make (0)                    room := r
        end                                          r.join (Current)
    join (a: USER)                           end
        do                                   send (s: STRING)
            users.extend (a)                     do
        end                                          room.send (s)
    send (s: STRING)                         end
        do                                   receive (s: STRING)
            across users as u loop               do
                u.item.receive (s)                   io.put_string (s)
            end                                      io.put_new_line
        end                                      end
end                                      end
```

Fig. 3. Example of a mediator pattern (in Eiffel)

```
class List {                            // For data node.
    Node! sentinel;                     Node(Node! prev, Node! next,
    List () {sentinel =                     Object? data) {
        new Node(this);}                    parent = prev.parent;
    void insert (Object? data)              this.prev = prev;
        {sentinel.                          this.next = next;
            insertAfter (data);}            this.data = data;
}                                       }
class Node {                            void insertAfter
    List! parent; Object? data;             (Object? data) {
    Node! prev; Node! next;             Node newNode = new Node
    // For sentinel.                        (this, next, data);
    Node(List! parent) {                next.prev = newNode;
        this.parent = parent;           next = newNode;
        prev = this; next = this;       }
}                                   }
```

Fig. 4. Example of circular object creation [5] (in Spec#)

However, when a new list is constructed, a special sentinel node is created instead. The sentinel should reference the original list object. In other words, an incompletely initialized list object has to be passed to a sentinel node constructor as an argument. An attempt to access the field `sentinel` in this `Node` constructor would compromise null safety, so there should be means to prevent such accesses or to make them safe (e.g., by treating field values as possibly null and as referring to uninitialized objects).

A particular case of circular references concerns an object that references itself rather than another object. Qi and Myers [16] give the example of a binary tree where every node has a parent, and the root is a parent to itself. At a binary node creation, left and right nodes should get a new parent and the parent should reference itself. With any initialization order there are states where the new binary node should be used to initialize either its own field or the field `parent` of its left or right nodes before it is completely initialized. Therefore, arbitrary accesses to this node should be protected like in the list example from Fig. 4.

3   Overview

3.1   Language Conventions and Terminology

Meyer [14] points out that some design principles of languages can simplify or make it more difficult to achieve null safety guarantees. E.g., in Java or C# a superclass constructor has to be called before the current constructor can be executed. This leads to the inability to initialize non-null fields of the subclass before the call to the superclass constructor. Without such restrictions, field initialization can be carried out in any suitable order that allows for fixing examples I and II without any need for new types. The enforcement to call superclass constructors before executing any code in the current constructor makes void-safe programming in such languages more verbose. A developer should rely either on additional annotations or on a convention to invoke special initialization methods from the top-level constructors.

This is different in Eiffel, an object oriented language designed with the goal to increase reliability of software. It does not enforce any special policy on object initialization, such as the requirement to call superclass constructors mentioned above. Unfortunately, Java and C# that borrowed several concepts from Eiffel did not incorporate this one. I implemented the proposed solution for Eiffel, and it is now in production with the goal to include it in the language standard. Applying the solution to other object-oriented languages such as Java and C# could require more efforts due to the restrictions mentioned above.

In Eiffel, all class types without any type marks are **attached**, i.e., non-null. The current object (`this` in Java and C#) is named **Current** and constructors are called creation procedures. They can also be used as regular (non-creation) procedures, and, therefore, are checked twice: as creation procedures for safe object initialization, and as regular procedures for "normal" program execution, not related to object initialization. Data members of a class are called attributes.

Some language constructs are specific to Eiffel: loops use exit conditions in the **until** part, this is the inverse of continuation conditions found in `while` loops of other languages. An object test expression **attached** {*TYPE*} *expr* **as** *var* tests whether the value of *expr* is attached and whether the type of this value conforms to the type *TYPE*. The effect of the object test expression is to initialize the local variable *var* when the test gives **True**.

The language standard [9] introduces a notion of a *properly set* variable and demands that all attributes of a class are properly set at the end of every creation procedure of this class. For object initialization, this means that all attributes of attached types should be initialized at this point using either assignment or creation instructions. Until properly set, a field of an attached reference type does not reference an existing object, or is **Void**. If **Void** is used as a target of a call, the run-time raises an exception *"Access on void target"*. A compile-time guarantee that a system never causes such an exception is called *Void safety*.

3.2   Solution Outline

All examples from the previous section can be divided into 2 major groups:

(A) Examples I to III: Can the code be reordered so that all fields are initialized before use?
(B) Example IV: Can compile-time rules ensure that an object with recursive references to itself is not used as a completely initialized one?

The issue in group (A) arises when **Current** object is passed before all its attributes are properly set. The simplest rule to fix this issue would be to forbid the usage of **Current** until all attributes are properly set:

Validity rule 1 (Creation procedure, strong). *A creation procedure is void-safe if it satisfies all the following conditions:*

1. *All (i.e., immediate and inherited) attributes of the class are properly set at the end of the creation procedure.*
2. *Every attribute is properly set before it is used.*
3. *All attributes of the current class are properly set at the execution point where an expression **Current** is used inside the creation procedure or a feature to which the creation procedure (directly or indirectly) makes an unqualified call.*

The remark in the last condition about unqualified calls to features (i.e., the calls that do not specify an explicit target as in my_method(), whereas qualified calls specify the target: expr.my_method()) ensures that access on void target does not happen in a feature called from the creation procedure if this feature accesses **Current**. In particular, for the class *CHILD* from Fig. 2 not only the creation procedure *make* is checked, but also the parent's creation procedure that passes **Current** to the window toolkit.

The rule is sufficient to deal with the group (A). The corrected version of the class *CHILD* from example II (only changed code) is shown in Fig. 5b. The main difference is in the order of initialization. The attributes of the child class are set before calling a parent's creation procedure. This ensures that at the time **Current** is used, all attributes are properly set and are safe for access. The similar fix (Fig. 5a) applies to example I.

But the rule is too strong for the group (B) the code will be rejected. If a reference to an incompletely initialized object is leaked, the task to identify such an object becomes almost intractable because it requires a complex alias analysis that is difficult to implement correctly [22]. Explicit type annotations [4, 5, 16, 20]

```
class B inherit A redefine m end
create make_b feature
   path: attached STRING               class CHILD ...
   make_b (p: STRING; s: STRING)          make (original_text: STRING)
   do                                      do
      path := p                               create text
      make_a (s)                              default_text := original_text
   end                                        make_parent
   m (x: INTEGER)                          end
   do                                      ...
      io.put_string (path)             end
   end
end
```

(a) Example from Fig. 1   (b) Example from Fig. 2

Fig. 5. Corrected versions of examples I and II (in Eiffel)

move detection of incompletely initialized objects from static analysis methods
to the type system. I avoid performing alias analysis and extending the type
system by preventing the usage of incompletely initialized objects in the first
place.

To weaken the Validity rule 1, I have to deal carefully with the polymorphism,
which is the core of information loss in the situation under consideration. Creation procedures are associated with specific classes, hence, no polymorphism is
involved here. If a creation procedure makes an unqualified call to a feature, this
feature can be checked for creation validity because the call is not polymorphic.
But qualified calls are still an issue for two reasons:

- a call on an incompletely initialized object cannot assume that all attributes
  are properly set, and
- a qualified call does not allow seeing whether there are calls on an incompletely initialized object.

The solution is given by the following validity rule that disallows qualified
calls in the contexts where some objects are incompletely initialized:

Validity rule 2 (Creation procedure, weak). *A creation procedure is void-
safe if it satisfies all the following conditions:*

1. *All attributes of the class are properly set at the end of the creation procedure.*
2. *Every attribute is properly set before it is used.*
3. *Any of the following is true at every execution point:*
   3.1. All attributes are properly set.
   *3.2. **Current** is unused before or at the current execution point.*
   3.3. The expression at the execution point is neither of
      – a qualified feature call;
      – a creation expression that makes a qualified call.

```
deferred class NODE feature
   parent: NODE assign set_parent
   set_parent (p: NODE)
      do
         parent := p
      end
end


class LEAF inherit NODE create
   make, set_parent
feature
   make
      do
         parent := Current
      end
end
```

```
class BINARY inherit NODE create
   make_root
feature
   left, right: NODE
   make_root (l, r: NODE)
      do
         left := l
         right := r
         parent := Current
         l.parent := Current
         r.parent := Current
      end
end
```

Fig. 6. Adapted example of a binary tree from [16] (in Eiffel)

Unlike Validity rule 1, the weak version assumes that there is information about other classes, whether their creation procedures make direct or indirect qualified feature calls. This information could be explicitly or implicitly specified in the signatures of creation procedures. In the proposed solution, whether a feature makes qualified calls is inferred from the feature code. The example in Fig. 4 literally translated into Eiffel compiles with Validity rule 2 without any further changes because the creation procedures do not make any qualified calls.

Similarly, an adapted version of the binary tree example from [16] only moves the assignment to the attribute *parent* from the client code inside the creation procedure of the class *BINARY* and sets the same attribute in the creation procedure of the class *LEAF* to reference **Current** (Fig. 6).

4   Related Work

Raw types (solve example I with 2+ annotations). Fähndrich and Leino [4] denote attached types with T^- and detachable types with T^+ and propose to add raw types T^{raw-} to be used for partially initialized objects. If a class C has an attribute of type T and some entity has type C^{raw-} then a qualified call on the entity to this attribute has type T^+ regardless of the original attachment status of the attribute. An assignment to a variable of a raw type is allowed only with a source expression of a non-raw non-null type to ensure that if an object becomes fully initialized, it cannot be uninitialized. Also, by the end of every constructor, every non-null field should be assigned.

Raw types are refined with class frames corresponding to superclasses. Inside a constructor of a class C, the special entity this has type C^{raw-}, and when the constructor finishes, the type becomes C^-. In a constructor of a super-class A the type of this is $C^{raw(A)-}$. The authors also specify conformance rules in this type system. Unfortunately, rules for super-class constructors, e.g., for $T^{raw(R)-}$, may not be directly applicable to the languages with multiple class inheritance like Eiffel. Moreover, the creation of circular references is supported.

A prototype implementation of the proposal demonstrated that further extensions are required to deal with real code, in particular, to access fields that have been initialized and to indicate that a method initializes certain fields.

Masked types (solve examples I to IV with many annotations). Qi and Myers [16] propose an approach that addresses the complete object life cycle, not just object initialization. They instrument the type system with so called "masks" representing sets of fields that are not currently initialized. For example, the notation Node\parent!\Node.sub[1.parent] -> *[this.parent] for an argument 1 tells that it has a type Node and requires that its field parent is not set on entry to the method and at the same time fields declared in subclasses of Node are not set unless 1.parent is initialized. On exit the actual argument conforms to the type Node*[this.parent] meaning that the node object will be completely initialized as soon as its field parent is set.

The notation is very powerful and goes far beyond void safety. However, the authors complain that even this complexity is insufficient for real programs. For information hiding, they propose abstract masks that are updated automatically in descendant classes. The idea seems similar to the data groups approach proposed by Leino in [12]. For modular processing of abstract masks, subclass masks and mask constraints are introduced with union and difference operations.

Like with masked types, the Validity rule 2 depends on what class attributes are properly set and whether a reference to **Current** object escapes before all attributes have been set. In both cases, a flow-sensitive type analysis is performed without special annotations. However, with masked types the type analysis results are checked against provided specifications, while in my approach these results are used to check validity rule conditions.

Free and committed types (solve examples I and IV with 1+ annotations). Summers and Müller propose a solution [20] which distinguishes just two object states: under initialization and completely initialized. A newly allocated object has a so called "free" type. A deeply initialized object, i.e., with all its fields set to deeply initialized objects, is said to have a "committed" type. The commitment point logically changes the type of an object from free to committed and is defined as the end of a constructor that takes only committed arguments. Unlike the case with raw types discussed above, possible aliasing between free and committed types is prevented by not having a subtyping relation between them.

The Validity rule 2 is very close in spirit to the idea of free and committed types. However, the rule relies on a flow-sensitive static analysis for class attributes and does not allow for propagating the free type status beyond the point when all attributes are set. This allows for creating cyclic data structures without explicit annotations.

A variant of committed and free types is implemented in the Checker Framework (see footnote 2) with annotations `@UnknownInitialization` and `@UnderInitialization`. The tool supports type frames `@UnderInitialization` (`A.class`) to tell that all fields specified in a (super)class `A` have been initialized. Authors of the Checker Framework claim that `this` cannot be used in a class constructor as `@Initialized`. This rules out examples II and III.

Other approaches (solve examples I to IV with 0 annotations, but are non-modular). Meyer [14] avoids additional type annotations for solving the null pointer dereference problem by using so called "targeted expressions" and creation-involved features. The analysis is somewhat similar to the abstract interpretation approach used by Spoto [17] and should be applied to the system as a whole, thus sacrificing modularity. This makes it difficult (if possible) to develop self-contained libraries. The advantage of "targeted expressions" is in selective detection of attributes that are not (completely) initialized whereas my approach flags the current object as a whole as unsafe and can reject more code.

5   Formalization

5.1   Initialization State

For formalization, I use a simplified version of an Eiffel-like abstract syntax (omitted here) with the following naming convention: e (possibly with an index) stands for an expression, es – for a list of expressions, $e \cdot es$ – for e prepended to es, t – for a type, n – for a name of a local variable or a feature, not including *Current* which denotes the current object, v – for a literal constant value.

I formalize the predicate that reports if all attributes are properly set at a particular execution point with the transfer function $\cdot \gg \cdot$ whose equations are specified in Fig. 7. The function takes 2 arguments: an expression and a set of attributes V that may be unattached before the expression. It returns a set of attributes that may be unattached after the expression. At the beginning of a creation procedure the set of unattached attributes is a set of all current class attributes of attached reference types.

If the expression is a sequence or an argument list, the set of unattached attributes for a subsequent expression is computed starting from the set computed for the first expression. For assignment to an attribute, firstly the set is computed for the source expression, then the attribute name is removed from the set of unattached attributes, because the attribute is set after the assignment.

For a creation expression, the set is computed using an associated list of actual arguments starting from the initial set. For a qualified call the rule is similar except that the set computed for the target of the call is used as a starting one.

For a conditional expression, the computation is done for both branches like for a sequence and then their union is used as a result. The rationale is that even though every branch can set some attributes, if these attributes are not set in the other branch, the attributes should not be considered set because the

$V \gg e_1 \; ;; \; e_2$	$= V \gg e_1 \gg e_2$	– Sequence
$V \gg n :=_L e$	$= V \gg e$	– Local assignment
$V \gg n :=_A e$	$= V \gg e - \{n\}$	– Attr. asssignment
$V \gg create \; \{t\} \, . \, n \; (es)$	$= V \gg es$	– Creation
$V \gg e \, . \, n \; (es)$	$= V \gg e \gg es$	– Qual. call
$V \gg if \; e \; then \; e_1 \; else \; e_2 \; end$	$= V \gg e \gg e_1 \cup V \gg e \gg e_2$	– Conditional
$V \gg until \; e \; loop \; e_1 \; end$	$= V \gg e$	– Loop
$V \gg attached \; t \; e \; as \; n$	$= V \gg e$	– Object test
$V \gg Exception$	$= \varnothing$	– Exception
$V \gg \_$	$= V$	– Val., loc., att., cur.
$V \gg []$	$= V$	– Empty arg. list
$V \gg (e \cdot es)$	$= V \gg e \gg es$	– Arg. list

Fig. 7. A function to compute a set of unattached attributes

branch to be taken at execution time is unknown at compile time. For a loop, only the exit condition is taken into account and the loop body is completely ignored. The loop body might be not executed at all, so any attributes the loop body sets cannot reduce the set of unattached attributes.

For an exception, the set of unattached attributes is empty because execution never goes after this point, so any assumptions are valid. Using an empty set signals to the compiler that no more attributes have to be initialized. For the rest of expressions, if there are subexpressions, the function returns sets for these subexpressions, otherwise it returns the initial set.

The function is monotone, i.e., the more attributes are set before an expression, the more are set after the expression:

Lemma 1 (Monotonicity of $\gg$). $A \subseteq B \Longrightarrow A \gg e \subseteq B \gg e$.

5.2   Safe Uses of *Current*

The predicate *safe* formalizes the conditions 3.1 and 3.2 of the Validity rule 2. Its inductive definition over the expression syntax is given in Fig. 8. The intuitive explanation of the different cases of this definition follows.

If *Current* is never referenced in a creation procedure, the potentially incompletely initialized object is not passed anywhere, so access on void target, caused by this object, is impossible. If *Current* is referenced when all attributes are set, there is no issue as well: once an object is completely initialized, it remains completely initialized. Finally, if *Current* is referenced when not all attributes of the current class are set, but can escape only at the current execution point (i.e., all previous expressions do not make any qualified calls, thus excluding the

$$safe\ Current\ V \qquad\qquad = V = \varnothing$$
$$safe\ (e_1\ ;;\ e_2)\ V \qquad\qquad = safe\ [e_1,\ e_2]\ V$$
$$safe\ (n :=_L e)\ V \qquad\qquad = safe\ e\ V$$
$$safe\ (n :=_A e)\ V \qquad\qquad = safe\ e\ V \vee V \gg n :=_A e = \varnothing$$
$$safe\ (create\ \{t\}\ .\ n\ (es))\ V \quad = safe\ es\ V$$
$$safe\ (e\ .\ n\ (es))\ V \qquad\qquad = safe\ (e\ \cdot\ es)\ V$$
$$safe\ (if\ e\ then\ e_1\ else\ e_2\ end)\ V = safe\ [e,\ e_1]\ V \wedge safe\ [e,\ e_2]\ V$$
$$safe\ (until\ e\ loop\ e_1\ end)\ V \qquad = safe\ [e,\ e_1]\ V$$
$$safe\ (attached\ t\ e\ as\ n)\ V \qquad = safe\ e\ V$$
$$safe\ \_\ V \qquad\qquad\qquad = True \qquad - \text{Value, local, attribute}$$

$$safe\ []\ V \qquad = True$$
$$safe\ (e\ \cdot\ es)\ V = safe\ e\ V \wedge safe\ es\ (V \gg e) \vee V \gg (e\ \cdot\ es) = \varnothing$$

Fig. 8. Function that tells if uses of *Current* (if any) are safe

possibility to access this incompletely initialized object), where all attributes are set, the object is completely initialized and can be safely used from now on.

An expression *Current* is safe if and only if all attributes are properly set (i.e., the set of unattached attributes is empty). If the expression is an assignment to an attribute, it is possible that the attribute would be the last one to initialize, so the result of the function *safe* will be *True* if either the source expression is safe or there are no unattached attributes left after the assignment.

Basically, if all attributes are set after an expression, it is safe to use *Current* afterwards. If this is not the case, *Current* should be used safely (if at all). For a list of expressions, the first expression should be safe in the initial context, and the subsequent expressions should be safe in the context of unattached attributes obtained for the first expression.

For a conditional expression, the checks should be done for both branches, and only when they both succeed, the use of *Current* is safe. For a loop the check is done for its exit condition and its body like for a sequence of expressions. For an expression with just one subexpression, this subexpression is checked for safety. And for the remaining expressions the function returns *True*.

The function *safe* is monotone: if more attributes are set for a given expressions, the chances to use *Current* unsafely are lower.

The function specifies only safe uses of *Current*, not safe uses of attributes of the current object. The cases with disjunctions describe situations when *Current* was not used or was used safely in previous expressions or subexpressions and is not used or is used safely in the current expression where all attributes of the current class appear to be properly set.

5.3   Detection of Qualified Feature Calls

This section formalizes the condition 3.3 of the Validity rule 2. The formalization is based on two functions that are defined by induction on the expression syntax (omitted) and apply to an expression e:

- A function $\mathcal{Q}$ evaluates to *True* if e has an immediate (i.e., syntactical, not as a result of an unqualified call to some other feature) qualified call in at least one of its subexpressions. Otherwise, it evaluates to *False*.
- A function $\mathcal{S}$ computes a set of creation procedures that can be called by the given creation procedure. It returns a set of pairs *(c, f)* of class types and feature names corresponding to all creation sub-expressions of e where f is used as a creation procedure and c is used as a creation type.

I also assume there is a function *routine_body* which returns an optional expression representing the routine body (*None* when the body is missing) for a feature of name f in a class c of a system S given as arguments. With these functions, I define the predicate *has_qualified (S, (c, f))* which returns *True* iff a creation procedure f of a class c in a system S can (indirectly) lead to a qualified call. The predicate searches in the set of all creation procedures reachable from the given one (this set is obtained using $\mathcal{S}$ and *routine_body*) a qualified call expression (detected using $\mathcal{Q}$) as follows.

In a given system S, the predicate *has_immediate_qualified_in_routine* tells whether a creation procedure f in a class c makes an immediate qualified feature call. It calls $\mathcal{Q}$ for the corresponding creation procedure body:

$$has\_immediate\_qualified\_in\_routine\ S\ (c, f)$$
$$= \textbf{case}\ routine\_body\ S\ c\ f\ \textbf{of}\ None\ \Rightarrow\ False \mid \lfloor b \rfloor\ \Rightarrow\ \mathcal{Q}\ b$$

The function *creation_reachable$_1$* computes a set of creation procedures that can be called from the creation procedure of a given name f from a given class c:

$$creation\_reachable_1\ S\ (c, f)$$
$$= \textbf{case}\ routine\_body\ S\ c\ f\ \textbf{of}\ None\ \Rightarrow\ \varnothing \mid \lfloor x \rfloor\ \Rightarrow\ \mathcal{S}\ x$$

Because the set of classes is known at compile time and is bounded, all recursively reachable creation procedures can be computed as a least fixed point using the previous function:

$$creation\_reachable\ S\ (c, f)$$
$$= lfp\ (\lambda x.\{(c, f)\} \cup\ x\ \cup (\bigcup_{y\ \in\ x} creation\_reachable_1\ S\ y))$$

The definition of the predicate *has_qualified* completes the formalization of the condition 3.3 of the Validity rule 2:

$$has\_qualified\ S\ c$$
$$= \exists\ x \in creation\_reachable\ S\ c.\ has\_immediate\_qualified\_in\_routine\ S\ x$$

5.4   Validity Predicate

The formal predicate for the conditions 2 and 3 of the Validity rule 2 is defined in Fig. 9. (The condition 1 is formalized by a predicate describing well-formed programs like for free and committed types [20] and is not considered here.) The conditions of the validity rule are encoded in the judgment $S,\ V \vdash\ e\ \sqrt{c}$ meaning that an expression e is valid in a creation procedure of a system S in the context of a set of unattached attributes V. The rule ATTR ensures that an attribute can be used only after it is set. The rule CURRENT for an expression *Current* tells that this expression is always valid.

The rule CREATE for a creation expression has a premise that *Current* should be used safely or, alternatively (if *Current* is used before all attributes of the current class are properly set), the called creation procedure should not make any qualified calls. In the same vein, the rule CALL for a qualified call has a premise that *Current* should be used safely. The remaining the rules are defined inductively making sure that all subexpressions satisfy the validity predicate in the corresponding context.

Lemma 2 (Validity predicate monotonicity)

$$A \subseteq B \wedge S, B \vdash e \sqrt{c} \Longrightarrow S, A \vdash e \sqrt{c}$$

$$\frac{}{S,\ V \vdash\ Value\ v\ \sqrt{c}}\ \text{VALUE} \qquad \frac{}{S,\ V \vdash\ Current\ \sqrt{c}}\ \text{CURRENT}$$

$$\frac{}{S,\ V \vdash\ Local\ n\ \sqrt{c}}\ \text{LOCAL} \qquad \frac{n \notin V}{S,\ V \vdash\ Attribute\ n\ \sqrt{c}}\ \text{ATTR}$$

$$\frac{S,\ V \vdash e_1\ \sqrt{c} \wedge S,\ V \gg e_1 \vdash e_2\ \sqrt{c}}{S,\ V \vdash e_1\ ;;\ e_2\ \sqrt{c}}\ \text{SEQ}$$

$$\frac{S,\ V \vdash e\ \sqrt{c}}{S,\ V \vdash n :=_L e\ \sqrt{c}}\ \text{ASSIGNLOCAL} \qquad \frac{S,\ V \vdash e\ \sqrt{c}}{S,\ V \vdash n :=_A e\ \sqrt{c}}\ \text{ASSIGNATTR}$$

$$\frac{S,\ V \vdash es\ [\sqrt{c}] \wedge (safe\ es\ V\ \vee\ \neg\ has\_qualified\ S\ (t, n))}{S,\ V \vdash create\ \{t\} \cdot n\ (es)\ \sqrt{c}}\ \text{CREATE}$$

$$\frac{S,\ V \vdash e\ \sqrt{c} \wedge S,\ V \gg e \vdash es\ [\sqrt{c}] \wedge safe\ (e \cdot es)\ V}{S,\ V \vdash e \cdot n\ (es)\ \sqrt{c}}\ \text{CALL}$$

$$\frac{S,\ V \vdash e\ \sqrt{c} \wedge S,\ V \gg e \vdash e_1\ \sqrt{c} \wedge S,\ V \gg e \vdash e_2\ \sqrt{c}}{S,\ V \vdash if\ e\ then\ e_1\ else\ e_2\ end\ \sqrt{c}}\ \text{IF}$$

$$\frac{S,\ V \vdash e\ \sqrt{c} \wedge S,\ V \gg e \vdash e_1\ \sqrt{c}}{S,\ V \vdash until\ e\ loop\ e_1\ end\ \sqrt{c}}\ \text{LOOP}$$

$$\frac{S,\ V \vdash e\ \sqrt{c}}{S,\ V \vdash attached\ t\ e\ as\ n\ \sqrt{c}}\ \text{TEST} \qquad \frac{}{S,\ V \vdash\ Exception\ \sqrt{c}}\ \text{EXCEPTION}$$

$$\frac{}{S,\ V \vdash []\ [\sqrt{c}]}\ \text{ARG}_{Nil} \qquad \frac{S,\ V \vdash e\ \sqrt{c} \wedge S,\ V \gg e \vdash es\ [\sqrt{c}]}{S,\ V \vdash e \cdot es\ [\sqrt{c}]}\ \text{ARG}_{Cons}$$

Fig. 9. Predicate $S,\ V \vdash\ e\ \sqrt{c}$ implementing the Validity rule 2

The monotonicity of the predicate is an important property for the soundness proof and for the implementation. Indeed, it allows analyzing loops and unqualified feature calls just once, because any subsequent iterations or recursive feature calls would be analyzed with a larger set of properly-set attributes.

The soundness proof for object initialization is similar to the one given by Summers and Müller [19] with two major differences. Firstly, the *free* status of a current object does not last until the end of a creation procedure, but only up to the point where all attributes are set, with the proviso that the creation procedure is not called by another one with an incompletely initialized *Current*. Secondly, annotations are replaced with the requirement to avoid qualified feature calls in the context with incompletely initialized objects.

For initialization of *Current* two situations are possible. In the first case all attributes of the current class are set and there are no incompletely initialized objects in the current context. Then the current object is deeply initialized and satisfies the void-safe type system expectations before the creation procedure finishes. In the second case either some attributes of the current class are not properly set or the context has references to objects that are not completely initialized. Because qualified calls are disallowed in these conditions, the uninitialized attributes cannot be accessed and therefore access on void target is impossible. Due to the requirement to have all attributes properly set at the end of a creation procedure, the current object will have all attributes set when the control is returned to the caller. In the context where all attributes of the class are set and no callers passed an uninitialized *Current*, the only reachable objects are either previously fully initialized or new ones but with all attributes pointing to old or new objects, i.e., also fully initialized. Therefore, under these conditions, all objects satisfy the void-safe type system expectations where all attributes of attached types evaluate to existing objects.

6   Practical Results

Although the Validity rule 1 looks pretty restrictive, 4254 classes of public Eiffel libraries were successfully converted by *Eiffel Software* and contributors relying on this rule. This comprises 822487 lines of code and 3194 explicit creation procedures. 1894 (59%) of these creation procedures perform regular direct or indirect qualified calls and might be in danger if not all attributes were set before **Current** was used. However, it was possible to refactor all the classes manually to satisfy the rule.

On average, 60% of creation procedures make qualified calls (Table 1). The remaining 40% do not use any qualified calls and set attributes using supplied arguments or by creating new objects. They could be unconditionally marked with annotations as safe for use with incompletely initialized objects.

In contrast to this, just a tiny fraction of all creation procedures – 77 creation procedures from two libraries, i.e., less than 2% – do pass uninitialized objects

Table 1. Creation procedures classified by use of qualified calls and incompletely initialized objects

Library	Creation	Qualified		Uninitialized	
		abs.	rel.	abs.	rel.
Docking	2062	1365	66.2%	16	0.8%
Gobo	1258	726	57.7%	61	4.8%
Others	3194	1894	59.3%	0	0.0%
Total (cumulative)	4045	2442	**60.4%**	77	**1.9%**

Legend:
Creation – number of explicit creation procedures
Qualified – number and percentage of creation procedures with qualified calls
Uninitialized – number and percentage of creation procedures passing **Current** before all attributes are set

and take advantage of the weaker Validity rule 2. In other words, if specific annotations were used, at most 5% of them would be useful, the rest would just clutter the code. Closer look reveals the following major families of uses:

Internal cursors are used in 59 of 61 cases in *Gobo*. Internal cursors perform traversal abstracting away container implementation and avoiding object creation for traversal. They continue working when the underlying container changes [1]. In *Gobo*, external cursors are aware about changes in the associated containers, so they can replace internal cursors altogether. The same functionality can also be provided without any additional classes, directly by containers.

Domain structure is used in 2 of 61 cases in *Gobo*. The classes are designed according to the XML specification [3] where an XML document has exactly one root element that could have nested elements. A parent of a root element is the document to which it belongs. In theory, the root element can be a descendant of a general element class with properties specific to a document, i.e., removing separation of concern can remove the need for two different classes.

Helper classes are used in all cases in *Docking*. The library deals with many aspects of a user interface, allows for storing and retrieving layout, animates placeholders, etc. All the code related to these different groups of functionality could be moved to just one class, but for maintainability it was distributed among different classes.

The checks for creation procedure validity rules are pretty light in time. The libraries were compiled with and without checks for the Validity rule 2 on a machine with 64-bit *Windows 10 Pro*, *Intel® Core^{TM} i7-3720QM*, 16 GB of RAM and SSD hard drive using *EiffelStudio 16.11 rev.99675*. The compilation involved only parsing and type checking, but not code generation. The maximum relative increase of compilation time was 1.5% for the *Docking* library.

For all libraries, the slowdown was just 0.7% that is absolutely acceptable. Sets of unattached attributes are encoded with bit vectors that in most scenarios fit a fixed-width integer variable. The number of the sets kept in memory during analysis is limited by the depth of branching instructions nesting which is insignificant in practice.

7   Conclusion

I propose a solution for the object initialization issue based on static analysis with the following advantages:

No annotations. Validity rules do not require any other type annotations in addition to attachment marks.

Flexibility. Creation of objects mutually referencing other objects is possible.

Simplicity. The analyses require only tracking for attributes that are not properly set, for use of **Current** and for checking whether certain conditions are satisfied when (direct or indirect) qualified feature calls are performed.

Coverage. It was possible to refactor all libraries to meet the requirements of the rules without changing design decisions. The rules solve all examples from the motivation section.

Modularity. The Validity rule 2 depends on properties of creation procedures from other classes. Because these creation procedures are known at compile time, the checks do not depend on classes that are not directly reachable from the one being checked. Consequently, it is possible to check a library as a standalone entity without the need to recheck it after inclusion in some other project.

Performance. Experiments demonstrate very moderate increase of total compilation time, below 1% on sample libraries with more than 2 millions lines of code.

Incrementality. Fast recompilation is supported by my approach if, for every class, the analyzer stores information about the creation procedures reachable from other creation procedures and information about the creation procedures performing qualified calls.

The main drawbacks of the solution detailed here are the following:

Certain coding pattern. A certain initialization order has to be followed.

Disallowing legitimate qualified calls. Lack of special annotations prevents from distinguishing between legitimate and non-legitimate qualified calls. To preserve soundness, all qualified calls are considered as potentially risky.

Special convention for formal generics. If a target type of a creation expression is a formal generic parameter, special convention (e.g., that the corresponding creation procedure makes qualified calls) should be used to indicate whether the creation procedure of an actual generic parameter satisfies the validity rule requirements.

References

1. Arnout, K., Meyer, B.: Finding implicit contracts in .NET components. In: de Boer, F.S., Bonsangue, M.M., Graf, S., de Roever, W.-P. (eds.) FMCO 2002. LNCS, vol. 2852, pp. 285–318. Springer, Heidelberg (2003). https://doi.org/10.1007/978-3-540-39656-7_12. ISBN: 978-3-540-39656-7

2. Barnett, M., Fähndrich, M., Leino, K.R.M., Müller, P., Schulte, W., Venter, H.: Specification and verification: the Spec# experience. Commun. ACM **54**(6), 81–91 (2011)

3. Bray, T., Paoli, J., Sperberg-McQueen, C.M., Maler, E., Yergeau, F.: Extensible Markup Language (XML) 1.0 (Fifth Edition). Fifth Edition of a Recommendation. W3C (2008). http://www.w3.org/TR/2008/REC-xml-20081126/

4. Fähndrich, M., Leino, K.R.M.: Declaring and checking non-null types in an object-oriented language. In: Proceedings of the 18th Annual ACM SIGPLAN Conference on Object-Oriented Programming, Systems, Languages, and Applications, OOPSLA 2003, Anaheim, California, USA, pp. 302–312. ACM (2003)

5. Fähndrich, M., Xia, S.: Establishing object invariants with delayed types. In: Proceedings of the 22nd Annual ACM SIGPLAN Conference on Object-Oriented Programming Systems and Applications, OOPSLA 2007, Montreal, Quebec, Canada, pp. 337–350. ACM (2007)

6. Flanagan, C., Leino, K.R.M., Lillibridge, M., Nelson, G., Saxe, J.B., Stata, R.: Extended static checking for Java. In: Proceedings of the ACM SIGPLAN 2002 Conference on Programming Language Design and Implementation, PLDI 2002, Berlin, Germany, pp. 234–245. ACM (2002)

7. Gamma, E., Helm, R., Johnson, R., Vlissides, J.: Design Patterns: Elements of Reusable Object-oriented Software. Addison-Wesley Longman Publishing Co., Inc., Boston (1995)

8. Hoare, T.: Null references: the billion dollar mistake. Presentation at QCon London (2009)

9. ISO: ISO/IEC 25436:2006(E): Information technology — Eiffel: Analysis, Design and Programming Language. ISO (International Organization for Standardization) and IEC (International Electrotechnical Commission), Geneva, Switzerland (2006)

10. JetBrains: Kotlin Language Specification (2017). https://jetbrains.github.io/kotlin-spec/kotlin-spec.pdf. Accessed 31 Jan 2017

11. Kogtenkov, A.: Mechanically proved practical local null safety. Proc. Inst. Syst. Program. RAS **28**(5), 27–54 (2016)

12. Leino, K.R.M.: Data groups: specifying the modification of extended state. In: Proceedings of the 13th ACM SIGPLAN Conference on Object-oriented Programming, Systems, Languages, and Applications, OOPSLA 1998, Vancouver, British Columbia, Canada, pp. 144–153. ACM (1998)

13. Mediator pattern (2016). https://en.wikipedia.org/wiki/Mediator_pattern. Accessed 23 Dec 2016

14. Meyer, B.: Targeted expressions: safe object creation with void safety (2012). http://se.ethz.ch/~meyer/publications/online/targeted.pdf. Accessed 8 May 2017

15. Pearce, D.J.: On flow-sensitive types in whiley (2010). http://whiley.org/2010/09/22/on-flow-sensitive-types-in-whiley/. Accessed 7 May 2017

16. Qi, X., Myers, A.C.: Masked types for sound object initialization. In: Proceedings of the 36th Annual ACM SIGPLAN-SIGACT Symposium on Principles of Programming Languages, POPL 2009, Savannah, GA, USA, pp. 53–65. ACM (2009)

17. Spoto, F.: Precise null-pointer analysis. Softw. Syst. Model. **10**(2), 219–252 (2011)

18. Stata, R.: ESCJ 2: improving the safety of Java (1995). http://kindsoftware. com/products/opensource/ESCJava2/ESCTools/docs/design-notes/escj02.html. Accessed 27 Apr 2017

19. Summers, A.J., Müller, P.: Freedom before commitment. Simple flexible initialisation for non-full types. Technical report 716, Zurich, Switzerland: ETH Zurich, Department of Computer Science (2010)

20. Summers, A.J., Müller, P.: Freedom before commitment: a lightweight type system for object initialisation. In: Proceedings of the 2011 ACM International Conference on Object Oriented Programming Systems Languages and Applications, OOPSLA 2011, Portland, Oregon, USA, pp. 1013–1032. ACM (2011)

21. Volpano, D., Irvine, C., Smith, G.: A sound type system for secure flow analysis. J. Comput. Secur. 4(2–3), 167–187 (1996)

22. Wu, J., Hu, G., Tang, Y., Yang, J.: Effective dynamic detection of alias analysis errors. In: Proceedings of the 2013 9th Joint Meeting on Foundations of Software Engineering, ESEC/FSE 2013, Saint Petersburg, Russia, pp. 279–289. ACM (2013)

Memory-Efficient Tactics for Randomized LTL Model Checking

Kim Larsen[1(✉)], Doron Peled[2], and Sean Sedwards[3]

[1] Department of Computer Science, University of Aalborg, Aalborg, Denmark
kgl@cs.aau.dk
[2] Department of Science, Bar Ilan University, Ramat Gan, Israel
[3] National Institute of Informatics, Tokyo, Japan

Abstract. We study model checking of LTL properties by means of random walks, improving on the efficiency of previous results. Using a randomized algorithm to detect accepting paths makes it feasible to check extremely large models, however a naive approach may encounter many non-accepting paths or require the storage of many explicit states, making it inefficient. We study here several alternative tactics that can often avoid these problems. Exploiting probability and randomness, we present tactics that typically use only a small fraction of the memory of previous approaches, storing only accepting states or an arbitrarily small number of "token" states visited during executions. Reducing the number of stored states generally increases the expected execution time until a counterexample is found, but we demonstrate that the trade-off is biased in favor of our tactics. By applying our memory-efficient tactics to scalable models from the literature, we show that the increase in time is typically less than proportional to the saving in memory and may be exponentially smaller.

1 Introduction

Automatic verification of systems has become an essential part of the development of many software and hardware projects. Complete verification of systems is rarely possible because of time and space complexity results, yet there are many techniques that help in applying verification to critical parts of the system. For example, heuristics for SAT solving, abstraction, decomposition, symbolic execution, partial order reduction and other techniques are all used to variously speed up the verification of systems. Despite these, the problem of automatic verification is asymptotically hard, and difficult cases often occur in practice.

We study here a randomized verification algorithm for LTL properties of finite state nondeterministic systems, based on repeated random walks. Given a

D. Peled—Partly supported by Israeli Science Foundation grant 2239/15: *Runtime Measuring and Checking of Cyber Physical Systems.*
S. Sedwards—Partly supported by Japanese Science and Technology agency ERATO project JPMJER1603: *HASUO Metamathematics for Systems Design.*

A. Paskevich and T. Wies (Eds.): VSTTE 2017, LNCS 10712, pp. 152–169, 2017.
https://doi.org/10.1007/978-3-319-72308-2_10

large enough number of such walks, this *Monte Carlo model checking* (MC^2) procedure [5] will eventually find a violation of the specification, if one exists, with probability one, i.e., *almost surely*. MC^2 is different to *statistical* model checking applied to inherently probabilistic systems (DTMC, CTMC, etc.) [6,16], where the goal is to estimate or bound the true probability of a property. We also distinguish MC^2 from algorithms that use randomization to improve memory consumption of standard model checking algorithms [2].

The principal advantage of MC^2 is that it deliberately avoids an explicit construction of the state space of a system and is thus usable when the size of the state space is intractable. The price of this tractability is the probabilistic uncertainty that a violation exists if none is found. There is also a potential cost in time: the worst case expectation of the number of experiments to find an existing error is exponential in the size of the state space. This upper bound can be avoided because error traces are typically short with respect to the size of the state space and often also occur quite densely among the system executions. Nevertheless, "rare event" errors, e.g., in the form of a *combination lock*, where only the right combination of choices reveals the erroneous sequence among a huge number of choices, can be induced by a particular randomized search tactic. This problem, previously identified in [5,11], is the motivation of the present work.

The effective rarity of error traces is dependent both on their inherent rarity among all execution traces and the search tactic used to find them. To overcome problems with the original search tactic of [5], in [11] the authors propose to optimize the randomized search by performing a preliminary analysis of the state space. The detailed structure of the state space is typically unknown and in using MC^2 we presume that its traversal is computationally expensive. Hence, as a more plausible approach, we suggest here several different tactics for forming random walks to search for error traces. These tactics generally avoid the problems identified in [11], without the need for a priori knowledge or analysis of the system, and have individual characteristics that may be optimal under different circumstances. This is demonstrated in the various examples given in Sect. 6. We also show that bounded memory versions of the same tactics are typically more efficient when considering the product of the space and time they require.

The principal random walk tactic suggested in [5] by Grosu and Smolka, which we denote GS, hashes the states encountered during the search, storing an enumeration of their appearance order. When the random walk hits the same state again for the first time it terminates. In this case it has generated an *ultimately periodic* path, also called a "lasso", i.e., a prefix followed by a simple cycle. If the periodic part includes an accepting state of the property automaton, the path forms a counterexample. Otherwise, the data structures are reset and a new random walk is required. GS is thus sensitive to the existence of non-accepting lassos, working best when there are few. Unfortunately, this is often not the case.

In [5] the authors also suggested an alternative tactic they call *multi-lasso*, which we denote here ML. They described its superiority over the GS tactic on a specific pathological (though not necessarily uncommon) example, but do not report experiments comparing these tactics. We provide experimental results here. ML detects all lassos, but if the current edge forms a loop that does not include an accepting state, it chooses an alternative edge. If it exhausts the alternatives, it starts a new random walk. In comparison to GS, we expect ML to work well when the prefix of an accepting lasso is long or there are many non-accepting lassos to avoid.

We propose two new tactics. Our tactic CW, for *continue walking*, does not abandon a walk after encountering an edge that closes a cycle that is not accepting, but rather continues the walk by revisiting the earlier state. CW can be seen as a compromise between always resetting (like GS) and always exploring deeper (like ML). Informally, we expect CW to work well when the prefix of an accepting lasso is not long and there are also many non-accepting lassos.

Our new tactic OA is similar to CW, but stores *only accepting* states. This tactic will generally require less memory to store an accepting lasso than other tactics and uses substantially less memory when accepting states are rare, which is often the case. We expect OA to work well under the same circumstances that CW works well, but the fact that it inherently uses less memory can give it an advantage when the state space is large relative to available memory.

The tactics GS, ML, CW and OA do not use an explicit stack to store the random walk, but make use of a hash table that may be of substantial size, noting that clearing the hash table after each random walk contributes to the overhead. We thus propose alternative bounded memory versions of GS, ML, CW and OA that store only a finite number of states as *tokens*, potentially using just a small fraction of the memory. We denote these tactics GS-NH, ML-NH, CW-NH and OA-NH, where suffix -NH signifies *no hash*. When the finite space to store tokens is fully occupied and a new state occurs along the walk, these tactics randomly replace an existing token or simply discard the new state. The tactics will nevertheless detect an existing counterexample given enough random walks.

In what follows, we compare the performance of GS, ML, CW and OA with the tokenized variants ML-NH, CW-NH and OA-NH. We show through qualitative analysis and experiments on standard case studies that our tactics often make substantial improvements over GS and do not share its pathological behavior with certain models. We note here, however, that it is possible to construct difficult examples for all the tactics. In general, the behavior of the tactics vary considerably between different examples, suggesting that in the lack of further knowledge about particular properties of the state space of a model, making a particular tactic superior, one may want to run an assortment of different tactics. A major advantage of randomized tactics is that they can be easily parallelized, especially when their memory is bounded. If a counterexample exists, the running time is then that of the fastest tactic to find it.

2   Preliminaries

Definition 1. *The* state space *of a transition system is defined by the following components:*

– *A finite set of states S.*

- *Initial state $\iota \in S$.*
- *A finite set of events E.*
- *Transitions $T \subseteq S \times E \times S$. We also write $s \xrightarrow{e} s'$ instead of $(s, e, s') \in E$. In this case we say that e is* enabled *from s.*
- *A finite set AP of propositions (representing atomic properties of a state).*
- *A labeling function $L : S \mapsto 2^{AP}$.*

Definition 2. *An* execution *of a transition system is a maximal path $s_0, s_1, s_2, \ldots$ such that s_0 is the initial state, and for each s_i on the path, either for some event e, $s_i \xrightarrow{e} s_{i+1}$ or there is no enabled event from s_i. In the latter case, $s_i = s_{i+1} = s_{i+2} = \ldots$ (for convenience of dealing only with infinite sequences).*

Definition 3. *A* strongly connected component *(SCC) G in a state space is a maximal subset of states such that there is a path from each state in G to each other state in G. A* bottom strongly connected component *(BSCC) is an SCC that has no exits.*

LTL and Büchi automata. We assume the use of linear temporal logic (LTL) as a specification formalism. One can express in LTL properties such as $\Box p$ ("p always happens" i.e., in every state), $\Diamond p$ ("p will happen eventually") and $\Box \Diamond p$ ("p will always eventually happen", i.e., will happen infinitely many times). For LTL syntax and semantics, see e.g., [10]. LTL formulas are interpreted over infinite sequences $\sigma = s_0 s_1 s_2 \ldots$ of *evaluations* of the atomic propositions; that is, each s_i is a subset of AP, denoting the atomic propositions that hold at position i of the sequence.

The simplest class of ω automata over infinite words is that of Büchi automata [14]. We will describe a variant of it, where the labels are defined on the states rather than on the transitions. A Büchi automaton $\mathcal{A}$ is a sextuple $\langle \Sigma, Q, \Delta, Q_0, L, F \rangle$ such that

- Σ is the finite *alphabet*. In our case, $\Sigma = 2^{AP}$.
- Q is the finite set of *states*.
- $\Delta \subseteq Q \times Q$ is the *transition relation*.
- $Q_0 \subseteq Q$ are the *initial states*.
- $L : Q \to \Sigma$ is a *labeling* of the *states*.
- $F \subseteq Q$ is the set of *accepting states*.

Let v be a word over Σ^ω. A *run* ρ of $\mathcal{A}$ on v corresponds to an infinite path in the automaton graph from an initial state, where the nodes on this path are labeled according to the letters in v. Let $\inf(\rho)$ be the set of states that appear infinitely often in the run ρ. A run ρ of a Büchi automaton $\mathcal{A}$ over an infinite word is *accepting* exactly when $\inf(\rho) \cap F \neq \emptyset$. That is, when some accepting state appears in ρ infinitely often.

Model checking (see, e.g., [3]) an LTL property φ can commence by first transforming $\neg \varphi$ into a Büchi automaton $\mathcal{B}$ that recognizes exactly the executions that are *not* satisfied by φ [4,15]. The translation may incur an exponential blowup on the size of the LTL property, however, in practice the LTL property is usually quite small. The intersection of $\mathcal{B}$ with an automaton $\mathcal{A}$ that represents the state space is checked for a satisfying example. An accepted run of the intersection is a *counterexample* for the state space satisfying φ. The intersection of these two automata includes pairs of states from $\mathcal{A}$ and $\mathcal{B}$ that agree on their labeling. Initial states are those that consist of a pair of initial components. Accepting states have a $\mathcal{B}$ accepting component. Because of finiteness, an occurrence of an accepting sequence (a counterexample for the checked property) implies that there is also one that has the following *ultimately periodic* form: a finite prefix, followed by a simple cycle that includes an accepting state (see, e.g., [10,14]). The cycle must exist entirely within one of the SCCs of the state space, not necessarily a BSCC. The prefix may cross several SCCs to reach the cycle.

One can use depth first search (DFS) to find such a path. Generating the state space in advance, before the start of the search can be prohibitively intractable. Instead, one can generate the state space "on-the-fly", i.e., on demand, when progressing from one state to another. A hash table and a stack can be used to keep the states that were generated so far and the current search path for the DFS algorithm [8].

3   Monte Carlo Model Checking

Monte Carlo search [5] can be used to exploit randomization in order to follow different execution paths. A random walk is a path in a graph, where at each step the next state is drawn at random from the possible successors. In our case we consider random walks over an *isotropic probabilistic abstraction* of a nondeterministic system. We define this to mean that an outgoing transition from a state is chosen with probability equal to the reciprocal of the state's out-degree (the number of enabled outgoing transitions), which we assume to be finite. The graph in our case is the intersection of the Büchi automaton and the state space for the checked system. The random walks start from the initial state, and the successors are generated by the set of transitions enabled at the current state. There is no need to generate the entire state space in advance: this will defy the advantage of using random walks and will be in many cases too large. What we need is a generator that can produce the successor for the current state given an enabled transition of the intersection. We will henceforth loosely use the term *state space* to refer to this intersection.

The original GS random search tactic uses a hash that is cleared after each unsuccessful random walk. It keeps a counter l of the steps in the search. The counter value is hashed with the current state. The variable f holds the largest counter value of an accepting state that the search has encountered. Upon returning to a state again, which happens when the current state is already hashed, we check if its hash value is smaller than f. If this is the case, we have found an ultimately periodic counterexample. Otherwise, we restart the random walk. The GS tactic is described by Algorithm 1, using the following notation.

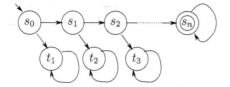

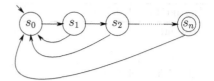

Fig. 1. A difficult case for GS.

Fig. 2. Case where ML needs only one random walk.

d. Diameter of the graph, i.e., the maximum shortest path between any two states. One can over-approximate d by the size of the state space, which can often be estimated.

l. A variable that holds the distance of the path in the current random walk.

f. The maximal distance of an accepting state found in the random walk from the initial state.

guess_succ. A function that randomly returns one of the successors for the current state. It returns void if there is no successor for the current state.

init. The initial state.

accepting. A Boolean function that returns *true* if its argument is an accepting state.

current. The current state.

Evaluation. The maximal length of an accepting lasso is $d + 1$ steps, in the case that the unique accepting state is maximally far from the initial state. The algorithm requires d steps to reach the accepting state, followed by one further step to close the loop of the lasso. The expected number of random walks to see an accepting lasso (if one exists) is thus bounded by $\mathcal{O}(m^d)$, where m is the maximal number of transitions enabled at any state. In what follows we will refer to this bound as the worst case expectation. Figure 1 shows an example, with $m = 2$, where the original GS algorithm is expected to behave according to this bound.

Algorithm 1 runs forever if no error is found. We can run the algorithm for an extended period, or a number of times

---

Algorithm 1. GS tactic of [5]

repeat
   $l := 0$;
   $f := -1$;
   clear hash table;
   $current := init$;
   repeat
      hash($current$, l);
      if $accepting(current)$ **then**
         $f := l$;
      $l := l + 1$;
      $current :=$
      $guess\_succ(current)$;
   until $current =$
      void $\lor$ hashed($current$);
   if hash_value($current$) $<= f$
   then
      print "error found";
      terminate
until *true*;

---

related to the worst case expectation calculated above. But note that the size of a counter that counts up to the worst time expectation is in the order of magnitude of the state space.

Algorithm 2. ML tactic

```
repeat
    l := 0;
    f := −1;
    clear hash table;
    current:=init;
    repeat
        hash(current, l);
        if accepting(current) then
            ⌊ f := l;
        l := l + 1 ;
        I := ∅;
        old := current
        repeat
            current := guess_new_succ(current, I);
            if current ≠ void ∧ hashed(current) then
                if hash_value(current) <= f then
                    print "error found";
                    ⌊ terminate
                else if l <= d then
                    I := I ∪ {current};
                    ⌊ current := old;
        until current = void ∨ ¬hashed(current) ∨ l > d;
    until current = void ∨ l > d;
until true;
```

For concurrent systems, it is tempting to use commutativity based reduction to limit the executions that are considered (e.g., partial order reduction). Such methods benefit model checking by restricting it to *representatives* of equivalence classes of executions. However, in the context of MC², there is no reason to suppose that such a reduction will necessarily increase the density of errors among the overall executions. The density could in fact be reduced and thus make errors more difficult to find.

Since a path potentially runs through all possible states, the size of the hash is of the same order of magnitude as the number of states. Practically, it makes sense to start with a much smaller hash table and grow it when too many hash conflicts make it inefficient. We do not necessarily need to clear the entire hash table at the end of each random walk, but can keep information about the random walk number in which a value is hashed, clearing a hashed location upon encountering this value in a later walk.

In [5] the authors bound the number of random walks using an hypothesis test, with user-specified parameters ϵ and δ. The value of ϵ is the supposed maximum probability of detecting an accepting lasso, and $1 - \delta$ is the desired maximum probability that an accepting lasso exists but is not observed, given ϵ. The true value of the probability of observing an accepting lasso is dependent on their inherent rarity, the structure of the state space and the efficiency of the particular tactic being used. All three of these are generally unknown (worst case expectation of a tactic is not useful in this regard) so it is important to note that δ only expresses statistical confidence with respect to the (arbitrarily) chosen value of ϵ. If no accepting lasso is seen, it is not possible to distinguish whether no counterexample exists or whether ϵ is too large. Such an hypothesis test is equally applicable to our own tactics, but specifies a somewhat arbitrary and thus meaningless level of confidence. We therefore do not consider it further.

4   Variants of the GS Tactic

To address problems with certain pathological models, the authors of [5] suggested the "multi-lasso" approach, which we refer to as ML. Upon returning to a value that is on the stack, but where the cycle does not contain an accepting state, it makes another choice of a successor, when possible.

The ML tactic is described by Algorithm 2. Function *guess_new_succ* (*current*, I) has two parameters: the current state, and the set of successors to ignore.[1] If all the successors of *current* appear in the set of successors I, then it returns the special value void. The additional memory that it requires is just storing a set of successors of the current state.

For the state space in Fig. 2, a single random walk of ML will find the accepting cycle, whereas GS is expected to need a number of random walks exponential in the length of the longest path (which is also the number of states).

We suggest here a variant of the GS algorithm, not considered in [5], which we call CW. It simply *continues walking* if the current closed cycle does not contain an accepting state. As with GS, the worst case random walk is bounded by $d + 1$ steps, however we expect CW to perform much better in practice. The CW tactic is described by Algorithm 3.

The tactic CW differs from GS in that when an edge in the random walk points back to a state that does not close an accepting cycle, the search continues, and

---

Algorithm 3. CW tactic

repeat
    $l := 0$;
    $f := -1$;
    clear hash table;
    current := *init*;
    hash(*current*, l);
    repeat
        if *accepting*(*current*) **then**
          $f := l$;
        $l := l + 1$;
        current := *guess_succ*(*current*);
        if *current* $\neq$ void **then**
          if hashed(*current*) **then**
            if
              hash_value(*current*) $\leq f$
            then
              print "error found";
              terminate
        else
          hash(*current*, l);
    until *current* = void $\lor\ l > d$;
until *true*;

---

[1] By ordering the transitions, we do not need to keep the actual states in I, but only a counter for the next enabled transition that was not tried from the previous state.

different choices can (eventually) be made. This saves on the amount of work it takes to set up a new random walk. The savings are particularly meaningful when an essential common prefix for the error trace is a combination lock.

As a variant of both GS and CW, we introduce the tactic OA that continues walking in the manner of CW, but stores *only accepting* states in the hash. This tactic can avoid storing many states that are irrelevant to the property, but must nevertheless step through them on its random walk, and can only close a loop when it observes an accepting state twice. The consequence of this latter feature is that the worst case random walk requires $2 \times d + 1$ steps. This occurs when the only accepting lasso contains a single accepting state that is reached after a maximal path from the initial state, and the cycle of the lasso returns to the initial state. OA then requires d steps to first reach the accepting state, one step to close the loop and a further d steps to reach the accepting state again. The worst case expectation therefore grows quadratically from that of GS, but as with CW, we expect OA to perform significantly better in practice.

We give details of OA in its bounded memory "no hash" form, OA-NH, in Sect. 5.

5   Token-Based Tactics Without Hashing

We describe here the tactic OA-NH, which does not use hashing. The memory required is a counter, and a fixed number of tokens that keep a fixed number of accepting states that appeared on the current walk. The OA-NH tactic is described by Algorithm 4, using the following notation.

K. The set of accepting states kept as "tokens".
k. The constant maximal number of tokens.
$drop\_one(M, r)$. A function that randomly drops one element from a set M if $|M| = r$, otherwise returns M.

The algorithm makes a random walk of size $2 \times d + 1$ for an ultimately periodic path (lasso). Whenever a new accepting state is found, it is added to the set K. A lasso is identified when the current state appears in K. However, we keep a maximum of k accepting states as tokens. If we already hold k tokens and encounter another accepting state, we discard one of the $k + 1$ states at random. Note that keeping just the first k accepting states is useless if they happen to appear before a cycle begins. Likewise, keeping only the most recent k accepting states would also not guarantee to catch an ultimately periodic error trace, as we may have more than k accepting states on the cyclic part and thus repeatedly throw away the token of an accepting state before we meet it again on the run. Discarding tokens at random guarantees that a run will always have positive probability of detecting an accepting lasso, if one exists.

Suppose that the maximal out-degree in the graph is m. If we can keep all the encountered accepting states, the worst case expectation of finding a counterexample is bounded by $\mathcal{O}(m^{2 \times d})$. If there are more than k accepting states in a path, then after storing k such states as tokens, an existing token will be retained with probability $k/(k+1)$ every time a new accepting state is encountered. The worst case expectation for the number of random walks to find a counterexample is thus bounded by $\mathcal{O}((m \times (k+$

Algorithm 4. OA-NH tactic

repeat
  $l := 0$;
  $K := \emptyset$;
  $current := init$;
  repeat
    if $accepting(current)$ **then**
      $K := drop\_one(K \cup$
      $\{current\}, k+1)$;
    $l := l+1$;
    $current := guess\_succ(current)$;
    if $current \neq$ void $\land$ $current \in K$
    then
      print "error found";
      terminate
  until $current =$ void $\lor l > 2 \times d$;
until $true$;

$1)/k)^{2 \times d})$. It is sufficient to have $k = 1$, i.e., one token, but note that the expectation is now (also) exponential in the size of $(k+1)/k$. Hence one may choose to increase the number of tokens used.

In Sect. 6 we give the results of simulation experiments that compare GS, OA and OA-NH, however we itemize here some key differences between these tactics.

- The GS algorithm has more chances of closing a cycle.
- The GS algorithm produces a counterexample that has length bounded by $d + 1$, rather than $2 \times d + 1$ with the OA algorithm. Thus, the worst case expectation of the number of random walks is quadratically better.
- The GS algorithm wastefully generates random walks that terminate with a cycle that does not contain an accepting state.
- The GS algorithm requires a hash table that can potentially store values (counters) for all the reachable states. On the other hand, the OA-NH algorithm uses $\mathcal{O}(\log d)$ memory, for storing the counter l and a fixed number of tokens.

Tokenizing GS, ML and CW

In a similar way, we can modify the tactics GS, ML and CW to use only a finite number of tokens, instead of the hash table. In this case, a token is a pair, consisting of a state s and its distance from the initial state l. We denote these tactics GS-NH, ML-NH and CW-NH, respectively. The worst case expectation of the number of random walks for these tactics is bounded by $\mathcal{O}((m \times (k+1)/k)^d)$, which follows from the analysis of GS and OA-NH. The CW-NH tactic is described by Algorithm 5. In Sect. 6 we compare the performance of the various hash-based and tokenized tactics.

Lemma 1. *Given an isotropic probabilistic abstraction of a nondeterministic automaton representing the product of a system and the negation of a property,*

Algorithm 5. CW-NH tactic

```
repeat
    l := 0 ;
    K := ∅;
    f := -1;
    current := init;
    repeat
        if accepting(current) then
            └ f := l;
        K := drop_one(K ∪ {⟨current, l⟩}, k + 1);
        l := l + 1 ;
        current := guess_succ(current);
        if current ≠ void ∧ ∃x ⟨current, x⟩ ∈ K ∧ x <= f then
            │ print "error found";
            └ terminate
    until current = void ∨ l > d;
until true;
```

the worst case expectation of the number of random walks necessary to detect an existent counterexample for tactics GS, ML and CW is bounded by $\mathcal{O}(m^d)$, and by $\mathcal{O}((m \times (k+1)/k)^d)$ for tokenized tactics GS-NH, ML-NH and CW-NH, where m is the maximal out-degree of the automaton graph, d is the diameter of the graph and k is the number of tokens. The worst case expectation of the number of random walks necessary to detect an existent counterexample for tactics OA and OA-NH is bounded by $\mathcal{O}(m^{2 \times d})$ and by $\mathcal{O}((m \times (k+1)/k)^{2 \times d})$, respectively.

Proof. The proof is immediate from the definitions of the upper bound expectations. □

Theorem 1. *Given an isotropic probabilistic abstraction of a nondeterministic automaton representing the product of a system and the negation of a property, the probabilistic measure of paths from an initial state that demonstrate a counterexample is non-zero iff there exists a counterexample.*

Proof. From automata theory we know that the Büchi automaton forms a graph comprising strongly connected components of states and transitions. A counterexample will be a trace starting in the initial state and having the general form of a finite "lasso", with an ultimately periodic cycle that includes an accepting state (see, e.g., [14]). By virtue of finite branching and our definition of an isotropic probabilistic abstraction, all transitions have non-zero probability and all lassos (not just counterexamples) therefore have non-zero probability. It has been shown in [5] that such lassos from a probability space, hence any subset of lassos will have positive measure. If no counterexample exists, no lassos will exist to demonstrate a counterexample. If one or more counterexamples exists there will be a subset of lassos that demonstrate them and these will have positive measure. □

Corollary 1. *Given sufficient random walks, all of the presented tactics* (GS, ML, CW, OA, GS-NH, ML-NH, CW-NH, OA-NH) *will find a counterexample almost surely, if one exists.*

Savitch construction for binary search [12] is used to show that model checking is in PSPACE. The construction uses space that is quadratic in a logarithm of the size of the state space (and polynomial in the size of the LTL property [13]). The time required is exponential in that (hence, the *space* efficient binary search is quadratically worse in *time* than the explicit state space search). Using randomization and our no-hash tactics provides an extremely compact representation, which is quadratically smaller than the one needed for the binary search. Moreover, our randomized search progresses from one reachable state to its successor, rather than blindly enumerating reachable and unreachable states. It thus has the potential to be significantly more efficient than the binary search, although the worst case expectation analysis, which is related to the time complexity, is exponential in the size of the state space and therefore exponentially worse than the binary search. In practice, however, the effectiveness of randomization depends on the particular properties of the state space. For example, any first order theory over dense graphs holds with probability of either one or zero (zero-one laws), but does not hold for graphs in general. Thus, the result of applying randomized methods to graphs can highly depend on their properties.

The Binary search algorithm does not produce a counterexample for the checked property: such a path can potentially be as long as the number of states of the system, exponentially larger than the amount of memory used by the binary search. The no-hash random walk tactics presented here also do not produce such a path, for the same reason; they do not keep enough memory to store the states that were reached during the execution. One can consider these algorithms as highly memory efficient checks for the existence of errors. Note that if an error is found and an error trace is needed, it is possible to make use of the properties of pseudo-random number generators to simply re-simulate the desired counterexample, or to invest in a more memory-heavy algorithm that would produce the desired counterexample.

6   Experimental Results

To compare the behavior of the tactics, we first apply them to multiple instances of three scalable models:

- The dining philosophers of [9], as also used in [5],
- The shared memory consensus model of [1], and
- A linear model with self loops [11].

We chose well known probabilistic algorithms because they are only correct with probability one, hence they include incorrect execution paths. We abstract random choice by nondeterminism then use randomized model checking to find these paths, noting that our method is *not* a statistical evaluation of these algorithms.

An *experiment* consists of performing random walks (we also write "walks") until an error is found (we know that erroneous executions exist in these algorithms). For each model and tactic we perform 100 experiments searching for accepting ultimately periodic cycles. Since the number and length of the walks used by each tactic is different, we report on the average number of *steps* used per experiment (successful and failed ones), which is the *sum of the lengths of the random walks*. The number of steps is a good measure to compare the time required by the tactics to find the counterexample.

For the tactics with unbounded memory, we also calculated the maximum number of states stored per walk in the hash table. In the case of tactics with a fixed number of tokens, we used 100 tokens. For reference, we also calculated the total number of states in each model using Prism [7].

Our -NH tactics trade reduced space for increased time, but the trade-off is biased in their favor. To demonstrate this we also plot the product of steps and states for increasing model size, showing that this product is typically less with a bounded number of states stored as tokens. One reason for this is that an accepting lasso may contain more than one accepting state. In such a case, if all but one of the accepting states is randomly discarded, the lasso nevertheless remains valid and the number of steps in the random walk is unaltered. Space has been saved, but with no increase in time.

6.1   Dining Philosophers

We consider models with 3 to 10 philosophers, with approximately 10^3 to 10^{10} states, respectively. We look for counterexamples for the property that an arbitrarily chosen philosopher will be hungry and then fed, infinitely often, i.e., $\varphi = \Box\Diamond(hungry \wedge \Diamond eat)$.

We first describe the performance of the unbounded tactics, then summarize what happens when we bound the memory. The results of our experiments are summarized in Fig. 3.

GS. The average number of steps grows approximately an order of magnitude larger than the total number of states in the model, which, in turn, grows exponentially with the number of philosophers. Due to this quick growth, we were only able to test models up to 6 philosophers. Our 100 experiments in this case took approximately 16 h. The poor performance is because these models contain a lot of non-accepting loops that cause the algorithm to start new walks, rather than continue exploring further. Walks of GS are therefore generally short.

ML. The average number of steps grows at an exponential rate, but at a significantly lower rate than the number of states in the model. Hence, on this example, ML performs exponentially better in time than GS. Intuitively, this is because ML continues rather than stops at the first repeated state, allowing the algorithm more chances to explore potentially good transitions.

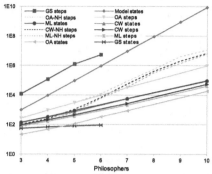
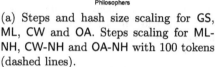
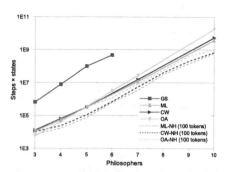

(a) Steps and hash size scaling for GS, ML, CW and OA. Steps scaling for ML-NH, CW-NH and OA-NH with 100 tokens (dashed lines).

(b) Overall performance (steps×states) of GS, ML, CW and OA vs ML-NH, ML-NH and OA-NH with 100 tokens (dashed lines).

Fig. 3. Performance of tactics with dining philosophers protocol.

CW. The average number of steps grows at a similar exponential rate as ML, hence CW is also exponentially faster than GS. The intuition behind the performance of CW is similar to ML, however in these experiments it requires approximately 10% more steps.

OA. The average number of steps grows at a lower (exponential) rate than the growth of states in the model, but it grows at a slightly higher rate than CW. Since OA only stores accepting states, it inherently requires less memory than the other tactics, however it pays by having to wait longer to close a cycle.

Due to the fact that CW and ML store all explored states, not only accepting states, they require approximately three times more memory than OA. However, the time performance of the bounded variants of these tactics, using 100 tokens, seems largely unrelated to their unbounded memory requirements. In general, as expected, when the number of tokens is bounded, the time performance worsens, but the relative performance between the tactics remains the same as the unbounded versions: ML (ML-NH) is better than CW (CW-NH), which is better than OA (OA-NH). For up to 5 philosophers, OA-NH requires fewer than 100 tokens, so its performance is actually identical to OA. CW-NH and ML-NH require more than 100 tokens with 3 philosophers, so their performance is consistently worse than the unbounded versions.

6.2 Shared Memory Consensus Protocol

We consider models containing from 2 to 12 processes, with approximately 10^3 to 10^{12} states, respectively. The negated property we check is $\neg\varphi = (\square\lozenge heads \wedge \square\lozenge tails)$. That is, the processes reach different consensuses infinitely often without terminating. The checked models contain a BSCC that includes the state in which the processes do reach a consensus and recognize that they

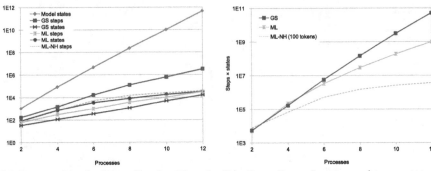

(a) Steps and hash size scaling for **GS** and **ML** compared to steps of **ML-NH** with 100 tokens (dashed line).

(b) Overall performance (steps×states) of **GS**, **ML** and **ML-NH** with 100 tokens (dashed line).

Fig. 4. Performance of tactics with shared memory consensus protocol.

have done so, hence φ holds. The protocol almost always reaches a consensus, which corresponds to falling into this BSCC, which contains no accepting states.

The tactics **CW** and **OA** (similarly, **CW-NH** and **OA-NH**), whose walks have a long a priori bound, tend to very quickly fall into this BSCC, where the property can not be satisfied. In contrast, when **GS** (similarly, **GS-NH**) falls into the BSCC, it rapidly discovers a non-accepting loop and starts a new walk. Likewise, when **ML** (similarly **ML-NH**) falls into the BSCC, it rapidly explores the extent of the component and starts a new walk. The consequence is that only **GS**, **ML** (and **GS-NH**, **ML-NH**) are feasible tactics for these models. The results of our experiments are summarized in Fig. 4.

GS. The average number of steps grows at a lower exponential rate than the total number of states in the model.

ML. The average number of steps grows at a lower exponential rate than **GS**.

MLNH. With 100 tokens the performance deteriorates towards that of **GS** up to 6 processes, but then converges to that of **ML** by 12 processes.

CW, OA. These tactics tend to lead the random walk into the BSCC that has no accepting state. Our experiments show that with very few processes one would need a huge number of random walks, significantly outside the scale we use to plot the results for the other tactics.

6.3 Pathological Linear Model

These models are illustrated in Fig. 5 and consist of a linear sequence of n states, where each state has a self loop. The negated property we use is $\neg\varphi = \Diamond p$. The

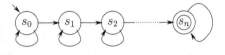

Fig. 5. A linear state space with local loops.

final (accepting) state satisfies p and happens to have a self loop. The results of our experiments are summarized in Fig. 6. The simplicity of the models allows us to include analytical results in the following description.

GS. Every encountered self loop causes the algorithm to reset to the beginning. Hence the average number of steps grows exponentially. Analysis reveals that the expected number of steps to reach the accepting state is $2^n - 2$. The maximum number of states that are stored is the entire state space.

ML. This tactic does not complete loops, but nevertheless takes the first step of a loop to discover it. The expected number of steps to pass from one state to the next is 1.5, so the expected number of steps to reach the accepting state is $1.5 \times (n - 1)$. The maximal number of states that are stored is the entire state space.

CW. Allowing simulations to follow the self loops gives multiple chances to get to the next state. The infinite sum of all such chances makes the expected number of moves to reach the next state equal to 2. Hence the expected number of steps to reach the accepting state is $2 \times (n - 1)$. The maximum number of stored states is the state space.

OA. The expected number of steps is the same as CW, but there is only one accepting state to store.

Bounding the memory to 100 tokens has minimal effect. In the case of OA-NH, for any model size it has no effect, since there is only ever one accepting state. In the case of ML-NH and CW-NH with $n \leq 100$ it has no effect. In the cases of ML-NH and CW-NH with $n > 100$, there is a $1/101$ chance that the accepting state will not be stored when it is first encountered, however every subsequent step will find the accepting state again and it will be stored with probability $100/101$.

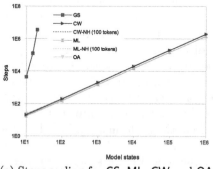 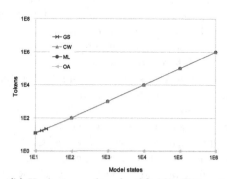

(a) Steps scaling for GS, ML, CW and OA with unbounded hash and for CW-NH and ML-NH with 100 tokens (dashed lines, but hidden).

(b) Hash size scaling for GS, ML, CW and OA. Plots for ML and CW are coincident.

Fig. 6. Performance of tactics with pathological model.

7   Conclusions and Further Work

Our new tactics can make significant improvements in efficiency over those of [5], especially GS. We have demonstrated this by considering the number of steps necessary to detect a counterexample, but our tactics also avoid the repeated setup cost of GS. Our bounded-memory tactics are particularly modest in their memory requirement, as they dispense with the hash (and stack). They require less memory even compared with the memory efficient binary search that establishes that model checking is in PSPACE [15]. However, as we have only a finite number of tokens and the execution path can be as large as the state space (so in the limit the eliminated hash table is of that magnitude), we risk throwing away good states in favor of useless states. This increases the expected number of steps needed to find an existing error, since a random walk that is a counterexample may not be detected as such if key states are randomly discarded. Our experiments demonstrate, however, that the increase in the required number of random walks is typically less than the memory saving and may be exponentially less. One explanation of this phenomenon is that accepting lassos can contain more than one accepting state. Removing all but one of the accepting states within the loop saves memory without invalidating it as a counterexample and without increasing the number of steps in the random walk.

Our experiments suggest that while GS is not necessarily the worst performing tactic under all circumstances, it is most likely to give poor or very poor performance in terms of the number of steps required to detect a counterexample. It is nevertheless possible to construct examples where GS requires fewer steps than some of the alternatives. For example, models whose non-accepting paths contain many loops and whose accepting paths contain no non-accepting loops. In these cases GS will quit non-accepting paths at the first encountered loop, while other tactics will pursue the paths to their maximum extent. In general, the performance of all tactics is strongly dependent on the model, whose detailed structure is usually unknown. Given that our tactics are memory-efficient and may be easily parallelized, we thus advocate running multiple tactics simultaneously. The running time will then always be that of the fastest tactic.

As future work we propose to study additional strategies. For example, ML and ML-NH effectively use single step backtracking and it is possible to extend them to multiple steps. Another promising approach is to exploit information about the structure of the SCCs in the state space of a system and a property. It is well known that random execution traces work their way down through the SCCs and eventually arrive in the BSCC. This affects the performance of randomized verification when accepting lassos are in intermediate SCCs, as demonstrated by the example in Sect. 6.2. Each SCC of the global state space comprises a combination of states in local SCCs of individual processes. We can use this knowledge to limit searches within specific global SCCs, avoiding the problem of wasting time in BSCCs with no accepting states.

References

1. Aspnes, J., Herlihy, M.: Fast randomized consensus using shared memory. J. Algorithms **11**(3), 441–461 (1990)
2. Brim, L., Černá, I., Nečesal, M.: Randomization helps in LTL model checking. In: de Alfaro, L., Gilmore, S. (eds.) PAPM-PROBMIV 2001. LNCS, vol. 2165, pp. 105–119. Springer, Heidelberg (2001). https://doi.org/10.1007/3-540-44804-7_7
3. Clarke, E.M., Grumberg, O., Peled, D.A.: Model Checking. The MIT Press, Cambridge (2000)
4. Gerth, R., Peled, D., Vardi, M.Y., Wolper, P.: Simple on-the-fly automatic verification of linear temporal logic. In: Protocol Specification, Testing and Verification XV, Proceedings of the Fifteenth IFIP WG6.1 International Symposium on Protocol Specification, Testing and Verification, Warsaw, Poland, pp. 3–18 (1995)
5. Grosu, R., Smolka, S.: Monte Carlo model checking. In: 11th International Conference on Tools and Algorithms for the Construction and Analysis of Systems, TACAS 2005, pp. 271–286 (2005)
6. Hérault, T., Lassaigne, R., Magniette, F., Peyronnet, S.: Approximate probabilistic model checking. In: Steffen, B., Levi, G. (eds.) VMCAI 2004. LNCS, vol. 2937, pp. 73–84. Springer, Heidelberg (2004). https://doi.org/10.1007/978-3-540-24622-0_8
7. Hinton, A., Kwiatkowska, M., Norman, G., Parker, D.: PRISM: a tool for automatic verification of probabilistic systems. In: Hermanns, H., Palsberg, J. (eds.) TACAS 2006. LNCS, vol. 3920, pp. 441–444. Springer, Heidelberg (2006). https://doi.org/10.1007/11691372_29
8. Holzmann, G.J.: The SPIN Model Checker. Pearson Education, Boston (2003)
9. Lehmann, D.J., Rabin, M.O.: On the advantages of free choice: a symmetric and fully distributed solution to the dining philosophers problem. In: Conference Record of the Eighth Annual ACM Symposium on Principles of Programming Languages, Williamsburg, Virginia, USA, January 1981, pp. 133–138 (1981)
10. Manna, Z., Pnueli, A.: How to cook a temporal proof system for your pet language. In: Conference Record of the Tenth Annual ACM Symposium on Principles of Programming Languages, Austin, Texas, USA, January 1983, pp. 141–154 (1983)
11. Oudinet, J., Denise, A., Gaudel, M., Lassaigne, R., Peyronnet, S.: Uniform Monte-Carlo model checking. In: 14th International Conference on Fundamental Approaches to Software Engineering, FASE 2011, pp. 127–140 (2011)
12. Savitch, W.J.: Relationships between nondeterministic and deterministic tape complexities. J. Comput. Syst. Sci. **4**(2), 177–192 (1970)
13. Sistla, A.P., Clarke, E.M.: The complexity of propositional linear temporal logics. J. ACM **32**(3), 733–749 (1985)
14. Thomas, W.: Automata on infinite objects. In: van Leeuwen, J. (ed.) Handbook of Theoretical Computer Science, Volume B: Formal Models and Semantics, pp. 133–192. MIT Press, Cambridge (1990)
15. Vardi, M.Y., Wolper, P.: An automata-theoretic approach to automatic program verification. In: Proceedings of IEEE Symposium on Logic in Computer Science, Boston, July 1986, pp. 332–344 (1986)
16. Younes, H.L.S., Simmons, R.G.: Probabilistic verification of discrete event systems using acceptance sampling. In: Brinksma, E., Larsen, K.G. (eds.) CAV 2002. LNCS, vol. 2404, pp. 223–235. Springer, Heidelberg (2002). https://doi.org/10.1007/3-540-45657-0_17

Reordering Control Approaches to State Explosion in Model Checking with Memory Consistency Models

Tatsuya Abe[1]($\boxtimes$), Tomoharu Ugawa[2], and Toshiyuki Maeda[1]

[1] STAIR Lab, Chiba Institute of Technology, Narashino, Japan
{abet,tosh}@stair.center
[2] Kochi University of Technology, Kami, Japan
ugawa@plas.info.kochi-tech.ac.jp

Abstract. The relaxedness of memory consistency models, which allows the reordering of instructions and their effects, intensifies the state explosion problem of software model checking. In this paper, we propose three approaches that can reduce the number of states to be visited in software model checking with memory consistency models. The proposed methods control the reordering of instructions. The first approach controls the number of reordered instructions. The second approach specifies the instructions that are reordered in advance, and prevents the other instructions from being reordered. The third approach specifies the instructions that are reordered, and preferentially explores execution traces with the reorderings. We applied these approaches to the McSPIN model checker that we have been developing, and reported the effectiveness of the approaches by examining various concurrent programs.

Keywords: Software model checking
Relaxed memory consistency model · State explosion
Instruction reordering control · Concurrent program examination

1 Introduction

Relaxed memory consistency models (MCMs) promote parallel processing on computer architectures that consist of multiple processors by allowing the reordering of instructions and their effects. Modern computing systems that include computer architectures and programming languages typically adopt relaxed MCMs [14, 16, 17, 22, 28].

A substantial problem with the relaxedness of MCMs is that it intensifies the state explosion problem of software model checking because reordering increases the number of execution traces to be explored. For example, consider a simple program $(\texttt{x=1; r0=y}) \, \| \, (\texttt{y=1; r1=x})$, where ; and $\|$ denote sequential and parallel compositions, respectively. Many relaxed MCMs allow load operations to overtake store operations because, in many cases, store operations do not need to be completed before load operations are executed, and relaxing the order

A. Paskevich and T. Wies (Eds.): VSTTE 2017, LNCS 10712, pp. 170–190, 2017.
https://doi.org/10.1007/978-3-319-72308-2_11

	x=1	y=1	r0=y	r1=x	x's effect	y's effect
the buffer on the left thread	x	x	x	x		
the buffer on the right thread		y	y	y		
the shared memory					x	x, y

Fig. 1. An execution trace on a computer architecture with store buffers

of executions in this way may enhance computational performance. In model checking with such relaxed MCMs, the right-hand thread can observe not only an execution trace (x=1; r0=y), but also (r0=y; x=1) on the left-hand thread. Similarly, the left-hand thread can observe not only an execution trace (y=1; r1=x), but also (r1=x; y=1) on the right-hand thread. These can be seen on computer architectures with store buffers. Figure 1 denotes that the two store instructions are invoked, but their reflects to the shared memory are delayed. Thus, model checking with relaxed MCMs requires more execution traces to be explored than conventional model checking, which ignores MCMs.

In our four-year study of relaxed MCMs (since [2]) and development of the model checker with relaxed MCMs, McSPIN, which utilizes SPIN [13], however, *we observed that counterexamples, that is, execution traces that violate the properties to be verified, often reorder a small number of instructions.* This observation implies that counterexamples can be detected efficiently by performing a state-space search in which the number of reordered instructions is controlled. For example, an assertion r0==1 or r1==1 for the above example program, which is violated by an execution trace (r0=y, r1=x, x=1, y=1) with *two* reorderings of (x=1; r0=y) and (y=1; r1=x), can be violated by another execution trace (r0=y, y=1, r1=x, x=1) with just *one* reordering of (x=1; r0=y).

In this paper, we propose three approaches to control the reordering of instructions for software model checking with MCMs. These approaches focus on the improvement of the efficiency of the counterexample detection, whereas our previous approaches are general-purpose [3,5].

The first approach controls the number of reordered instructions. Let us suppose that *one* reordering between two instructions is allowed. Under this restriction, the execution trace (r0=y, r1=x, x=1, y=1) is not allowed because there is a point at which *two* reorderings occur. However, (r0=y, x=1, r1=x, y=1) is allowed because the latter reordered instructions are executed after the former reordered instructions have been completed, that is, the *two* reorderings do not occur. The second approach specifies the instructions to be reordered in advance. We specify an arbitrary set of instructions which is given to a model checker with MCMs. For example, suppose that the first and second instructions (x=1; r0=y) on the left-hand thread can be reordered, and the other reordering is prohibited. Whereas (x=1, r0=y, y=1, r1=x) and (r0=y, x=1, y=1, r1=x) are allowed under this definition, (x=1, r0=y, r1=x, y=1) is not allowed because the pair (y=1; r1=x) is reordered. This approach also enables the parallel processing of model checking with MCMs. The third approach specifies the instructions that are reordered, and preferentially explores execution traces with the reorderings. A difference from the second approach is that the reorderings of the other instructions are not prohibited but postponed. We would like to note that the former two approaches restrict explored execution traces. For example, if the number of pairs of reordered instructions is limited to one, then no counterexample on an execution trace which has two pairs of reordered instructions is detected. The third approach is not a restriction of an exploration but a change of an exploration.

As a proof of concept, we implement the approaches in McSPIN and report on their effectiveness by examining various concurrent programs, including some popular mutual exclusion algorithms, such as Dekker's algorithm [25] and concurrent copying protocols for garbage collection [21,23,24]. Properties to be verified in this paper are whether mutual exclusions and concurrent copies work correctly or not. The experimental results show that the proposed approaches successfully mitigate the state explosion caused by the relaxedness of MCMs when counterexamples are found. In a few cases, our approaches can detect counterexamples that the original exploration of McSPIN could not detect. Also, in other cases, some of our approaches can detect counterexamples more quickly than the original exploration of McSPIN. We would like to note that their effectiveness disappears when there is no counterexample (i.e., the property to be verified holds) because it becomes necessary to consider all the reorderings of instructions allowed under MCMs.

The remainder of this paper is organized as follows: In Sect. 2, we formally define the reordering of instructions. In Sect. 3, we introduce the three proposed approaches. In Sect. 4, we explain the implementation of the approaches in McSPIN. In Sect. 5, we present case studies and experimental results obtained by applying McSPIN to these approaches. In Sect. 6, we discuss related work, and in Sect. 7, we conclude this paper by identifying future work.

2   Preliminaries

In this section, we formally define reorderings of instructions.

2.1   Instructions and Concurrent Programs

A program is defined by an N-tuple of sequences of labeled instructions. A labeled instruction i is a pair of a label and instruction $\langle L, \iota \rangle$, where

$$\iota ::= \texttt{Move}\, r\, t \mid \texttt{Load}\, r\, x \mid \texttt{Store}\, x\, t \mid \texttt{Fence} \mid \texttt{Jump}\, L\, \texttt{if}\, t \mid \texttt{Nop}$$
$$t ::= r \mid v \mid t + t \mid t - t \mid \cdots$$

and N is the number of processes. We write the set of labeled instructions that occur in a program P as $I(P)$. A label L denotes an instruction in a program. Distinct instructions have distinct labels. In this paper, L is a natural number. In the definitions of instructions and terms, r denotes a variable local to a process and $x, \ldots,$ are shared variables. The term v denotes an immediate value.

The terms $t_0 + t_1, t_0 - t_1, \ldots$, denote arithmetic expressions in a standard manner. Note that term t contains no shared values.

In this paper, we omit to explain arrays, pointers, and functions for simplicity. However, McSPIN (introduced in Sect. 4) supports them, and the programs used in experiments in Sect. 5 contain them.

Instructions are defined as follows: Move $r\,t$ denotes the assignment of an evaluated value of a term t to r, which does not affect the other processes. Load $r\,x$ denotes loading x from its own store buffer if a value of x is buffered in it, or from shared memory otherwise, and assigning its value to r. Store $x\,t$ denotes storing an evaluated value of t to x in its own store buffer. Fence denotes a memory fence, which separates preceding memory operations from succeeding memory operations, and guarantees the completion of preceding memory operations before succeeding memory operations are invoked. Various fence instructions are considered to control memory operations more delicately (e.g., lwsync and hwsync of POWER [14]). However, in this paper, we define the so-called *full fence*, which separates memory operations without distinguishing load and store instructions, since the variety of fence instructions is out of the scope of this paper, although McSPIN (introduced in Sect. 4) supports various fence instructions. Jump L if t denotes a conditional jump to L depending on the evaluated value of t. Because t contains no shared values by definition, to jump to L depending on x, it is necessary to perform Load $r\,x$ in advance. Nop denotes no operation.

2.2   Reorderings of Instructions Under Relaxed MCMs

Suppose that a sequence of labeled instructions $i_0; i_1$ is included in a program. We say that i_0 and i_1 are ordered in *program order*. We call i_0 and i_1 *reordered* if a thread performs the two instructions in program order while another thread *observes* that i_0 and i_1 have been invoked in the reverse order.

To manage this case, we introduce *operations* for each instruction as follows:

$$o ::= \text{Issue}^j\,i \mid \text{Effect}^j\,i$$

where superscript j denotes the j-th dynamic instance of labeled instruction i. A labeled instruction *may* be executed multiple times because our language has jump instructions. To take reorderings into account under relaxed MCMs, one operation has to be distinguished from another. Although the j-th dynamic instance is defined for any $j \geqslant 0$, all the instances are not invoked in general.

For any labeled instruction i, its issue $\text{Issue}^j\,i$ operation is defined. This represents the issue of the instruction, as its name suggests. For load and store instructions, which deal with shared variables, additional operations are defined. $\text{Effect}^j\,i$ denotes an effect of i, that is, a change of state in shared memory. For load/store instruction i, its execution $\text{Effect}^j\,i$ denote load/store from/to shared memory, respectively.

Although fence instructions themselves do not access shared variables and are separators for the effects of load/store instructions, we define $\text{Effect}^j\,i$ for any fence instruction i. This is because delays in the effects of memory fences by separating executions from issues can be separators for delays of the effects of load/store instructions.

Execution traces are defined as sequences of *operations*.

2.3   Representations of Memory Consistency Models

The formalized MCMs used as inputs in model checking are defined as constraints. An execution trace that follows constraints corresponding to an MCM $\mathfrak{M}$ is called $\mathfrak{M}$-*admissible*. An execution trace that does not follow constraints corresponding to an MCM $\mathfrak{M}$, is called $\mathfrak{M}$-*inadmissible*.

Constraints are defined as equational first-order predicate formulas consisting of operations and the unique predicate symbol $\leqslant$, which denotes an order between operations. We write $o < o'$ as $o \leqslant o' \wedge o \not\equiv o'$. An atomic formula $\texttt{Issue}^j\, i < \texttt{Issue}^{j'}\, i'$ means that the j-th dynamic instance of instruction i is issued before the j'-th dynamic instance of instruction i'.

We can easily define constraints to control the reordering of operations of instructions. Such constraints are called *integrations* in our previous paper [4]. Let i be a labeled instruction whose instruction is $\texttt{Store}$. The instruction i is split into two operations: $\texttt{Issue}$ and $\texttt{Effect}$. Operation $\texttt{Effect}$ must be performed after the other operations. To prohibit the splitting of i, it is sufficient to force the operations of instructions that are issued after $\texttt{Issue}$ of i to wait for $\texttt{Effect}$ of i: $\texttt{Issue}^j\, i < o \supset \texttt{Effect}^j\, i < o$ where the logical connective $\supset$ is the implication in a standard manner, and o is an arbitrary operation except $\texttt{Effect}^j\, i$.

3   Reordering Control

In this section, we propose three approaches for controlling the reordering of instructions to address the state explosion problem in model checking with MCMs.

Because an execution trace that is inadmissible under a non-relaxed MCM may be admissible under a relaxed MCM, the relaxedness of MCMs intensifies the state explosion problem in model checking. A key idea in addressing the problem is to control the reordering of instructions, that is, to control splits of instructions into operations and exploring strategies of operations. Splits of instructions into operations form a hierarchical structure. Execution traces that allow the splits into operations on at most $n - 1$ instructions are contained in the set of execution traces that allow the splits into operations for at most n instructions. Therefore, exploring execution traces in ascending order of the supremums seems promising.

3.1   Restriction of the Number of Issued Instructions

The first approach is based on the idea of controlling the *number* of issued instructions. Let n be the number of instructions that are split into operations. For example, $n = 0$ means that no instruction can be issued, that is, no issue

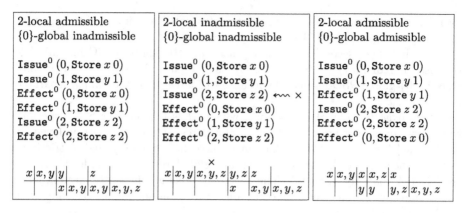

Fig. 2. Example execution traces which are PSO-admissible/inadmissible

operation can be performed while an operation of an instruction is delayed. In the following, the restriction by the number of instructions that are split into operations is called *the n-local restriction*. Execution traces that are admissible under *the n-local restriction* are called *n-local admissible*. By definition, explorations with the $(n-1)$-local restriction are contained by explorations with n-local restrictions.

We explain the n-local restriction using a simple example program $(\mathrm{x=0};$ $\mathrm{y=1};$ $\mathrm{z=2})\|\mathrm{r0=z}$ under partial store ordering (PSO), which allows load and store operations to overtake store operations. The statements on the left-hand thread are translated into $\langle 0, \mathtt{Store}\ x\ 0\rangle; \langle 1, \mathtt{Store}\ y\ 1\rangle; \langle 2, \mathtt{Store}\ z\ 2\rangle$.

The three execution traces in Fig. 2 are PSO-admissible. The first trace is at most 2-local PSO-admissible because it does not violate the restriction that two instructions are split into operations. The figure below the trace denotes the effects of the store instructions within the two buffers and memory. However, the second trace violates the 2-local restriction, that is, it is 2-local PSO-inadmissible because $\langle 2, \mathtt{Store}\ z\ 2\rangle$ is issued before either the effect of $\langle 0, \mathtt{Store}\ x\ 0\rangle$ or $\langle 1, \mathtt{Store}\ y1\rangle$ has been performed (denoted by $\times$). The third trace is 2-local PSO-admissible even under the 2-local restriction because the effect of $\langle 1, \mathtt{Store}\ y\ 1\rangle$ is completed before $\langle 2, \mathtt{Store}\ z\ 2\rangle$ is issued.

3.2 Restriction of Separations of Specified Instructions

Another proposed approach is based on the idea of specifying the instructions that are reordered. Specifically, we specify the instructions that are allowed to be split into two types of operations. Instructions that are not specified are not allowed to be split into operations. In the following, we call this *the L-global restriction*, where L is a set of labels of instructions. Execution traces that are admissible under the *L-global restriction* are called *L-global admissible*. The global restriction can control the reordering more delicately than the local restriction. For example, consider the {0}-global restriction of the example program described in Sect. 3.1.

The first and second execution traces are {0}-global PSO-inadmissible because $\langle 1, \text{Store } y\ 1 \rangle$ ($\not\equiv \langle 0, \text{Store } x\ 0 \rangle$) is a separated instruction. The third trace is {0}-global PSO-admissible because $\langle 0, \text{Store} x\ 0 \rangle$ is the *unique* separated instruction.

There exist 2^M global restrictions, where M is the number of instructions that occur in a program, including M global restrictions that are indexed by singletons $\{\, L \mid 0 \leqslant L < M \,\}$, which are called the *singular* global restrictions. We will check these M models under the global restrictions indexed by the singletons in parallel in Sect. 5. Thus, we can make a sufficiently large number of explorations by focusing on reorderings, and conduct model checking with MCMs *in parallel*.

3.3   Reordering-Oriented Explorations

The third approach is based on the idea of changing the exploration strategies of execution traces. Because model checking with relaxed MCMs has the problem of which instructions are reordered, unlike conventional model checking with non-relaxed MCMs, we can try exploration strategies of execution traces that focus on the reordering of instructions. In this paper, we try two exploration strategies: increasing and decreasing the number of reordered instructions. The purpose of the increasing strategy is first to try model checking under sequential consistency (SC), which prohibits all reorderings, and then to increment the number of instructions that are reordered. The decreasing strategy is the converse.

We would like to note the relations among the approaches introduced in this section. Since the approach in Sect. 3.1 controls the number of instructions that are reordered, the exploration strategy to increment the number of instructions that are reordered is the increasing strategy in Sect. 3.3. Conversely, the exploration strategy to decrement the number of instructions that are reordered is the decreasing strategy in Sect. 3.3. Since the approach in this subsection ignores *which* instructions are reordered, the approach in Sect. 3.2 can control reorderings more delicately than the approaches in Sects. 3.1 and 3.3.

4   Implementation for a Model Checker McSPIN

In this section, we explain how to implement the approaches proposed in Sect. 3 to McSPIN.

4.1   PROMELA Code Generated by McSPIN

McSPIN takes a program written in a subset of the C programming language and generates a code written in PROMELA (the modeling language of SPIN [13]), which represents an N-tuple of sequences of instructions. An operation is represented as a *clause* of PROMELA. SPIN chooses and performs one of the clauses nondeterministically. Each clause has a *guard* that determines whether the operation can be performed, in which case, the operation is called *executable*. Specifically, multiple clauses are generated on *each* thread p in Fig. 3 where $i_0, \ldots, i_n, \ldots, i_{M_p-1}$ are instructions on the thread p, and $prologue_{n,k}^j$ and $epilogue_{n,k}^j$ ($k = 0, 1$) are pre/post-processings of the j-th dynamic instances of operations of i_n, respectively, such as setting a program counter and turning on a flag ($end_o = 1$) denoting that an operation o has been executed. We write J_p as the supremum of loop iterations on thread p in model checking. Model checking that considers the reordering of instructions distinguishes instructions that may be operated multiple times. In this sense, McSPIN is implemented as a bounded model checking protocol with respect to the supremums of loop iterations (for more details, see [4]).

From the constraints that define an MCM $\mathfrak{M}$, McSPIN automatically generates guards, which are carefully designed to promote *partial order reduction* on SPIN (for more details, see [3]). For example, the following guard $(\neg end_{\text{Issue}^j\,i}) \vee end_{\text{Effect}^j\,i}$ (corresponding to the integration constraint introduced in Sect. 2.3) denotes that the effect of the j-th dynamic instance of i has to be performed if the j-th dynamic instance of i is issued, where 1 and 0 are interpreted as *true* and *false*, respectively. Example constraints, Itanium and Unified Parallel C MCMs [15,30] are fully formalized in [4]. Additionally, the full constraints for total store ordering (TSO), PSO, relaxed memory ordering (RMO) [6], and other relaxed MCMs are formalized in McSPIN's public repository. SPIN chooses an executable operation, and the execution traces that SPIN generates are $\mathfrak{M}$-admissible because they follow guards that McSPIN generates.

Thus, McSPIN adopts *constraint-based* reorderings of instructions. Therefore, generating appropriate constraints enables implementing the reordering controls of instructions. In the following subsections, we introduce implementations of the approaches in Sect. 3.

4.2   Implementation of Local Restrictions

We explain an implementation of the n-local restriction introduced in Sect. 3.1. Under the n-local restriction, the number of instructions that are reordered is limited to n. For an instruction i on thread p, an additional guard to its issue operation is an implementation of the n-local restriction:

$$|\{ \langle i', j \rangle \mid i' \in I(P) \setminus \{i\}, 0 \leqslant j < J_p, separated(p, i', j) = 1 \}| \leqslant n$$

where $separated(p, i', j)$ denotes $end_{\text{Issue}^j\,i'} - end_{\text{Effect}^j\,i'}$, and $|A|$ denotes the cardinality of A. The equation $separated(p, i', j) = 1$ means that the j-th dynamic instance of instruction i' on thread p is split into operations. The n-local restriction is represented as their summation is less than n.

To be precise, a trace that is prohibited under the n-local restriction can be generated at some point in time. However, at the next time step, the trace is

```
do
:: ...
:: (guard^j_{n,0}) && (prologue^j_{n,0}) ->
     (operation of Issue of i_n);
     (epilogue^j_{n,0});
:: (guard^j_{n,1}) && (prologue^j_{n,1}) ->
     (operation of Effect of i_n);
     (epilogue^j_{n,1});
:: ...
od;
```

Fig. 3. A PROMELA code of thread p

```
active proctype main() {
  int i,x;
  do
  :: atomic { i<1 -> i++; x=1; }
  :: atomic { i<2 -> i++; }
  :: else -> break;
  od;
  assert(x==1);
}
```

Fig. 5. Another example code

```
do
:: false -> (the first clause);
:: true  -> (the second clause);
:: false -> (the third clause);
:: true  -> (the fourth clause);
od;
```

Fig. 4. An example code

```
do
:: (clause of Issue^0 of i_0);
:: (clause of Effect^0 of i_0);
:: ...
:: (clause of Issue^{J_p-1} of i_{M_p-1});
:: (clause of Effect^{J_p-1} of i_{M_p-1});
od;
```

Fig. 6. A simplification of Fig. 3

determined to be inadmissible, and is removed from the list of admissible traces that are explored.

4.3 Implementation of Global Restrictions

Next, we consider an implementation of L-global restriction introduced in Sect. 3.2. By definition, the L-global restriction does not split an instruction indexed by L into operations for any $L \notin \boldsymbol{L}$, that is, it requires them to behave sequentially consistently. We introduce a new Boolean variable $specified_i$ for each instruction i to denote whether i on thread p is specified by the L-global restriction. An additional guard is simply

$$\bigwedge \{ specified_i \vee \bigwedge \{ \neg separated(p,i,j) \mid 0 \leqslant j < J_p \} \mid i \in I(P) \}$$

which denotes that i is allowed to be split into operations, that is, $separated(p,i,j)$ is ignored if i is specified, and vice versa, where 1 and 0 are interpreted as the truth values true and false, respectively.

4.4 Implementation of the Increasing and Decreasing Exploration Strategies

In this section, we explain how to implement the increasing and decreasing strategies introduced in Sect. 3.3. The straightforward approach is to modify the implementation of SPIN, but it is hard because the exploration strategy of SPIN is fixed and embedded in its implementation. To workaround the problem, we modify McSPIN to generate PROMELA code so that (unmodified) SPIN can explore execution traces with the increasing and decreasing exploration strategies. More specifically, in this section, we first explain the exploration strategy for do loops of SPIN and then explain how to generate PROMELA code which achieves the increasing and decreasing strategies on top of the strategy.

As explained in Sect. 4.1, clauses in do loops written in PROMELA are nondeterministically chosen according to the semantics of SPIN. We explain the exploration strategy for do loops with the example code shown in Fig. 4. Please note that the following explanation strongly depends on the semantics of SPIN, and may be not applicable to the other model checkers for PROMELA such as SPINJA [9].

SPIN adopts the so-called depth-first search by default [13]. That is, when exploring a do loop, SPIN chooses the first executable clause in the loop, fully explores the chosen clause, and then moves to the next executable clause. For example, when exploring the do loop in Fig. 4, SPIN first chooses the *second* clause because, in the semantics of SPIN, false is not executable, whereas true is executable. After exploring all the execution traces following the first executable clause, SPIN chooses the second executable clause in the do loop, that is, the *fourth* clause. Thus, SPIN eventually explores all the execution traces by choosing all the executable clauses in the do loop.

Because of the above-mentioned exploration strategy of SPIN, the order of clauses in a do loop can affect the number of states to be explored to find a counterexample. For example, let us consider the PROMELA code in Fig. 5. In the do loop, the first and second clauses are executable. According to the exploration strategy, SPIN chooses the first clause and explores all the execution traces that follow it. Because x is set to 1 in the first clause, the assertion x==1 holds in the following execution traces. Then, SPIN chooses the second clause and explores all the execution traces that follow it. Because i<1 is not an executable statement in the following execution traces, x retains the initial value 0. Thus, SPIN finds that the assertion is violated. More concretely, SPIN (version 6.4.6) explores *nine* states to find the violation of the assertion.

Next, let us suppose that the first and second clauses are exchanged in the PROMELA code of Fig. 5. SPIN first chooses the first clause (i.e., the second clause in the original code) and explores all the execution traces that follow it. In this case, SPIN immediately finds that the assertion is violated. More concretely, SPIN (version 6.4.6) explores *four* states to find the counterexample.

By exploiting the exploration strategy and the sensitivity to the order of clauses of SPIN, we implement the increasing and decreasing exploration strategies on McSPIN. More specifically, we implement them by reordering clauses in do loops in the generated PROMELA code. As explained in Sect. 4.1, McSPIN generates PROMELA code that has do loops as instructions that are nondeterministically chosen under relaxed MCMs. By default, the loops have clauses that

```
do
:: (clause of Effect^{J_p−1} of i_{M_p−1});
:: (clause of Effect^{J_p−1} of i_{M_p−2});
:: ...
:: (clause of Effect^0 of i_0);
:: (clause of Issue^{J_p−1} of i_{M_p−1});
:: (clause of Issue^{J_p−1} of i_{M_p−2});
:: ...
:: (clause of Issue^0 of i_0);
od;
```

Fig. 7. A loop for the increase strategy

```
do
:: (clause of Issue^0 of i_0);
:: (clause of Issue^0 of i_1);
:: ...
:: (clause of Issue^{J_p−1} of i_{M_p−1});
:: (clause of Effect^{J_p−1} of i_{M_p−1});
:: ...
:: (clause of Effect^0 of i_1);
:: (clause of Effect^0 of i_0);
od;
```

Fig. 8. A loop for the decrease strategy

correspond to instructions. More specifically, their issues and effects on thread p are placed in order as shown in Fig. 6, as explained in Sect. 4.1.

To implement the increasing exploration strategy, McSPIN generates a code written in PROMELA as shown in Fig. 7. The point is that the issues of the instructions follow their effects in do loops, that is, if an issue of an instruction is chosen to be explored, its corresponding effect tends to be chosen first before the issues of the other instructions. Thus, SPIN first explores execution traces as in sequential consistency (that is, no reorderings), and gradually increases the number of reorderings of instructions.

To implement the decreasing exploration strategy, McSPIN generates a code written in PROMELA as shown in Fig. 8. The point is that the issues of the instructions precede their effects in do loops, that is, if an issue of an instruction is chosen to be explored, the issues of the other instructions tend to be chosen first before its corresponding effect. Thus, SPIN first reorders instructions as much as possible, then gradually decreases the number of reorderings.

5   Case Studies of Various Concurrent Programs

In this section, we demonstrate the effectiveness of the proposed approaches through various case studies.

5.1   MCMs, Programs, and the Experimental Environment

We formalize several MCMs as inputs of McSPIN. A key characteristic of MCMs is the reordering between load/store instructions from/to shared memory. In this paper, we considered the following MCMs:

SC no operation can overtake the other operations,
TSO load operations can overtake store operations,
PSO load and store operations can overtake store operations, and
RMO load and store operations can overtake load and store operations,

where the above describes operations that have neither a data nor control dependency.

These MCMs are theoretical and actually arranged to be specific MCMs for practical use. For example, the Intel 64 [16] and POWER [14] MCMs are based on TSO and RMO, respectively. The SPARC specification manual [28] also defines multiple MCMs based on TSO, PSO, and RMO.

We used three types of program sets. The first included the following popular mutual exclusion algorithms: Dekker's, Lamport's bakery, Peterson and Fischer's tournament-based, Peterson's, Lamport's fast, and Aravind's algorithms [25]. The second set included the SV-COMP competition benchmarks [29]. We selected six programs: X_true-unreach-call where

$$X \in \{\texttt{fib\_bench}, \texttt{indexer}, \texttt{queue}, \texttt{stack}, \texttt{stateful01}, \texttt{sync01}\}$$

from the 32 programs in the pthread directory that collects C programs with POSIX threads, which (1) work correctly under SC, (2) have more than two instructions for each thread, and (3) are the simplest programs among similar programs. In the following, we omit the postfix _true-unreach-call, for short. Because this work considers the reordering of instructions, we did not choose any program that worked incorrectly under SC and had fewer than three instructions. We were not concerned with conducting a stress test of McSPIN. Therefore, we ignored duplicated programs whose only difference was the data size, and simply reduced the data size. For example, we did not choose fib_bench_longer under the third criterion because it was almost the same as fib_bench except for the value of the loop length NUM. We also reduced NUM in the program to two for the same reason. The third set contained concurrent copying protocols that are used in concurrent copying garbage collection algorithms, Chicken [24], Staccato [21], and Stopless [23], which are larger than the mutual exclusion algorithms described above. We already modeled these algorithms in our previous work [5]. Chicken and Staccato are essentially the same algorithm, although they were developed independently. The only difference is their target MCMs: Chicken is designed for the MCMs of Intel CPUs, whereas Staccato's main target appears to be POWER MCM. Staccato works correctly under RMO. Stopless is a different algorithm from the other two, which is designed for x86-TSO.

The experimental environment was as follows: CPU was Intel Xeon E5-2620 2.10 GHz, memory was DDR4-2400 128 GB, OS was Ubuntu 16.10, SPIN version was 6.4.6, and GCC version was 5.4.0.

5.2   How to Read the Tables of Experiments

Table 1 presents the experimental results. The first column lists the program names. The second column lists the MCMs under which the experiments were conducted. The third, fourth, and fifth columns list whether the assertions, that is, verified properties, held or were violated, the memory consumed, and time elapsed with no reordering control with model checking on a single core. More specifically, ✓ denotes that an assertion held, whereas × denotes that an assertion was violated by detecting a counterexample execution trace. A dash "—"

denotes that the experiment could not be completed because of a lack of memory. N/A denotes that McSPIN was unable to perform the experiment. McSPIN could not manage indexer. The reason is explained in Sect. 5.4.

The sixth, seventh, and eighth columns in Table 1 refer to the 1-local restriction. The sixth column states whether the assertions held or were violated. When an assertion was violated, the seventh and eighth columns list the memory consumed and time elapsed, respectively, until the execution trace that violated the assertion was detected. In the case that the assertion held, the seventh column lists the *supremum* of the memory consumed with the 1-local restriction and no restriction because we *retried* to conduct model checking with the original PROMELA code in our experimental environment. The eighth column lists the *sum* of the elapsed times with the 1-local restriction and no restriction.

We note that we *retried* experiments with no restriction in cases in which assertions held with the 1-local restriction. This is because, even if no counterexample was determined with the 1-local restriction, this does not ensure that an assertion held. Therefore, in the case in which an assertion held, its experimental result was necessarily *worse*. Thus, the local restrictions – and the global restrictions, as described later – have the penalty of retries unlike the increasing and decreasing exploration strategies.

A reason of such retries is that our implementation is not sufficient. In this paper, we developed a prototype implementation of the proposed approaches, and did not implement the exploration of execution traces with no restriction using the experimental results with the 1-local restriction. We conducted the experiment with no restriction when we did not detect an execution trace that violated the assertion in the experiment with the 1-local restriction.

The ninth, tenth, and eleventh columns in Table 1 state whether the assertions held or were violated, the memory consumed, and the time elapsed under the singular global restriction. The singular global restriction enables the parallel processing of model checking. The × symbol denotes that there existed *at least one* counterexample in the experiments that was processed in parallel. The tenth and eleventh columns present the memory consumed and the time elapsed in the experiment for which a counterexample was detected in the smallest time.

A checkmark ✓ denotes that an assertion held in all the experiments. Similarly to the experiments with the 1-local restriction, we *retried* to conduct model checking with the original PROMELA code. The tenth and eleventh columns are similar to the seventh and eighth columns, respectively. The tenth column provides the *supremum* of the memory consumed with the singular global restrictions and the original code. The eleventh column then provides the *sum* of the largest of elapsed times with the singular global restrictions and the original code. Similarly to the experiments with the original code, the 12–17th columns show experimental results under the increasing and decreasing strategies.

5.3   Experimental Results

We show overall comparisons of the performances by our approaches, and compare counterexample detectabilities of the approaches.

Table 1. Experimental results by our approaches

Algorithm	MCM	The original mem. (MB)	time (sec.)	The 1-local Sects. 3.1 and 4.2 mem. (MB)	time (sec.)	The singular global Sects. 3.2 and 4.3 mem. (MB)	time (sec.)	The increasing Sects. 3.3 and 4.4 mem. (MB)	time (sec.)	The decreasing Sects. 3.3 and 4.4 mem. (MB)	time (sec.)
dekker	SC	✓ 101	**0.37**	✓ 101	0.77	✓ 101	0.81	✓ 101	**0.37**	✓ 101	0.39
	TSO	× 101	0.69	× 101	0.61	× 99	0.28	× 101	0.71	× 101	**0.23**
	PSO	× 101	0.84	× 101	0.68	× 99	**0.31**	× 101	0.86	× 101	0.39
	RMO	× 101	1.10	× 101	0.88	× 99	**0.36**	× 101	1.12	× 101	0.53
bakery	SC	✓ 1487	**25.86**	✓ 1487	54.17	✓ 1609	62.48	✓ 1487	25.89	✓ 1487	**25.86**
	TSO	× 3423	74.14	× 2153	43.37	× 1075	21.22	× 3423	74.46	× 419	**7.77**
	PSO	× 6294	154.82	× 2821	63.00	× 741	**13.68**	× 6294	159.30	× 1020	29.28
	RMO	— —	—	— —	—	× 941	**18.28**	— —	—	× 66267	1814.29
tournament	SC	✓ 99	2.22	✓ 99	4.49	✓ 99	4.50	✓ 99	**2.20**	✓ 99	2.24
	TSO	✓ 99	2.22	✓ 99	4.50	✓ 99	4.48	✓ 99	2.22	✓ 99	**2.13**
	PSO	✓ 99	**2.22**	✓ 99	4.46	✓ 99	4.50	✓ 99	**2.22**	✓ 99	2.24
	RMO	✓ 99	3.96	✓ 99	7.98	✓ 99	7.96	✓ 99	**3.94**	✓ 99	3.98
peterson	SC	✓ 101	**0.96**	✓ 101	1.99	✓ 101	2.10	✓ 101	0.97	✓ 101	**0.96**
	TSO	× 101	0.96	× 101	0.91	× 99	0.72	× 101	1.00	× 101	**0.37**
	PSO	× 101	1.37	× 101	1.14	× 99	**0.74**	× 101	1.37	× 101	0.90
	RMO	× 101	2.07	× 101	1.54	× 99	**0.98**	× 101	2.05	× 101	1.18
fast	SC	✓ 224	**2.79**	✓ 224	6.03	✓ 224	5.95	✓ 224	2.98	✓ 224	2.94
	TSO	× 224	3.66	× 156	1.73	× 81	**0.98**	× 224	3.64	× 157	2.60
	PSO	× 424	8.24	× 223	3.21	× 82	**1.00**	× 424	8.16	× 625	14.28
	RMO	× 492	11.22	× 224	3.94	× 82	**1.17**	× 492	11.12	× 692	18.23
aravind	SC	✓ 225	2.88	✓ 225	6.05	✓ 225	6.37	✓ 225	**2.83**	✓ 225	2.85
	TSO	× 359	6.72	× 291	4.81	× 151	**2.79**	× 359	6.69	× 225	4.57
	PSO	× 493	13.32	× 358	6.60	× 151	**2.80**	× 493	13.37	× 426	10.53
	RMO	× 28739	905.12	× 9374	222.56	× 218	**3.56**	× 28739	894.59	× 9308	313.70
fib_bench	SC	✓ 89	0.51	✓ 89	1.07	✓ 89	1.07	✓ 89	0.53	✓ 89	**0.39**
	TSO	✓ 89	**1.80**	✓ 89	3.06	✓ 89	2.78	✓ 89	**1.80**	✓ 89	1.82
	PSO	✓ 89	2.52	✓ 89	4.05	✓ 89	3.68	✓ 89	2.50	✓ 89	**2.34**
	RMO	✓ 891	**47.38**	✓ 891	64.33	✓ 891	49.34	✓ 891	47.92	✓ 891	47.84
indexer	*	N/A		N/A		N/A		N/A		N/A	
queue_ok	SC	✓ 83	0.24	✓ 83	0.50	✓ 83	0.53	✓ 83	**0.23**	✓ 83	0.24
	TSO	✓ 83	**0.51**	✓ 83	0.98	✓ 83	0.89	✓ 83	0.67	✓ 83	0.67
	PSO	✓ 150	1.63	✓ 150	2.39	✓ 150	2.08	✓ 150	**1.59**	✓ 150	1.60
	RMO	✓ 151	1.92	✓ 150	2.78	✓ 150	2.46	✓ 150	1.78	✓ 150	**1.62**
stack	SC	✓ 84	0.94	✓ 84	1.94	✓ 84	1.97	✓ 84	**0.92**	✓ 84	**0.92**
	TSO	✓ 150	1.25	✓ 150	2.41	✓ 150	2.27	✓ 150	**1.24**	✓ 150	1.26
	PSO	✓ 151	1.40	✓ 151	2.70	✓ 151	2.42	✓ 151	**1.38**	✓ 151	1.42
	RMO	✓ 151	**1.78**	✓ 151	3.40	✓ 151	2.94	✓ 151	1.80	✓ 151	1.79
state-ful01	SC	✓ 92	0.03	✓ 92	0.06	✓ 92	0.08	✓ 92	0.03	✓ 92	**0.02**
	TSO	✓ 92	**0.03**	✓ 92	0.05	✓ 92	0.07	✓ 92	0.04	✓ 92	0.05
	PSO	✓ 92	**0.02**	✓ 92	0.05	✓ 92	0.06	✓ 92	0.03	✓ 92	0.04
	RMO	✓ 92	**0.03**	✓ 92	0.07	✓ 92	0.09	✓ 92	0.05	✓ 92	0.04
sync01	SC	✓ 92	**0.04**	✓ 92	0.08	✓ 92	0.09	✓ 92	**0.04**	✓ 92	**0.04**
	TSO	✓ 92	**0.03**	✓ 92	0.06	✓ 92	0.09	✓ 92	0.04	✓ 92	**0.03**
	PSO	✓ 92	**0.04**	✓ 92	0.08	✓ 92	0.10	✓ 92	0.05	✓ 92	**0.04**
	RMO	✓ 92	**0.04**	✓ 92	0.09	✓ 92	0.10	✓ 92	0.05	✓ 92	0.05

(continued)

Table 1. (*continued*)

Algorithm	MCM	The original		The 1-local Sects. 3.1 and 4.2		The singular global Sects. 3.2 and 4.3		The increasing Sects. 3.3 and 4.4		The decreasing Sects. 3.3 and 4.4	
		mem. (MB)	time (sec.)	mem. (MB)	time (sec.)	mem. (MB)	time (sec.)	mem. (MB)	time (sec.)	mem. (MB)	time (sec.)
chicken	SC	✓ 26522	369.69	✓ 26522	768.32	✓ 26522	929.13	✓ 26522	**367.57**	✓ 26522	379.39
	TSO	✓ 48163	709.24	✓ 48163	1333.47	✓ 48163	1372.40	✓ 48163	**707.45**	✓ 48163	712.32
	PSO	× 29328	455.63	× 19240	300.38	× 8586	**175.73**	× 29328	456.79	× 29662	460.57
	RMO	—	—	—	—	× 9792	**194.73**	—	—	—	—
staccato	SC	✓ 51050	697.99	✓ 51050	1443.83	✓ 51050	1756.46	✓ 51050	697.98	✓ 51050	**696.74**
	TSO	✓ 82596	1198.35	✓ 82596	2365.73	✓ 82596	2391.03	✓ 82596	**1197.39**	✓ 82590	1202.74
	PSO	✓ 84669	1243.83	✓ 84669	2432.60	✓ 84669	2463.15	✓ 84669	**1238.68**	✓ 84663	1245.15
	RMO	—	—	—	—	—	—	—	—	—	—
stopless	SC	✓ 24361	438.72	✓ 24487	937.88	✓ 24361	1407.18	✓ 24361	457.30	✓ 24361	**386.11**
	TSO	✓ 37472	658.28	✓ 37472	1349.94	✓ 37472	1755.94	✓ 37472	715.72	✓ 37472	**636.66**
	PSO	× 2543	42.64	× 1934	**33.18**	× 1653	38.54	× 2543	39.40	× 2409	39.94
	RMO	× 15330	262.49	× 11309	193.97	× 1669	**35.61**	× 15330	264.55	× 15129	249.82

Overall Comparisons of Performances by the Approaches. In all the experiments where assertions held, the elapsed times of the experiments without the penalties were smaller than those of the experiments with the penalties, as expected and explained in Sect. 5.2. Memory consumptions are similar to those at the experiments with the original codes.

In the following, we focus on the experiments in which assertions were violated. All the experiments with the singular global restrictions were the best with respect to their elapsed times, for example, aravind under RMO and chicken under PSO as follows:

Algorithm	MCM	The original		The 1-local Sects. 3.1 and 4.2		The singular global Sects. 3.2 and 4.3		The increasing Sects. 3.3 and 4.4		The decreasing Sects. 3.3 and 4.4	
		mem. (MB)	time (sec.)	mem. (MB)	time (sec.)	mem. (MB)	time (sec.)	mem. (MB)	time (sec.)	mem. (MB)	time (sec.)
aravind	RMO	× 28739	905.12	× 9374	222.56	× 218	**3.56**	× 28739	894.59	× 9308	313.70
chicken	PSO	× 29328	455.63	× 19240	300.38	× 8586	**175.73**	× 29328	456.79	× 29662	460.57

except for the following four cases: dekker, bakery, and peterson under TSO, and stopless under PSO. The memory consumptions are interrelated to the elapsed times. In the case of stopless under PSO, their counterexamples were identical. In the other cases, the counterexample had delays of effects of *identical* store instructions although the counterexamples themselves were *distinct*.

The decreasing exploration strategy was better than the increasing exploration strategy except in the following four cases: fast under PSO and RMO, and chicken and stopless under PSO. The model of fast (written the modeling language of McSPIN) differs from the other models with respect to containing jump instructions natively, while the other models do not have jump instructions but `if` and `while` statements, which are compiled into `Jump` instructions introduced in Sect. 2.1. The experiments of `chicken` and `stopless` under PSO with the original, and the increasing and decreasing strategies had similar performances, and we have confirmed that their counterexample had delays of effects of identical store instructions, although the counterexamples were distinct.

In this settings of the paper, we cannot specify the best exploration strategy with reordering control, which seems to *depend on* input programs and MCMs. Nevertheless, we can conclude that the singular global restrictions seems to be the best, followed by the decreasing exploration strategy, the 1-local restriction, and the increasing exploration strategy. More detailed investigations are necessary.

Comparisons of Counterexample Detectability. For all experiments except those that could not be completed because of a lack of memory (designated by —), the detectabilities of the approaches coincide, that is, the approaches detect the counterexamples which the experiments with the original PROMELA codes can detect. This means that just *one* reordering between instructions is sufficient to detect counterexamples in the experiments in this paper.

We focus on the experiments that could not be completed because of a lack of memory (designated by —). The singular global restriction can detect counterexamples that the original PROMELA code could not detect as seen at the experiments for `bakery` and `chicken` with RMO as follows:

Algorithm	MCM	The original		The 1-local Sects. 3.1 and 4.2		The singular global Sects. 3.2 and 4.3		The increasing Sects. 3.3 and 4.4		The decreasing Sects. 3.3 and 4.4	
		mem. (MB)	time (sec.)	mem. (MB)	time (sec.)	mem. (MB)	time (sec.)	mem. (MB)	time (sec.)	mem. (MB)	time (sec.)
bakery	RMO	—	—	—	—	—	—	× 941	**18.28**	—	—	× 66267	1814.29
chicken	RMO	—	—	—	—	—	—	× 9792	**194.73**	—	—	—	—

The experiments with the decreasing strategy for `bakery` could also detect a counterexample that the original code could not detect. However, at the experiment for `chicken` with RMO, the decreasing exploration strategy could not detect a counterexample. The experiments with the 1-local restriction and the increasing strategy could not detect a counterexample which the original code could not detect. Therefore, we can only conclude that reordering controls affect model checking with MCMs.

Careful readers may notice that in the setting of this paper, the experiments of `staccato` under RMO were not completed. In fact, the assertion held in the model checking of `staccato` under RMO. We conducted an additional experiment in another experimental environment with ample memory, the supercomputer system at Kyoto University as follows: CPU was Intel Xeon E7-8880

2.30 GHz, memory was DDR3-1600 3TB, SPIN version was 6.4.6, and GCC version was 4.8.5. The experiment was completed using in 1.17 TB memory and in 7.07 h, and we confirmed that the assertion in (the original PROMELA code of) staccato held under RMO.

5.4   Other Results Obtained Besides the Comparisons

We describe other results obtained besides the comparisons among the approaches through the experiments. In the experiments using the popular mutual exclusion algorithms, with the exception of Peterson and Fischer's tournament-based algorithm, the assertions were violated under TSO as would certainly be the case under PSO and RMO. The reason is that these algorithms have been organized delicately, and their behavior is sensitive to the relaxedness of MCMs. The sensitivity was so high that the assertions were violated in the experiments. As Peterson and Fischer's tournament-based algorithm is implemented by *locking*, it is independent of the relaxedness of MCMs.

The experiments using programs selected from the SV-COMP were independent of the relaxedness of MCMs for the following reasons. The assertion in fib_bench denotes that Fibonacci numbers computed by two threads cannot overtake a value. Therefore, the assertion is independent of delays to the effects of stores. The experiments on indexer could not be completed. The assertion concerns a property of using prime numbers on multiple threads. Therefore, we could not reduce the size of the program to complete the experiments, although we reduced the loop length NUM in fib_bench. The other experiments using programs selected from the SV-COMP were independent of the relaxedness of MCMs because they were all implemented by *locking*.

6   Related Work and Discussion

As the reordering of instructions under relaxed MCMs obviously intensifies the state explosion problem of software model checking, it is natural to attempt to reduce the state explosion by controlling the reordered instructions. Van der Berg [34] proposed an exploration strategy using the so-called *cost* [26] in directed model checking [12], which roughly relaxes an MCM (SC→TSO→PSO), and implemented it on a model checker LTSmin [7]. However, no previous work has considered more delicate optimization by focusing on the number of reordered instructions and controlling the execution traces that are explored. Additionally, no previous works have considered case studies to show the effectiveness of their approaches.

Edelkamp et al. provided *heuristic search* on SPIN, and developed HSF-SPIN [11], which is an extension of SPIN, in the context of directed model checking. However, they have not conducted heuristic searches as seen in our paper for model checking with relaxed MCMs. However, HSF-SPIN could not the take large guards (corresponding to constraints of MCM) which McSPIN generates. We have applied the reorderings approach in Sect. 4.4 through generating PROMELA codes without changing the exploration strategy of SPIN.

We believe there are two reasons for the absence of previous work. The first is that there has been little work on handling various MCMs within a uniform framework. Replacing the store buffers [20,31,32,35] is one method of defining model checkers with various MCMs. However, this approach cannot manage relatively strict relaxed MCMs, such as TSO and PSO. Although model checking with the more relaxed MCMs has been studied, these are specific to certain MCMs, namely the Unified Parallel C MCM [10] and POWER MCM [1], and do not manage various MCMs in a uniform way. Jonsson's seminal work [18] is similar to our work. He considered relaxed MCMs, including SPARC RMO [28], by translating the program into PROMELA. However, he did not conduct experiments as substantial as those presented in this paper.

Senftleben et al. [27] recently succeeded in specifying some MCMs with linear temporal logic (LTL). This is a significant contribution because several MCMs can be represented as inputs of nuXmv [8], a bounded model checker that takes LTL formulas. Thus, their approach does not embed MCMs into models, unlike our approach. In 2013, when we started to define the general model checking framework and develop McSPIN [2], we stopped specifying MCMs as temporal logic formulas in, for example, LTL and computational tree logic, and adopted standard first-order formulas. This led us to use the technique of program translation to follow non-intuitive behavior under relaxed MCMs. As a result, the general model checking framework covers a wide range of MCMs, whereas Senftleben et al. have not identified LTL formulas that specify TSO, which many computer architectures adopt. Our long-term development has also resulted in several approaches for the general model checking framework [2–5], whereas the work of Senftleben et al. has not yet presented substantial approaches or experiments. In their approach, every event is assigned to a global identifier, which may exacerbate the state explosion problem, whereas we have proposed an approach in which states are recalled by predicates to reduce the problem in [3]. Certainly, they have not proposed the approaches described in this paper.

The second reason is that the idea of reducing the state explosion by controlling the reordered instructions is too simple to have been explicitly described in the literature. Model checking with relaxed MCMs is a topic of great interest in the field of program verification, and some model checkers that manage relaxed MCMs are currently being developed (e.g., [19,20,31–33]). Although some of these may support the approaches proposed in this paper, it is not easy to survey their source code. This paper explicitly describes the approaches as simply and generally as possible using the general model checking framework, and evaluates their effects through case studies of various concurrent programs. The authors hope that this paper contributes to the development of other model checkers with relaxed MCMs with respect to the strategy of exploring the traces.

7   Conclusion and Future Work

In this paper we described model checking approaches by focusing on the control of the reordering of instructions, which affects the state explosion problem encountered by relaxed MCMs. This paper also showed the effects of these techniques through case studies using various concurrent programs, including popular mutual exclusion algorithms, benchmarks used for verification tools, and practical concurrent copying protocols. In some cases, our approaches can detect counterexamples that the original exploration of McSPIN could not detect, or detect counterexamples more quickly if the original exploration could detect.

There are four future areas of interest for this research. While model checking with MCMs is affected by the reordering controls, no uniform strategy is provided in this paper. The best exploration strategy depends on the input programs and MCM. Because the `fast` and `bakery` algorithms are sensitive to the increasing and decreasing strategies, more detailed investigations are significant to study exploration strategies with reordering control. This study dealt with the three simple approaches of reordering controls. It is significant to design and implement more complicated reordering controls, and investigate their effects. The present study shows that a counterexample can be detected quickly if the reordering instructions are specified. This opens the possibility of constructing a theory to specify such reordering instructions from programs, verified properties, and MCMs. As described in Sect. 6, Senftleben et al. [27] invented a new approach for handling several MCMs in LTL, which can be the input of nuXmv [8], whereas we adopted first-order logic. It would be interesting to implement the reordering control described in this paper using their approach.

Acknowledgments. The authors thank Gerard J. Holzmann, who has respectfully answered some questions at the SPIN forum http://spinroot.com/fluxbb/. In particular, the idea of the implementations of the exploration strategies in Sect. 4.4 is based on his comment to our questions about the exploring strategy of SPIN. The authors also thank the anonymous reviewers for several comments to improve the paper. This research partly used computational resources under Collaborative Research Program for Young Scientists provided by Academic Center for Computing and Media Studies, Kyoto University. This work was also supported by JSPS KAKENHI Grant Numbers 25330080 and 16K21335, and the Ogasawara Foundation for the Promotion of Science and Engineering in the form of an international travel grant.

References

1. Abdulla, P.A., Atig, M.F., Jonsson, B., Leonardsson, C.: Stateless model checking for POWER. In: Chaudhuri, S., Farzan, A. (eds.) CAV 2016. LNCS, vol. 9780, pp. 134–156. Springer, Cham (2016). https://doi.org/10.1007/978-3-319-41540-6_8
2. Abe, T., Maeda, T.: Model checking with user-definable memory consistency models. In: Proceedings of PGAS, short paper, pp. 225–230 (2013). https://bitbucket.org/abet/mcspin/
3. Abe, T., Maeda, T.: Optimization of a general model checking framework for various memory consistency models. In: Proceedings of PGAS (2014)

4. Abe, T., Maeda, T.: A general model checking framework for various memory consistency models. STTT (2017). https://doi.org/10.1007/s10009-016-0429-y
5. Abe, T., Ugawa, T., Maeda, T., Matsumoto, K.: Reducing state explosion for software model checking with relaxed memory consistency models. In: Fränzle, M., Kapur, D., Zhan, N. (eds.) SETTA 2016. LNCS, vol. 9984, pp. 118–135. Springer, Cham (2016). https://doi.org/10.1007/978-3-319-47677-3_8
6. Adve, S.V., Gharachorloo, K.: Shared memory consistency models: a tutorial. Computer **29**(12), 66–76 (1996)
7. Blom, S., van de Pol, J., Weber, M.: LTSMIN: distributed and symbolic reachability. In: Touili, T., Cook, B., Jackson, P. (eds.) CAV 2010. LNCS, vol. 6174, pp. 354–359. Springer, Heidelberg (2010). https://doi.org/10.1007/978-3-642-14295-6_31
8. Cavada, R., et al.: The NUXMV symbolic model checker. In: Biere, A., Bloem, R. (eds.) CAV 2014. LNCS, vol. 8559, pp. 334–342. Springer, Cham (2014). https://doi.org/10.1007/978-3-319-08867-9_22
9. de Jonge, M., Ruys, T.C.: The SPINJA model checker. In: van de Pol, J., Weber, M. (eds.) SPIN 2010. LNCS, vol. 6349, pp. 124–128. Springer, Heidelberg (2010). https://doi.org/10.1007/978-3-642-16164-3_9
10. Ebnenasir, A.: UPC-SPIN: a framework for the model checking of UPC programs. In: Proceedings of PGAS. ACM (2011)
11. Edelkamp, S., Lafuente, A.L., Leue, S.: Directed explicit model checking with HSF-SPIN. In: Dwyer, M. (ed.) SPIN 2001. LNCS, vol. 2057, pp. 57–79. Springer, Heidelberg (2001). https://doi.org/10.1007/3-540-45139-0_5
12. Edelkamp, S., Schuppan, V., Bošnački, D., Wijs, A., Fehnker, A., Aljazzar, H.: Survey on directed model checking. In: Peled, D.A., Wooldridge, M.J. (eds.) MoChArt 2008. LNCS (LNAI), vol. 5348, pp. 65–89. Springer, Heidelberg (2009). https://doi.org/10.1007/978-3-642-00431-5_5
13. Holzmann, G.J.: The SPIN Model Checker. Addison-Wesley, Boston (2003)
14. IBM Corp.: PowerPC Architechture Book, Version 2.02 (2005)
15. Intel Corp.: A Formal Specification of Intel Itanium Processor Family Memory Ordering (2002)
16. Intel Corp.: Intel 64 and IA-32 Architectures Software Developer's Manual (2016)
17. ISO/IEC 14882:2011: Programming Language C++ (2011)
18. Jonsson, B.: State-space exploration for concurrent algorithms under weak memory orderings: (preliminary version). SIGARCH Comput. Archit. News **36**(5), 65–71 (2008)
19. Kroening, D., Tautschnig, M.: CBMC – C bounded model checker. In: Ábrahám, E., Havelund, K. (eds.) TACAS 2014. LNCS, vol. 8413, pp. 389–391. Springer, Heidelberg (2014). https://doi.org/10.1007/978-3-642-54862-8_26
20. Linden, A., Wolper, P.: An automata-based symbolic approach for verifying programs on relaxed memory models. In: van de Pol, J., Weber, M. (eds.) SPIN 2010. LNCS, vol. 6349, pp. 212–226. Springer, Heidelberg (2010). https://doi.org/10.1007/978-3-642-16164-3_16
21. McCloskey, B., Bacon, D.F., Cheng, P., Grove, D.: Staccato: a parallel and concurrent real-time compacting garbage collector for multiprocessors. Research Report RC24504, IBM (2008)
22. Oracle Corp.: The Java Language Specification. Java SE 8 edn. (2015)
23. Pizlo, F., Frampton, D., Petrank, E., Steensgaard, B.: Stopless: a real-time garbage collector for multiprocessors. In: Proceedings of ISMM, pp. 159–172 (2007)
24. Pizlo, F., Petrank, E., Steensgaard, B.: A study of concurrent real-time garbage collectors. In: Proceedings of PLDI, pp. 33–44 (2008)

25. Raynal, M.: Concurrent Programming: Algorithms, Principles, and Foundations. Springer, Heidelberg (2013). https://doi.org/10.1007/978-3-642-32027-9
26. Reffe, F., Edelkamp, S.: Error detection with directed symbolic model checking. In: Wing, J.M., Woodcock, J., Davies, J. (eds.) FM 1999. LNCS, vol. 1708, pp. 195–211. Springer, Heidelberg (1999). https://doi.org/10.1007/3-540-48119-2_13
27. Senftleben, M., Schneider, K.: Specifying weak memory consistency with temporal logic. In: Proceedings of VECoS, pp. 107–122 (2016)
28. SPARC International, Inc.: The SPARC Architecture Manual, Version 9 (1994)
29. SV-COMP: The 6th International Competition on Software Verification. https://sv-comp.sosy-lab.org/
30. The UPC Consortium: UPC Language Specifications Version 1.3 (2013)
31. Tomasco, E., Truc Nguyen Lam, O.I., Fischer, B., Torre, S.L., Parlato, G.: Lazy sequentialization for TSO and PSO via shared memory abstractions. In: Proceedings of FMCAD, pp. 193–200 (2016)
32. Travkin, O., Mütze, A., Wehrheim, H.: SPIN as a linearizability checker under weak memory models. In: Bertacco, V., Legay, A. (eds.) HVC 2013. LNCS, vol. 8244, pp. 311–326. Springer, Cham (2013). https://doi.org/10.1007/978-3-319-03077-7_21
33. Travkin, O., Wehrheim, H.: Verification of concurrent programs on weak memory models. In: Sampaio, A., Wang, F. (eds.) ICTAC 2016. LNCS, vol. 9965, pp. 3–24. Springer, Cham (2016). https://doi.org/10.1007/978-3-319-46750-4_1
34. van der Berg, F.: Model checking LLVM IR using LTSmin: using relaxed memory model semantics. Master's thesis, University of Twente (2013)
35. Yang, Y., Gopalakrishnan, G., Lindstrom, G.: UMM: an operational memory model specification framework with integrated model checking capability. Concurr. Comput. Pract. Exper. 17(5–6), 465–487 (2005)

An Abstraction Technique for Describing Concurrent Program Behaviour

Wytse Oortwijn[1], Stefan Blom[1], Dilian Gurov[2], Marieke Huisman[1(✉)], and Marina Zaharieva-Stojanovski[1]

[1] University of Twente, Enschede, The Netherlands
{w.h.m.oortwijn,s.c.c.blom,m.huisman,m.zaharieva}@utwente.nl
[2] KTH Royal Institute of Technology, Stockholm, Sweden
dilian@csc.kth.se

Abstract. This paper presents a technique to reason about functional properties of shared-memory concurrent software by means of abstraction. The abstract behaviour of the program is described using process algebras. In the program we indicate which concrete atomic steps correspond to the actions that are used in the process algebra term. Each action comes with a specification that describes its effect on the shared state. Program logics are used to show that the concrete program steps adhere to this specification. Separately, we also use program logics to prove that the program behaves as described by the process algebra term. Finally, via process algebraic reasoning we derive properties that hold for the program from its abstraction. This technique allows reasoning about the behaviour of highly concurrent, non-deterministic and possibly non-terminating programs. The paper discusses various verification examples to illustrate our approach. The verification technique is implemented as part of the VerCors toolset. We demonstrate that our technique is capable of verifying data- and control-flow properties that are hard to verify with alternative approaches, especially with mechanised tool support.

1 Introduction

The major challenge when reasoning about concurrent or distributed software is to come up with an appropriate abstraction that provides sufficient detail to capture the intended properties, while at the same time making verification manageable. This paper presents a new powerful abstraction approach that enables reasoning about the intended properties of the program in a purely non-deterministic setting, and can abstract code at different levels of granularity. The presentation of the abstraction technique in this paper focuses on shared-memory concurrent programs and safety properties, but many extensions may be explored, for example for distributed programs or progress properties, as sketched in the paragraph on future work. The paper illustrates our approach by discussing multiple verification examples in which we verify various data- and control-flow properties. We demonstrate that the proposed technique can

© Springer International Publishing AG 2017
A. Paskevich and T. Wies (Eds.): VSTTE 2017, LNCS 10712, pp. 191–209, 2017.
https://doi.org/10.1007/978-3-319-72308-2_12

```
1  int x, y;                              17  |  if (y > x) { y := y − x; }
2                                         18  |    stop := x = y;
3  void threadx() {                       19  |    release lock;
4  |  bool stop := false;                 20  |  }
5  |  while ¬stop do {                    21  }
6  |  |  acquire lock;                    22
7  |  |  if (x > y) { x := x − y; }        23  int startgcd(int a, int b) {
8  |  |    stop := x = y;                 24  |  x := a;  y := b;
9  |  |    release lock;                  25  |  init lock;
10 |  }                                   26  |  handle t₁ := fork threadx();
11 }                                      27  |  handle t₂ := fork thready();
12                                        28  |  join t₁;
13 void thready() {                       29  |  join t₂;
14 |  bool stop := false;                 30  |  destroy lock;
15 |  while ¬stop do {                    31  |  return x;
16 |  |  acquire lock;                    32  }
```

Fig. 1. A parallel implementation of the Euclidean algorithm for finding the greatest common divisor of two (positive) integers x and y.

be used to verify program properties that are hard to verify with alternative approaches, especially in a practical manner via mechanised tools.

To motivate our approach, consider the program shown in Fig. 1. The figure shows a parallel version of the classical Euclidean algorithm for finding a greatest common divisor, $\gcd(x, y)$, of two given positive integers x and y. This is done by forking two concurrent threads: one thread to decrement the value of x whenever possible, and one thread to decrement the value of y.

We are interested in verifying deductively that this program indeed computes the greatest common divisor of x and y. To accomplish this in a scalable fashion requires that our technique be *modular*, or more precisely procedure-modular and thread-modular, to allow the individual functions and threads to be analysed independently of one another. The main challenge in achieving this lies in finding a suitable way of capturing the *effect* of function calls and threads on the shared memory in a way that is independent of the other functions and threads. Our proposal is to capture these effects as *sequences of exclusive accesses* (in this example increments and decrements) to shared memory (in this example the variables x and y). We abstract such accesses into so-called *actions*, and their sequences into process algebraic terms.

In our example above we abstract the assignments $x := x - y$ and $y := y - x$ needed to decrease the values of x and y into actions decrx and decry, respectively. Action behaviour is specified by means of *contracts* consisting of a guard and an effect; the explanation of the details of this are deferred to Sect. 3. Using these actions, we can specify the effects of the two threads by means of the process algebra terms tx and ty, respectively, which are defined as follows:

process tx() := decrx · tx() + done   **process** ty() := decry · ty() + done

Here the action done indicates termination of a process. The functional behaviour of the program can then be specified by the process pargcd defined as the term tx() ∥ ty(). Standard process algebraic reasoning can be applied to show that executing pargcd results in calculating the correct gcd.

Therefore, by proving that the implementation executes as prescribed by pargcd, we simultaneously establish its functional property of producing the correct result. The pargcd process thus describes the program behaviour.

Once the program has been specified, the access exclusiveness of the actions is verified by a suitable extension of separation logic with permission accounting [5, 19]. On top of it, we develop rules that allow to prove, in a thread-local fashion, that the program indeed follows its prescribed process. The details of our technique applied to the above program are presented in Sect. 3.

In previous work [4, 27] we developed an approach that records the actions of a concurrent program as the program executes. Reasoning with this approach is only suitable for terminating programs, and occurs at the end of its execution, requiring the identification of repeating patterns. In contrast, the current approach requires a process algebra term upfront that describes the patterns of atomic concurrent actions, which allows the specification of functional behaviour of reactive, non-terminating programs. For instance, we can verify properties such as "the values of the shared variables x and y will be equal infinitely often", expressed in LTL by the formula $\Box\Diamond(x = y)$, of a program that forks separate threads to modify x and y, similarly to the above parallel GCD program.

Compared to many of the other modern logics to reason about concurrent programs, such as CAP [9], CaReSL [26], Iris [17], and TaDA [7], our approach does the abstraction at a different level. Our abstraction connects program code with individual actions, while these other approaches essentially encode an abstract state machine, describing how program steps evolve from one abstract program state to the next abstract program state, and explicitly consider the changes that could be made by the thread environment. As a result, in our approach the global properties are specified in a way that is independent of the program implementation. This makes it easier for non-experts to understand the program specification. The main contributions of this paper are:

- An abstraction technique to specify and verify the behaviour of possibly non-terminating, shared-memory concurrent programs, where the abstractions are implementation-independent and may be non-deterministic;
- A number of verification examples that illustrate our approach and can mechanically be verified via the VerCors toolset; and thus
- Tool support for our model-based reasoning approach.

The remainder of this paper is organised as follows. Section 2 provides a brief background on separation logic and process algebras. Then, Sect. 3 illustrates in more detail how abstract models are used in the verification of the parallel GCD example. Section 4 elaborates on the proof rules as they are used by the VerCors tool set. Section 5 discusses two more verification examples that apply our approach: verifying a concurrent counter and verifying a locking protocol. Finally, Sect. 6 discusses related work and Sect. 7 concludes.

2   Background

Our program logic is an extension of Concurrent Separation Logic (CSL) with permission accounting [1,19,22]. The main difference with classical Hoare logic is that each allocated heap location is associated with a fractional permission π, modelled as a rational number in the range $(0,1]$ [5,6]. By allocating a heap location ℓ, the allocating thread gets *full* ownership over ℓ, represented by the $\ell \overset{1}{\hookrightarrow} v$ predicate. The $\hookrightarrow$ predicate gives writing permission to the specified heap location, whereas $\overset{\pi}{\hookrightarrow}$ for $\pi < 1$ only gives reading permission. The $\overset{\pi}{\hookrightarrow}$ predicates may be split and merged along π, so that $\ell \overset{\pi_1}{\hookrightarrow} v * \ell \overset{\pi_2}{\hookrightarrow} v \Leftrightarrow \ell \overset{\pi_1+\pi_2}{\hookrightarrow} v$. In this case, $\Leftrightarrow$ can be read as "splitting" from right to left, or "merging" from left to right. The $*$ connector is the *separating conjunction*; the assertion $\mathcal{P} * \mathcal{Q}$ means that the heap can be split into two disjoint parts, so that one part satisfies the assertion $\mathcal{P}$ and the other part satisfies $\mathcal{Q}$. CSL allows (splitted) points-to predicates that are separated via the $*$-connective to be distributed over concurrent threads (under certain conditions), thereby allowing to reason about race freedom and about functional behaviour of concurrent programs.

2.1   Dynamic Locking

To reason about dynamically allocated locks we use the program logic techniques proposed by Gotsman et al. [11]. Our language includes the **init** $\mathcal{L}$ statement, which initialises a new lock associated with the lock label $\mathcal{L}$. The program logic requires that a *resource invariant* is specified for each initialised lock. A resource invariant is a predicate that expresses the ownership predicates protected by the lock. In the program logic a $\mathsf{Lock}_1(\mathcal{L})$ predicate is produced by **init** $\mathcal{L}$, which represents the knowledge of the existence of a lock labelled $\mathcal{L}$ and this predicate is required to obtain the lock later. Obtaining a lock labelled $\mathcal{L}$ is done via the **acquire** $\mathcal{L}$ statement which, on the program logic level, consumes the $\mathsf{Lock}_\pi(\mathcal{L})$ predicate and exchanges it for the resource invariant that is associated to $\mathcal{L}$. Releasing a lock is done via the **release** $\mathcal{L}$ statement, which has the reverse effect: it takes the resource invariant of $\mathcal{L}$ and exchanges it for $\mathsf{Lock}_\pi(\mathcal{L})$. The **destroy** $\mathcal{L}$ statement destroys the lock $\mathcal{L}$ and thereby consumes $\mathsf{Lock}_1(\mathcal{L})$ in the program logic and gives back the resource invariant associated to $\mathcal{L}$.

2.2   Process Algebra Terms

The abstract models we use to reason about programs are represented as process algebra terms. A subset of the μCRL [12,13] language is used as a suitably expressive process algebra with data. The basic primitives are actions, each representing an indivisible process behaviour. Processes are defined by combining actions and recursive process calls, which both may be parameterised by data. Process algebra terms have the following structure:

$$P, Q ::= \ \varepsilon \mid \delta \mid a(\overline{E}) \mid p(\overline{E}) \mid P \cdot Q \mid P + Q \mid P \parallel Q \mid \textbf{if } B \textbf{ then } P \textbf{ else } P$$

where E are arithmetic expressions, B are Boolean expressions, a are action labels, and p are process labels. With $\overline{E}$ we mean a sequence of expressions.

The empty process is denoted ε and the deadlock process by δ. The process $a(\overline{E})$ is an action call and $p(\overline{E})$ a recursive process invocation, with $\overline{E}$ the argument sequence. Two process terms P and Q may compose either sequentially $P \cdot Q$ or alternatively $P + Q$. The parallel composition $P \parallel Q$ allows the actions of P and Q to be interleaved during execution. The conditional construct **if** B **then** P **else** Q resembles the classical "if-then-else"; it yields either P or Q, depending on the result of evaluating the expression B.

3   Motivating Example

This section demonstrates our approach by verifying functional correctness of the parallel GCD verification example that was discussed in the introduction. With *functional correctness* we mean verifying that, after the program terminates, the *correct* value has been calculated. In this example, the correct value is the mathematical GCD of the two (positive) values given as input to the algorithm.

Our approach uses the following steps:

(1) *Actions* and their associated *guards* and *effects* are defined that describe in what ways the program is allowed to make updates to shared memory.
(2) The actions are composed into *processes* by using the process algebraic connectives discussed in Sect. 2. These processes determine the desired behaviour of (parts of) the concrete program. Notably, processes that are composed in parallel correspond to forked threads in the program.
(3) All defined processes that have a *contract* are verified. Concretely, we automatically verify whether the postconditions of processes can be ensured by all traces that start from a state in which the precondition is satisfied.
(4) Finally we verify that every thread forked by the program *behaves as specified* by the process algebraic specification. If this is the case, the verification results that are established from *(3)* can be used in the program logic.

Tool support for model-based reasoning is provided as part of the VerCors verification tool set [2, 3]. The VerCors tool set aims to verify programs under various concurrency models, notably heterogeneous and homogeneous concurrency, written in high-level programming languages such as Java and C. Although most of the examples presented in this paper have been worked out and verified in PVL, the Prototypal Verification Language that we use to prototype new verification features, tool support is also provided for both Java and C.

All verification examples presented in this paper have been verified with the VerCors tool set. Moreover, all example programs are accessible via an online interface to VerCors, available at http://utwente.nl/vercors.

```
1  int x, y;                        11  guard x = y
2                                    12  action done;
3  guard x > 0 ∧ y > x              13
4  effect x = old(x) ∧ y = old(y) − old(x)   14  process tx() := decrx · tx() + done;
5  action decrx;                    15  process ty() := decry · ty() + done;
6                                    16
7  guard y > 0 ∧ x > y             17  requires x > 0 ∧ y > 0
8  effect x = old(x) − old(y) ∧ y = old(y)   18  ensures x = y
9  action decry;                    19  ensures x = gcd(old(x), old(y))
10                                   20  process pargcd() := tx() ∥ ty();
```

Fig. 2. The processes used for the *parallel GCD* verification example. Three actions are used: decrx, decry, and done; the first two actions capture modifications made to the (shared) variables x and y, and done indicates termination.

Parallel GCD. We demonstrate our model-based reasoning approach by capturing the functional behaviour of a parallel GCD algorithm. The parallel GCD verification problem is taken from the VerifyThis challenge held at ETAPS 2015[1] and considers a parallel version of the classical Euclidean algorithm.

The standard Euclidean algorithm is defined as a function gcd such that, given two positive integers x and y, $\gcd(x, x) = x$, $\gcd(x, y) = \gcd(x - y, y)$ if $x > y$, and $\gcd(x, y) = \gcd(x, y - x)$ if $y > x$. The parallel version of this algorithm uses two concurrent threads: the first thread continuously decrements the value of x when $x > y$, the second thread continuously decrements the value of y when $y > x$, and this process continues until x and y converge to the gcd of the two original input values. Model-based reasoning is used to describe the interleaving of the concurrent threads and to prove functional correctness of the parallel algorithm in an elegant way. Figure 2 presents the setup of the pargcd process, which models the behaviour of a parallel GCD algorithm with respect to the two global variables x and y. The pargcd process uses three different actions, named: decrx, decry, and done. Performing the action decrx captures the effect of decreasing x, provided that $x > y$ before the action is performed. Likewise, performing decry captures the effect of decreasing y. Finally, the done action may be performed when $x = y$ and is used to indicate termination of the algorithm.

The pargcd process is defined as the parallel composition of two processes; the process tx() describes the behaviour of the thread that decreases x, and ty() describes the behaviour of the thread that decreases y. The pargcd process requires that the shared variables x and y are both positive, and ensures that both x and y contain the gcd of the original values of x and y. Proving that pargcd satisfies its contract is done via standard process algebraic reasoning: first pargcd is converted to a linear process (i.e. a process without parallel constructs), which is then analysed (e.g. via model checking) to show that every thread interleaving leads to a correct answer, in this case $\gcd(\mathbf{old}(x), \mathbf{old}(y))$.

---

[1] See also http://etaps2015.verifythis.org.

```
 1  resource lock := ∃v₁, v₂ : v₁ > 0 ∗         9   init lock;
 2     v₂ > 0 ∗ x ⇀¹ₚ v₁ ∗ y ⇀¹ₚ v₂;          10   handle t₁ := fork threadx(m);
 3                                              11   handle t₂ := fork thready(m);
 4  requires a > 0 ∧ b > 0                      12   join t₁;
 5  ensures x = y ∧ x = gcd(a, b)               13   join t₂;
 6  void startgcd(int a, int b) {               14   destroy lock;
 7  │  x := a; y := b;                          15   finish m;
 8  │  model m := init pargcd() over x, y;      16  }
```

Fig. 3. The entry point of the *parallel GCD* algorithm. Two threads are forked and continuously decrement either x or y until $x = y$, which is when the threads converge. The functional property of actually producing a gcd is proven by analysing the process.

Verifying Program Correctness. Figure 3 shows the startgcd function, which is the entry point of the parallel GCD algorithm. According to startgcd's contract, two positive integers must be given as input and permission is required to write to x and y. On line 8 a model is initialised and named m, which describes that all further program executions behave as specified by the pargcd process. Since pargcd is defined as the parallel composition of the processes tx and ty, its definition may be *matched* in the program code by forking two concurrent threads and giving each thread one of the components of tx() ‖ ty(). In this case, the thread executing threadx() continues from the process tx() and the thread executing thready() continues from ty(). By later joining the two threads and finishing the model by using the ghost statement **finish** (which is only possible if pargcd has been fully executed), we may establish that startgcd satisfies its contract. However, we still have to show that the threads executing threadx and thready behave as described by the model m.

Figure 4 shows the implementation of threadx and thready. Both procedures require a $\mathsf{Lock}_\pi(lock)$ predicate, which gives the knowledge that a lock with resource invariant labelled $lock$ has been initialised, and gives the possibility to acquire this lock and therewith the associated resource invariant. Moreover, both procedures require one half of the splitted $\mathsf{Proc}_1(m, \mathsf{tx}() \| \mathsf{ty}())$ predicate that is established in Fig. 3 as result of initialising the model on line 8.

The connection between the process and program code is made via the **action** (ghost) statements. To illustrate, in the function threadx the decrement of x on line 13 is performed in the context of an action block, thereby forcing the tx() process in the $\mathsf{Proc}_{1/2}$ predicate to perform the decrx action. The **guard** of decrx specifies the condition under which decrx can be executed, and the **effect** clause describes the effect on the (shared) state as result of executing decrx. Eventually, both threads execute the done action to indicate their termination.

The VerCors tool set can automatically verify the parallel GCD verification example discussed above, including the analysis of the processes.

```
1  requires Lockπ(lock)                      1  requires Lockπ(lock)
2  requires Proc1/2(m, tx())                 2  requires Proc1/2(m, ty())
3  ensures Lockπ(lock)                       3  ensures Lockπ(lock)
4  ensures Proc1/2(m, ε)                      4  ensures Proc1/2(m, ε)
5  void threadx(model m) {                   5  void thready(model m) {
6  |  bool stop := false;                    6  |  bool stop := false;
7  |  loop-inv Lockπ(lock);                  7  |  loop-inv Lockπ(lock);
8  |  loop-inv ¬stop ⇒ Proc1/2(m, tx());     8  |  loop-inv ¬stop ⇒ Proc1/2(m, ty());
9  |  loop-inv stop ⇒ Proc1/2(m, ε);         9  |  loop-inv stop ⇒ Proc1/2(m, ε);
10 |  while ¬stop do {                       10 |  while ¬stop do {
11 |  |  acquire lock;                       11 |  |  acquire lock;
12 |  |  if (x > y) {                        12 |  |  if (y > x) {
13 |  |  |  action m.decrx() {               13 |  |  |  action m.decry() {
14 |  |  |  |  x := x − y;                    14 |  |  |  |  y := y − x;
15 |  |  |  }                                15 |  |  |  }
16 |  |  }                                   16 |  |  }
17 |  |  if (x = y) {                        17 |  |  if (x = y) {
18 |  |  |  action m.done() {                18 |  |  |  action m.done() {
19 |  |  |  |  stop := true;                 19 |  |  |  |  stop := true;
20 |  |  |  }                                20 |  |  |  }
21 |  |  }                                   21 |  |  }
22 |  |  release lock;                       22 |  |  release lock;
23 |  }                                      23 |  }
24 }                                         24 }
```

Fig. 4. The implementation of the procedures used by the two threads to calculate the gcd of x and y. The procedure `threadx` decrements x and `thready` decrements y.

4   Program Logic

This section shortly elaborates on the assertion language and the proof rules of our approach, as used internally by the VerCors tool set to reason about abstractions. We do not present a full formalisation, for full details we refer to [27]. Only the proof rules related to model-based reasoning are discussed.

4.1   Assertion Language

Our program logic builds on standard CSL with permission accounting [6] and lock predicates [11]. The following grammar defines its assertion language:

$$\mathcal{P}, \mathcal{Q} ::= B \mid \forall x.\mathcal{P} \mid \exists x.\mathcal{P} \mid \mathcal{P} \wedge \mathcal{Q} \mid \mathcal{P} * \mathcal{Q} \mid \mathsf{Lock}_\pi(\mathcal{L}) \mid \mathsf{Locked}_\pi(\mathcal{L}) \mid \cdots$$
$$\mid E \overset{\pi}{\hookrightarrow}_n E \mid E \overset{\pi}{\hookrightarrow}_p E \mid E \overset{\pi}{\hookrightarrow}_a E \mid \mathsf{Proc}_\pi(E, p, P)$$

where E are arithmetic expressions, B are Boolean expressions, x are variables, π are fractional permissions, $\mathcal{L}$ are lock labels, and p are process labels. Note that the specification language implemented in VerCors supports more assertion constructs; we only highlight a subset to elaborate on our approach.

Instead of using a single points-to ownership predicate, like in standard CSL, our extensions require three different points-to predicates:

- The $E \overset{\pi}{\hookrightarrow}_n E'$ predicate is the standard points-to predicate from CSL. It gives write permission to the heap location expressed by E in case $\pi = 1$, and gives read access in case $\pi \in (0, 1]$. This predicate also represents the knowledge that the heap contains the value expressed by E' at location E.
- The *process points-to predicate* $E \overset{\pi}{\hookrightarrow}_p E'$ is similar to $\hookrightarrow_n$, but indicates that the heap location at E is *bound* by an abstract model. Since all changes to this heap location must be captured by the model, the $\hookrightarrow_p$ predicate *only* gives read permission to E, even when $\pi = 1$.
- The *action points-to predicate* $E \overset{\pi}{\hookrightarrow}_a E'$ gives read- or write access to the heap location E in the context of an **action** block. As a precondition, **action** blocks require $\hookrightarrow_p$ predicates for all heap locations that are accessed in their body. These predicates are then converted to $\hookrightarrow_a$ predicates, which give reading permission if $\pi \in (0, 1]$, and writing permission if $\pi = 1$.

All three points-to ownership predicates can be split and merged along the associated fractional permission, to be distributed among concurrent threads:

$$E \overset{\pi_1+\pi_2}{\hookrightarrow}_t E' \Leftrightarrow E \overset{\pi_1}{\hookrightarrow}_t E' * E \overset{\pi_2}{\hookrightarrow}_t E' \qquad \text{for } t \in \{n, p, a\}$$

Essentially, three different predicates are needed to ensure soundness of the verification approach. When a heap location ℓ becomes bound by an abstract model, its $\ell \overset{\pi}{\hookrightarrow} E$ predicate is converted to an $\ell \overset{\pi}{\hookrightarrow}_p E$ predicate in the program logic. As an effect, the value at ℓ cannot just be changed, since the $\hookrightarrow_p$ predicate does not permit writing to ℓ (even when $\pi = 1$). However, the value at ℓ *can* be changed in the context of an action block, as the rule for action blocks in our program logic converts all affected $\hookrightarrow_p$ predicates to $\hookrightarrow_a$ predicates, and $\hookrightarrow_a$ again allows heap writes. The intuition is that, by converting $\ell \overset{\pi}{\hookrightarrow}_p E$ predicates to $\ell \overset{\pi}{\hookrightarrow}_a E$ predicates, all changes to ℓ *must* occur in the context of action blocks, and this allows us to describe all changes to ℓ as process algebra terms. Consequently, by reasoning over these process algebra terms, we may reason about all possible changes to ℓ, and our verification approach allows to use the result of this reasoning in the proof system.

The second main extension our program logic makes to standard CSL is the $\mathsf{Proc}_\pi(E, p, P)$ predicate, which represents the knowledge of the existence of an abstract model that: *(i)* is identified by the expression E, *(ii)* was initialised by invoking the process labelled p, and *(iii)* is described by the process term P. For brevity we omitted p from the annotations in all example programs, since this component is constant (it cannot be changed in the proof system). The third component P is the remaining process term that is to be "executed" (or "matched") by the program. The Proc_π predicates may be split and merged along the fractional permission and the process term, similar to the points-to ownership predicates:

$$\mathsf{Proc}_{\pi_1+\pi_2}(E, p, P_1 \parallel P_2) \Leftrightarrow \mathsf{Proc}_{\pi_1}(E, p, P_1) * \mathsf{Proc}_{\pi_2}(E, p, P_2)$$

4.2 Proof System

Figure 5 shows the proof rules for our model-based reasoning approach. For presentational purposes these rules are somewhat simplified: the rules [INIT], [FIN], and [ACT] require some extra side conditions that deal with process- and action arguments. We also omitted handing process arguments in [INIT]. More details on these proof rules can be found in [27].

The [ASS] rule allows reading from the heap, which can be done with any points-to permission predicate (that is, $\overset{\pi}{\hookrightarrow}_t$ for any permission type t). Writing to shared memory is only allowed by [MUT] with a *full* permission predicate that is *not* of type p; if the targeted heap location is bound by an abstract model, then all changes must be done in an action block (see the [ACT] rule). [INIT] handles the initialisation of a model, which on the specification level converts all affected $\overset{1}{\hookrightarrow}_n$ predicates to $\overset{1}{\hookrightarrow}_p$ and produces a *full* Proc_1 predicate. [FIN] handles model finalisation: it requires a fully executed Proc_1 predicate (holding the process ε) and converts all affected $\overset{1}{\hookrightarrow}_p$ predicates back to $\overset{1}{\hookrightarrow}_n$. Finally, [ACT] handles action blocks. If a proof can be derived for the body S of the action block that: *(i)* respects the guard and effect of the action, and *(ii)* with the $\overset{1}{\hookrightarrow}_p$ predicates of all heap locations accessed in S converted to $\overset{1}{\hookrightarrow}_a$, then a similar proof can be established for the entire action block. Observe that [ACT] requires and consumes the matching action call in the process term.

$$\frac{x \notin \mathsf{fv}(E, E')}{\vdash \{\mathcal{P}[x/E'] \wedge E \overset{\pi}{\hookrightarrow}_t E'\}\, x := [E]\, \{\mathcal{P} \wedge E \overset{\pi}{\hookrightarrow}_t E'\}}\ [\text{ASS}]$$

$$\frac{t \neq \mathsf{p}}{\vdash \{E \overset{1}{\hookrightarrow}_t -\}\, [E] := E'\, \{E \overset{1}{\hookrightarrow}_t E'\}}\ [\text{MUT}]$$

$$\frac{B = \mathsf{precondition}(p) \qquad P = \mathsf{body}(p)}{\vdash \{*_{i=0..n} E_i \overset{1}{\hookrightarrow}_n E_i' * B\}}\ [\text{INIT}]$$
$$\mathbf{model}\ m := \mathbf{init}\ p()\ \mathbf{over}\ E_0, \ldots, E_n$$
$$\{*_{i=0..n} E_i \overset{1}{\hookrightarrow}_p E_i' * \mathsf{Proc}_1(m, p, P)\}$$

$$\frac{\mathsf{locations}(m) = (E_0, \ldots, E_n) \qquad B = \mathsf{postcondition}(p)}{\vdash \{*_{i=0..n} E_i \overset{1}{\hookrightarrow}_p E_i' * \mathsf{Proc}_1(m, p, \varepsilon)\}\ \mathbf{finish}\ m\ \{*_{i=0..n} E_i \overset{1}{\hookrightarrow}_n E_i' * B\}}\ [\text{FIN}]$$

$$\frac{\mathsf{accessedlocs}(S) = (E_0, \ldots, E_n) \qquad B_1 = \mathsf{guard}(a) \qquad B_2 = \mathsf{effect}(a)}{\vdash \{*_{i=0..n} E_i \overset{1}{\hookrightarrow}_a E_i' * B_1\}\, S\, \{*_{i=0..n} E_i \overset{1}{\hookrightarrow}_a E_i'' * B_2\}}\ [\text{ACT}]$$
$$\vdash \{*_{i=0..n} E_i \overset{1}{\hookrightarrow}_p E_i' * \mathsf{Proc}_\pi(m, p, a(\overline{E}) \cdot P) * B_1\}$$
$$\mathbf{action}\ m.a(\overline{E})\ \{\ S\ \}$$
$$\{*_{i=0..n} E_i \overset{1}{\hookrightarrow}_p E_i'' * \mathsf{Proc}_\pi(m, p, P) * B_2\}$$

Fig. 5. The simplified proof rules of all model-related specification constructs.

5   Applications of the Logic

In this section we apply our approach on two more verification problems: *(i)* a concurrent program in which multiple threads increase a shared counter by one (see Sect. 5.1); and *(ii)* verifying control-flow properties of a fine-grained lock implementation (see Sect. 5.2). Also some interesting variants on these problems are discussed. For example *(i)* we verify the functional property that, after the program terminates, the correct value has been calculated. For *(ii)* we verify that clients of the lock adhere to the intended locking protocol and thereby avoid misusing the lock.

5.1   Concurrent Counting

Our second example considers a *concurrent counter*: a program where two threads concurrently increment a common shared integer. The basic algorithm is given in Fig. 6. The goal is to verify that **program** increments the original value of *counter* by two, given that it terminates. However, providing a specification for **worker** can be difficult, since no guarantees to the value of *counter* can be given after termination of **worker**, as it is used in a concurrent environment.

Existing verification approaches for this particular example [8] mostly require *auxiliary state*, a form of *rely/guarantee reasoning*, or, more recently, *concurrent abstract predicates*, which may blow-up the amount of required specifications and are not always easy to use. We show how to verify the program of Fig. 6 via our model-based abstraction approach. Later, we show how our techniques may be used on the same program but generalised to n threads.

Our approach is to protect all changes to *counter* by a process that we name parincr. The parincr process is defined as the parallel composition incr $\|$ incr of two processes that both execute the incr action once. Performing incr has the effect of incrementing *counter* by one. From a process algebraic point of view it is easy to see that parincr satisfies its contract: every possible trace of parincr indeed has the effect of increasing *counter* by two, and this can automatically be verified. We use this result in the verification of **program** by using model-based reasoning. In particular, we may instantiate parincr as a model m, split along its

---

```
1  int counter;                         8  void program(int n) {
2                                        9  |  counter := n;
3  void worker() {                      10  |  handle t₁ = fork worker();
4  |  atomic {                          11  |  handle t₂ = fork worker();
5  |  |  counter := counter + 1;        12  |  join t₁;
6  |  }                                 13  |  join t₂;
7  }                                    14  }
```

Fig. 6. The concurrent counting example program, where two threads forked by **program** increment the shared integer *counter*.

```
1  int counter;                       15  │ │ }
2                                      16  │ }
3  effect counter = old(counter) + 1; 17  }
4  action incr;                        18
5                                      19  ensures counter = c + 2;
6  ensures counter = old(counter) + 2; 20  void program(int c) {
7  process parincr() := incr ‖ incr;  21  │ counter := c;
8                                      22  │ model m := parincr();
9  requires Proc_π(m, incr);          23  │ handle t₁ := fork worker(m);
10 ensures Proc_π(m, ε);              24  │ handle t₂ := fork worker(m);
11 void worker(model m) {             25  │ join t₁;
12 │ atomic {                         26  │ join t₂;
13 │ │ action m.incr {                27  │ finish m;
14 │ │ │ counter := counter + 1;      28  }
```

Fig. 7. Definition of the parincr process that models two concurrent threads performing an atomic incr action, and the required annotations for worker and program.

parallel composition, and give each forked thread a fraction of the splitted Proc predicate. The interface specification of the worker procedure thus becomes:

$$\{\mathsf{Proc}_\pi(m, \mathsf{incr})\}\, \mathsf{worker}(m)\, \{\mathsf{Proc}_\pi(m, \varepsilon)\}$$

An annotated version of the concurrent counting program is presented in Fig. 7. The **atomic** statement is used as a construct for statically-scoped locking; for simplicity we assume that writing permissions for *counter* are maintained by its resource invariant. Indeed, by showing that both threads execute the incr action, the established result of incrementing *counter* by 2 can be concluded.

Generalised Concurrent Counting. The interface specification of worker is generic enough to allow a generalisation to n threads. Instead of the parincr process as presented in Fig. 7 one could consider the following process, which essentially encodes the process "incr $\‖ \cdots \‖$ incr" (n times) via recursion:

> **requires** $n \geq 0$;
> **ensures** *counter* = old(*counter*) + n;
> **process** parincr(**int** n) := **if** $n > 0$ **then** incr $\‖$ parincr(n − 1) **else** ε;

Figure 8 shows the generalised version of the concurrent counting program, in which we reuse the incr action and the worker procedure from Fig. 7. Here program takes an extra parameter n that determines the number of threads to be spawned. The spawn procedure has been added to spawn the n threads. This procedure is recursive to match the recursive definition of the parincr(n) process. Again, each thread executes the worker procedure. We verify that after running program the value of *counter* has increased by n.

```
 1  requires n ≥ 0;                         11
 2  requires Procπ(m, parincr(n));          12  requires n ≥ 0;
 3  ensures Procπ(m, ε);                     13  ensures counter = c + n;
 4  void spawn(model m, int n) {            14  void program(int c, int n) {
 5    if (n > 0) {                           15    counter := c;
 6      handle t := fork worker(m);          16    model m := parincr(n);
 7      spawn(m, n − 1);                      17    spawn(m, n);
 8      join t;                              18    finish m;
 9    }                                       19  }
10  }
```

Fig. 8. Generalisation of the concurrent counting verification problem, where `program` forks n threads using the recursive `spawn` procedure. Each thread executes the `worker` procedure and therewith increments the value of *counter* by one.

On the level of processes we may automatically verify that each trace of the process parincr(n) is a sequence of n consecutive incr actions. As a consequence, from the effects of incr we can verify that parincr(n) increases *counter* by n. On the program level we may verify that spawn(m, n) fully executes according to the parincr(n) process. To clarify, on line 6 the definition of parincr(n) can be unfolded to incr $\|$ parincr($n − 1$) and can then be split along its parallel composition. Then the forked thread receives incr and the recursive call to spawn receives parincr($n − 1$). After calling **join** on line 8, both the call to worker and the recursive call to spawn have ensured completing the process they received, thereby leaving the (merged) process $\varepsilon \| \varepsilon$, which can be rewritten to ε to satisfy the postcondition of spawn. As a result, after calling **finish** on line 18 we can successfully verify that *counter* has indeed been increased by n.

Unequal Concurrent Counting. One could consider an interesting variant on the two-threaded concurrent counting problem: one thread performing the assignment "*counter* = *counter* + v" for some integer value v, and the other thread concurrently performing "*counter* = *counter* * v". Starting from a state where *counter* = c holds for some c, the challenge is to verify that after running the program we either have *counter* = $(c + v) * v$ or *counter* = $(c * v) + v$.

This program can be verified using our model-based approach (without requiring for example auxiliary state) by defining corresponding actions for the two different assignments. The global model is described as the process count(**int** n) := plus(n) $\|$ mult(n), where the action plus(n) has the effect of incrementing *counter* by n and mult(n) has the effect of multiplying *counter* by n. The required program annotations are then similar to the ones used in Fig. 7.

All three variants on the concurrent counting problem can be automatically verified using the VerCors toolset.

5.2 Lock Specification

The third example demonstrates how our approach can be used to verify control-flow properties of programs, in this case the *compare-and-swap lock implementation* that is presented in the Concurrent Abstract Predicates (CAP) paper [9]. The implementation is given in Fig. 9. The $cas(x, c, v)$ operation is the *compare-and-swap* instruction, which atomically updates the value of x by v if the old value at x is equal to c, otherwise the value at x is not changed. A Boolean result is returned indicating whether the update to x was successful.

In particular, model-based reasoning is used to verify that the clients of this lock adhere to the intended locking protocol: clients may only successfully acquire the lock when the lock was unlocked and vice versa. Stated differently, we verify that clients may not acquire (nor release) the same lock successively.

The process algebraic description of the locking protocol is a composition of two actions, named acq and rel, that model the process of acquiring and releasing the lock, respectively. A third action named done is used to indicate that the lock is no longer used and can thus be destroyed. We use this process as a model to protect changes to the shared variable $flag$, so that all changes to $flag$ must either happen as an acq or as a rel action. The acq action may be performed only if $flag$ is currently false and has the effect of setting $flag$ to true. The rel action simply has the effect of setting $flag$ to false, whatever the current value of $flag$ (therefore rel does not need a guard). The locking protocol is defined by the processes $\mathsf{Locked}() := \mathsf{rel} \cdot \mathsf{Unlocked}()$ and $\mathsf{Unlocked}() := \mathsf{acq} \cdot \mathsf{Locked}() + \mathsf{done}$. This allows us to use the following interface specifications for the `acquire` and `release` procedures (with m a global identifier of an initialised model):

$$\{\mathsf{Proc}_\pi(m, \mathsf{Unlocked}())\}\, \texttt{acquire}()\, \{\mathsf{Proc}_\pi(m, \mathsf{Locked}())\}$$
$$\{\mathsf{Proc}_\pi(m, \mathsf{Locked}())\}\, \texttt{release}()\, \{\mathsf{Proc}_\pi(m, \mathsf{Unlocked}())\}$$

Specification-wise, clients of the lock may only perform `acquire` when they have a corresponding process predicate that is in an "Unlocked" state (and the same holds for `release` and "Locked"), thereby enforcing the locking protocol (i.e. the process only allows traces of the form: $\mathsf{acq}, \mathsf{rel}, \mathsf{acq}, \mathsf{rel}, \cdots$). The `acquire` procedure performs the acq action via the `cas` operation: one may define `cas` to update $flag$ as an acq action. Moreover, since `cas` is an atomic operation,

```
1  bool flag := false;                    7    |  }
2                                          8  }
3  void acquire() {                        9
4    |  bool b := false;                  10  void release() {
5    |  while ¬b {                        11    |  atomic { flag := false; }
6    |  |  b := cas(flag, false, true);   12  }
```

Fig. 9. Implementation of a simple locking system.

```
 1  bool flag;                              25  requires Proc_π(m, Locked());
 2  model m;                                26  ensures Proc_π(m, Unlocked());
 3                                          27  void release() {
 4  resource inv := flag ↪¹_p −;           28  │   atomic inv {
 5                                          29  │   │   action m.rel { flag := false; }
 6  guard ¬flag; effect flag; action acq;  30  │   }
 7  effect ¬flag; action rel;              31  }
 8                                          32
 9  process Unlocked() := acq · Locked();  33  requires flag ↪¹_n −;
10  process Locked() :=                    34  ensures Proc₁(m, Unlocked());
11      rel · Unlocked() + done;           35  void init() {
12                                         36  │   flag := false;
13  requires Proc_π(m, Unlocked());        37  │   m := model Unlocked();
14  ensures Proc_π(m, Locked());           38  │   init inv;
15  void acquire() {                       39  }
16  │   bool b := false;                   40
17  │   loop-inv ¬b ⇒                      41  requires Proc₁(m, Unlocked());
18  │       Proc_π(m, acq · Locked());     42  ensures flag ↪¹_n −;
19  │   loop-inv b ⇒ Proc_π(m, Locked());  43  void destroy() {
20  │   while ¬b {                         44  │   action m.done { }
21  │   │   b := cas(flag, false, true);   45  │   destroy inv;
22  │   }                                  46  │   finish m;
23  }                                      47  }
24
```

Fig. 10. The annotated implementation of the simple fine-grained locking system.

it can get all necessary ownership predicates from the resource invariant *inv*. Furthermore, calling `destroy()` corresponds to performing the done action on the process algebra level, which may only be done in the "Unlocked" state.

The full annotated lock implementation is presented in Fig. 10. The `init` and `destroy` procedures have been added to initialise and finalise the lock and thereby to create and destroy the corresponding model. The `init` consumes write permission to *flag*, creates the model, and transfers the converted write permission into the resource invariant *inv*. Both the atomic block (on line 28) and the `cas` operation (on line 21) make use of *inv* to get permission to change the value of *flag* in an action block. The `cas` operation on line 21 performs the acq action internally, depending on the success of the compare-and-swap (indicated by its return value). This is reflected upon in the loop invariant. The `destroy` procedure has the opposite effect of `init`: it consumes the (full) Proc predicate (in state "Unlocked"), destroys the model and the associated resource invariant, and gives back the converted write permission to *flag*.

In the current presentation, `init` returns a single Proc predicate in state Unlocked, thereby allowing only a single client. This is however not a limitation: to support two clients, `init` could alternatively initialise and ensure the Unlocked() ∥ Unlocked() process. Furthermore, to support n clients (or a dynamic number of clients), init could apply a construction similar to the one used in the generalised concurrent counting example (see Sect. 5.1).

Reentrant Locking. The process algebraic description of the locking protocol can be upgraded to describe a *reentrant lock*: a locking system where clients may acquire and release multiple times in succession. A reentrant lock that is acquired n times by a client must also be released n times before it is available to other clients. Instead of using the Locked and Unlocked processes, the reentrant locking protocol is described by the following process (with $n \geq 0$):

$$\textbf{process } \mathsf{Lock}(\textbf{int } n) := \mathsf{acq} \cdot \mathsf{Lock}(n+1) + (\textbf{if } n > 0 \textbf{ then } \mathsf{rel} \cdot \mathsf{Lock}(n-1))$$

Rather than describing the lock state as a Boolean flag, like done in the single-entrant locking example, the state of the reentrant lock can be described as a *multiset* containing thread identifiers. In that case, acq and rel protect all changes made to the multiset in order to enforce the locking protocol described by Lock. The interface specifications of acquire and release then become:

$$\{\mathsf{Proc}_\pi(m, \mathsf{Lock}(n))\} \texttt{ acquire() } \{\mathsf{Proc}_\pi(m, \mathsf{Lock}(n+1))\}$$
$$\{\mathsf{Proc}_\pi(m, \mathsf{Lock}(n)) \wedge n > 0\} \texttt{ release() } \{\mathsf{Proc}_\pi(m, \mathsf{Lock}(n-1))\}$$

Moreover, the $\mathsf{Lock}(n)$ process could be extended with a done action to allow the reentrant lock to be destroyed. The done action should then only be allowed when $n = 0$. Both the simple locking implementation and the reentrant locking implementation have been automatically verified using the VerCors toolset.

5.3   Other Verification Examples

This section demonstrated the use of process algebraic models in three different verification examples, as well as some interesting variants on them. We showed how model-based reasoning can be used as a practical tool to verify different types of properties that would otherwise be hard to verify, *especially with an automated tool*. We considered *data properties* in the parallel GCD and the concurrent counting examples, and considered *control-flow* properties in the locking examples. Moreover, we showed how to use the model-based reasoning approach in environments with a dynamic number of concurrent threads.

Our approach can also be used to reason about *non-terminating* programs. Notably, a *no-send-after-read* verification example is available that addresses a commonly used security property: if confidential data is received by a secure device, it will not be passed on. The concrete send- and receive behaviour of the device can be abstracted by send and recv actions, respectively. Receiving confidential information is modelled as the clear action. Essentially, we show that after performing a clear action the device can no longer perform send's.

6   Related Work

The abstraction technique proposed in this paper allows reasoning about functional behaviour of concurrent, possibly non-terminating programs. A related approach is (impredicative) Concurrent Abstract Predicates (CAP) [9,25], which also builds on CSL with permissions. In the program logic of CAP, *regions* of memory can be specified as being *shared*. Threads must have a consistent view of all shared regions: all changes must be specified as *actions* and all shared regions are equipped with a set of possible actions over their memory. Our approach uses process algebraic abstractions over shared memory in contrast to the shared regions of CAP, so that all changes to the shared memory must be captured as process algebraic actions. We mainly distinguish in the use of *process algebraic reasoning* to verify properties that could otherwise be hard to verify, and in the capability of doing this mechanically by providing tool support.

Other related approaches include TaDA [7], a program logic that builds on CAP by adding a notion of *abstract atomicity* via Hoare triples for atomic operations. CaReSL [26] uses a notion of shared regions similar to CAP, but uses *tokens* to denote ownership. These tokens are used to transfer ownership over resources between threads. Iris [17,18] is a reasoning framework that aims to provide a comprehensive and simplified solution for recent (higher-order) concurrency logics. Sergey et al. [24] propose *time-stamped histories* to capture modifications to the shared state. Our approach may both capture and model program behaviour and benefits from extensive research on process algebraic reasoning [12]. Moreover, the authors provide a *mechanised* approach to interactively verify full functional correctness of concurrent programs by building on CSL [23]. Popeea and Rybalchenko [21] combine abstraction refinement with rely-guarantee reasoning to verify termination of multi-threaded programs.

In the context of verifying distributed systems, Session Types [15] describe communication protocols between processes [14]. However, our approach is more general as it allows describing any kind of behaviour, including communication behaviour between different system components.

7   Conclusion

This paper addresses thread-modular verification of possibly non-terminating concurrent programs by proposing a technique to abstract program behaviour using process algebras. A key characteristic of our approach is that properties about programs can be proven by analysing process algebraic program abstractions and by verifying that programs do not deviate from these abstractions. The verification is done in a thread-modular way, using an abstraction-aware extension of CSL. This paper demonstrates how the proposed technique provides an elegant solution to various verification problems that may be challenging for alternative verification approaches. In addition, the paper contributes tool support and thereby allow mechanised verification of the presented examples.

Future Work. We are currently working on mechanising the formalisation and the soundness proof of the proposed technique using Coq. At the moment, verification at the process algebra level is non-modular. As a next step, we plan to achieve modularity at this level as well, by combining our approach with rely-guarantee [16] and deny-guarantee reasoning [10]. We also plan to investigate how to mix and interleave abstract and concrete reasoning. In the current set up, reasoning is done completely at the level of the abstraction. If this part of the program is used as a component in a larger program, we plan to investigate how the verification results for the components can be used to reason about the larger program, if reasoning about the larger program is not done at this level of abstraction. Finally, in a different direction, we plan to extend the abstraction technique to reason about distributed software. For example, abstractions may be used to capture the behaviour of a single actor/agent as a process term, allowing process algebraic techniques such as [20] to be used for further verification.

Acknowledgements. This work is partially supported by the ERC grant 258405 for the VerCors project and by the NWO TOP 612.001.403 project VerDi.

References

1. Amighi, A., Haack, C., Huisman, M., Hurlin, C.: Permission-based separation logic for multithreaded Java programs. LMCS **11**(1), 1–66 (2015)
2. Blom, S., Darabi, S., Huisman, M., Oortwijn, W.: The VerCors tool set: verification of parallel and concurrent software. In: Polikarpova, N., Schneider, S. (eds.) IFM 2017. LNCS, vol. 10510, pp. 102–110. Springer, Cham (2017). https://doi.org/10.1007/978-3-319-66845-1_7
3. Blom, S., Huisman, M.: The VerCors tool for verification of concurrent programs. In: Jones, C., Pihlajasaari, P., Sun, J. (eds.) FM 2014. LNCS, vol. 8442, pp. 127–131. Springer, Cham (2014). https://doi.org/10.1007/978-3-319-06410-9_9
4. Blom, S., Huisman, M., Zaharieva-Stojanovski, M.: History-based verification of functional behaviour of concurrent programs. In: Calinescu, R., Rumpe, B. (eds.) SEFM 2015. LNCS, vol. 9276, pp. 84–98. Springer, Cham (2015). https://doi.org/10.1007/978-3-319-22969-0_6
5. Bornat, R., Calcagno, C., O'Hearn, P.W., Parkinson, M.J.: Permission accounting in separation logic. In: POPL, pp. 259–270 (2005)
6. Boyland, J.: Checking interference with fractional permissions. In: Cousot, R. (ed.) SAS 2003. LNCS, vol. 2694, pp. 55–72. Springer, Heidelberg (2003). https://doi.org/10.1007/3-540-44898-5_4
7. da Rocha Pinto, P., Dinsdale-Young, T., Gardner, P.: TaDA: a logic for time and data abstraction. In: Jones, R. (ed.) ECOOP 2014. LNCS, vol. 8586, pp. 207–231. Springer, Heidelberg (2014). https://doi.org/10.1007/978-3-662-44202-9_9
8. da Rocha Pinto, P., Dinsdale-Young, T., Gardner, P.: Steps in modular specifications for concurrent modules. In: MFPS, EPTCS, pp. 3–18 (2015). https://doi.org/10.1016/j.entcs.2015.12.002
9. Dinsdale-Young, T., Dodds, M., Gardner, P., Parkinson, M.J., Vafeiadis, V.: Concurrent abstract predicates. In: D'Hondt, T. (ed.) ECOOP 2010. LNCS, vol. 6183, pp. 504–528. Springer, Heidelberg (2010). https://doi.org/10.1007/978-3-642-14107-2_24

10. Dodds, M., Feng, X., Parkinson, M., Vafeiadis, V.: Deny-guarantee reasoning. In: Castagna, G. (ed.) ESOP 2009. LNCS, vol. 5502, pp. 363–377. Springer, Heidelberg (2009). https://doi.org/10.1007/978-3-642-00590-9_26

11. Gotsman, A., Berdine, J., Cook, B., Rinetzky, N., Sagiv, M.: Local reasoning for storable locks and threads. In: Shao, Z. (ed.) APLAS 2007. LNCS, vol. 4807, pp. 19–37. Springer, Heidelberg (2007). https://doi.org/10.1007/978-3-540-76637-7_3

12. Groote, J.F., Mousavi, M.R.: Modeling and Analysis of Communicating Systems. MIT Press, Cambridge (2014)

13. Groote, J.F., Ponse, A.: The syntax and semantics of μCRL. In: Ponse, A., Verhoef, C., van Vlijmen, S.F.M. (eds.) Algebra of Communicating Processes, pp. 26–62. Springer, London (1995). https://doi.org/10.1007/978-1-4471-2120-6_2

14. Honda, K., Marques, E.R.B., Martins, F., Ng, N., Vasconcelos, V.T., Yoshida, N.: Verification of MPI programs using session types. In: Träff, J.L., Benkner, S., Dongarra, J.J. (eds.) EuroMPI 2012. LNCS, vol. 7490, pp. 291–293. Springer, Heidelberg (2012). https://doi.org/10.1007/978-3-642-33518-1_37

15. Honda, K., Yoshida, N., Carbone, M.: Multiparty asynchronous session types. In: POPL, pp. 273–284. ACM (2008)

16. Jones, C.B.: Tentative steps toward a development method for interfering programs. ACM Trans. Program. Lang. Syst. 5(4), 596–619 (1983)

17. Jung, R., Swasey, D., Sieczkowski, F., Svendsen, K., Turon, A., Birkedal, L., Dreyer, D.: Iris: monoids and invariants as an orthogonal basis for concurrent reasoning. In: POPL, pp. 637–650. ACM (2015)

18. Krebbers, R., Jung, R., Bizjak, A., Jourdan, J.-H., Dreyer, D., Birkedal, L.: The essence of higher-order concurrent separation logic. In: Yang, H. (ed.) ESOP 2017. LNCS, vol. 10201, pp. 696–723. Springer, Heidelberg (2017). https://doi.org/10.1007/978-3-662-54434-1_26

19. O'Hearn, P.W.: Resources, concurrency and local reasoning. Theoret. Comput. Sci. 375(1–3), 271–307 (2007)

20. Pang, J., van de Pol, J., Espada, M.: Abstraction of parallel uniform processes with data. In: SEFM, pp. 14–23. IEEE (2004)

21. Popeea, C., Rybalchenko, A.: Compositional termination proofs for multi-threaded programs. In: Flanagan, C., König, B. (eds.) TACAS 2012. LNCS, vol. 7214, pp. 237–251. Springer, Heidelberg (2012). https://doi.org/10.1007/978-3-642-28756-5_17

22. Reynolds, J.C.: Separation logic: a logic for shared mutable data structures. In: Logic in Computer Science, pp. 55–74. IEEE Computer Society (2002). https://doi.org/10.1109/LICS.2002.1029817

23. Sergey, I., Nanevski, A., Banerjee, A.: Mechanized verification of fine-grained concurrent programs. In: PLDI, pp. 77–87. ACM (2015)

24. Sergey, I., Nanevski, A., Banerjee, A.: Specifying and verifying concurrent algorithms with histories and subjectivity. In: Vitek, J. (ed.) ESOP 2015. LNCS, vol. 9032, pp. 333–358. Springer, Heidelberg (2015). https://doi.org/10.1007/978-3-662-46669-8_14

25. Svendsen, K., Birkedal, L.: Impredicative concurrent abstract predicates. In: Shao, Z. (ed.) ESOP 2014. LNCS, vol. 8410, pp. 149–168. Springer, Heidelberg (2014). https://doi.org/10.1007/978-3-642-54833-8_9

26. Turon, A., Dreyer, D., Birkedal, L.: Unifying refinement and hoare-style reasoning in a logic for higher-order concurrency. In: ICFP, pp. 377–390 (2013)

27. Zaharieva-Stojanovski, M.: Closer to reliable software: verifying functional behaviour of concurrent programs. Ph.D. thesis, University of Twente (2015). https://doi.org/10.3990/1.9789036539241

Author Index

Printed in the United States
By Bookmasters